U0085016

TEST 1 詳解

聽力測驗 (第 1-21 題，共 21 題)

第一部分：辨識句意 (第 1-3 題，共 3 題)

1. (**B**) (A)  (B)  (C)

Ronnie is taking a photograph of some butterflies.
蘭尼正在拍一些蝴蝶。

* photograph〔'fotə,græf〕*n.* 照片　　***take a picture of*** 給…照相
butterfly〔'bʌtə,flaɪ〕*n.* 蝴蝶

2. (**A**) (A)  (B)  (C)

Nick, Eric, and Tina are seated at a table.
尼克、艾瑞克及蒂娜坐在桌旁。

* ***be seated*** 坐 (= *sit*)　　***at a table*** 在桌子旁邊

3. (**A**) (A)  (B)  (C)

Carson is packing some of his belongings in a box.
卡爾森正在打包一些他的物品到一個箱子裡。

* pack〔pæk〕v. 打包　　belongings〔bɪ'lɔŋɪŋz〕n. pl. 所有物
  box〔baks〕n. 箱子

第二部分：基本問答（第 4-10 題，共 7 題）

4. (**A**) I'm in shock! I won 2,000 NT in the receipt lottery this
   month. 我好驚訝啊！我這個月中了統一發票 2,000 元的獎。

   (A) Wow, you're so lucky. 哇，你真幸運。

   (B) It was too expensive. 這太貴了。

   (C) What a terrible idea! 這想法糟透了！

   * *in shock* 驚訝的　　*NT* 新台幣（= *NTD* = *New Taiwan Dollar*）
     receipt〔rɪ'sit〕n. 收據　　lottery〔'latərɪ〕n. 彩券
     receipt lottery 統一發票抽獎　　terrible〔'tɛrəbl̩〕adj. 很糟的

5. (**C**) What's your email address, Vicki?
   維奇，你的電子郵件地址是什麼？

   (A) 555-0898. 555-0898。

   (B) V-I-C-K-I. V-I-C-K-I。

   (C) Stardreamer at Jmail dot com. Stardreamer@Jmail.com。

   * email〔'imel〕n. 電子郵件　　address〔ə'drɛs〕n. 地址
     dot〔dat〕n. 點　　com〔kam〕adj. 商業的（= *commercial*）

6. (**B**) Sorry, what did you say your name was?
   對不起，你說你的名字是什麼？

   (A) Thanks. 謝謝。

   (B) Edward. 艾德華。

   (C) She's over there. 她在那裡。

   * *over there* 在那裡

7. (**A**) Come on! Let's go. We'll miss the bus.

快點！我們走吧。我們要錯過公車了。

(A) I need one more minute. 我還要再一分鐘。

(B) They took the bus. 他們搭了巴士。

(C) All my friends will be there. 我所有的朋友都會在那裡。

* ***come on*** 快一點；加把勁   miss 〔 mɪs 〕 *v.* 錯過

8. (**A**) I'm kind of busy right now. Can I get back to you in a while? 我現在有點忙。我可以過一會兒回覆你嗎？

(A) Sure. Whenever you're free.

當然。你有空時隨時跟我說。

(B) Yes. I'm almost finished. 是，我幾乎完成了。

(C) They did? 他們有嗎？

* ***kind of*** 有點   ***right now*** 目前；現在
get back to 回覆   ***in a while*** 過一會兒
finished 〔 'fɪnɪʃt 〕 *adj.* 完成的

9. (**B**) Judy, I just mopped the kitchen floor and it's still wet, so don't go in there for a while. 茱蒂，我剛拖完廚房地板，地還是溼的，所以暫時不要走進廚房。

(A) Oops. Let me do it for you. 對不起！我來幫你做。

(B) OK, I won't. 好，我不會。

(C) I left it on the kitchen table. 我把它留在廚房桌上。

* just 〔 dʒʌst 〕 *adv.* 剛剛   mop 〔 mɑp 〕 *v.* 拖 (地)
floor 〔 flɔr 〕 *n.* 地板   wet 〔 wɛt 〕 *adj.* 潮溼的
for a while 一陣子
oops 〔 ʊps 〕 *interj.* (表示驚訝、道歉等) 啊呀；對不起

10. (**A**) Would you like to see a movie this afternoon?

你今天下午想要去看電影嗎？

(A) Maybe. What's playing? 或許。正在上映的是什麼？

(B) We have several colors to choose from.
我們有幾個顏色可以選。

(C) There's not enough gas left in the tank.
油箱裡沒有足夠的油。

* *would like to V.* 想要~　　*see a movie* 看電影
maybe (ˈmebɪ) *adv.* 或許；可能　　play (ple) *v.* 播放；上映
several (ˈsɛvərəl) *adj.* 幾個的　　*there + be* 有~
gas (gæs) *n.* 汽油　　tank (tæŋk) *n.* 缸；油箱

第三部分：言談理解（第 11-21 題，共 11 題）

11. (**A**) W : Fall is my favorite time of year.
　　　　女：秋天是我一年中最喜歡的時候。

　　　　M : Mine, too. The weather is cool and we don't need to use the air conditioner anymore.
　　　　男：我也是。天氣很涼爽，我們都不需要再使用冷氣。

　　　　W : Right. It saves a lot of money on electricity. Running the air conditioner during the summer is expensive.
　　　　女：沒錯。這樣可以省下很多電費。夏天開冷氣很貴。

　　　　M : I'm glad I don't have to pay the bills at home, that's for sure.
　　　　男：我很高興我不用付家裡的帳單，那是毫無疑問的。

　　　　Question : How do the speakers feel about the seasons?
　　　　這些說話者對於季節感到如何？

　　　　(A) They like autumn the best. 他們最喜歡秋天。

　　　　(B) They prefer warmer months. 他們喜歡溫暖的月份。

　　　　(C) They love it when it snows. 他們喜歡下雪的時候。

* fall〔fɔl〕*n.* 秋天　　favorite〔'fevərɪt〕*n.* 最喜愛的
air conditioner〔ɛr kən'dɪʃənə〕*n.* 空調設備；冷氣機
right〔raɪt〕*interj.* 對；沒錯　　save〔sev〕*v.* 節省
electricity〔ɪ,lɛk'trɪsətɪ〕*n.* 電　　run〔rʌn〕*v.* 開動（機器）
bill〔bɪl〕*n.* 帳單　　*for sure* 肯定的；毫無疑問的
season〔'sizn̩〕*n.* 季節　　autumn〔'ɔtəm〕*n.* 秋季
love it when S + V. 喜歡～的時候【it 為虛受詞，代替後面 when 的
名詞子句】　　snow〔sno〕*v.* 下雪

12. (**C**)　M：Do you have any exercise equipment at home?
　　　　　男：妳家裡有什麼運動器材嗎？
　　　　　W：We have a treadmill, but I rarely use it.
　　　　　女：我們有跑步機，但我很少使用它。
　　　　　M：Why is that?
　　　　　男：為什麼？
　　　　　W：If I need some exercise, I'd rather be outdoors in the
　　　　　　　fresh air.
　　　　　女：如果我要運動，我寧可在戶外有新鮮空氣的地方。
　　　　　Question：Where does the woman prefer to exercise?
　　　　　　　　　　這個女士運動時的偏好是什麼？
　　　　　(A) At the gym. 在健身房。
　　　　　(B) At home on the treadmill. 在家裡的跑步機上。
　　　　　(C) Outdoors. 在戶外。

* exercise〔'ɛksə,saɪz〕*n. v.* 運動
equipment〔ɪ'kwɪpmənt〕*n.* 設備
treadmill〔'trɛd,mɪl〕*n.* 跑步機
rarely〔'rɛrlɪ〕*adv.* 不常；很少　　use〔juz〕*v.* 使用
would rather V. 寧可～　　outdoors〔'aut'dɔrz〕*adv.* 在戶外
fresh〔frɛʃ〕*adj.* 新鮮的　　*in the fresh air* 在有新鮮空氣的地方
prefer〔prɪ'fɝ〕*v.* 偏好　　gym〔dʒɪm〕*n.* 體育館；健身房

13. (**B**) M : What are you reading, Fiona?

男：費歐娜，妳在讀什麼？

W : It's a novel by a Japanese writer, and I have to say, it's really good.

女：是一個日本作家寫的小說，而且我必須要說，這真的很好看。

M : Oh, which writer?

男：噢，哪位作家？

W : Haruki Murakami.

女：村上春樹。

M : I'm a big fan of his work, too. Have you read *The Wind-Up Bird Chronicle*?

男：我也是他的超級書迷。妳有讀過《發條鳥年代記》嗎？

W : That's next on my list.

女：我書單的下一本就是它。

Question : What do the speakers have in common?

這些說話者的共同之處是？

(A) They both like the same kind of movies.

他們喜歡同種類的電影。

(B) They like the same author. 他們喜歡相同的作家。

(C) They both like Korean pop music.

他們都喜歡韓國的流行樂。

* novel〔ˋnɑvḷ〕*n.* 小說　　Japanese〔͵dʒæpəˋniz〕*adj.* 日本的

I have to say （用於強調）我必須說

oh〔o〕*interj.* （表示驚訝、恐懼等）啊；哎呀

Haruki Murakami 村上春樹【日本小說家、美國文學翻譯家】

fan〔fæn〕*n.* 粉絲；迷　　work〔wɝk〕*n.* 工作；作品

wind-up〔ˋwaɪnd͵ʌp〕*adj.* 上發條的；用手柄操作的

chronicle〔ˋkrɑnɪkḷ〕*n.* 年代記　　list〔lɪst〕*n.* 一覽表；清單

have sth. in common 有共同之處　　author〔'ɔθə 〕*n.* 作者
Korean〔ko'riən 〕*adj.* 韓國的　　*pop music* 流行樂

14. (**B**)　W：Hi, I saw the advertisement for your one-bedroom apartment on Pine Street.　And I was wondering if it has an updated kitchen or not.

女：嗨，我看到你在松樹街的單人房公寓出租廣告。我在想這間公寓的廚房是否是新的。

M：As a matter of fact, the kitchen was just renovated last year.　However, it's quite small and there's not a lot of counter space.　I can arrange to meet and show you the place today if you'd like.

男：事實上，這個廚房去年才翻修過。不過，它有點小，流理台空間不大。如果妳想要的話，我今天可以安排帶看。

W：Thanks.　I'd definitely like to check it out.

女：謝謝。我當然想來看一看。

Question：What is the purpose of the woman's call?

這個女士來電的目的是什麼？

(A) To place an ad. 登廣告。

(B) To get information. 獲得資訊。

(C) To complain. 抱怨。

* advertisement〔ˌædvə'taɪzmənt〕*n.* 廣告
apartment〔ə'pɑrtmənt〕*n.* 公寓　　pine〔paɪn〕*n.* 松樹
wonder〔'wʌndə 〕*v.* 考慮；想
update〔ʌp'det〕*v.* 更新　　*as a matter of fact* 事實上
renovate〔'rɛnəˌvet〕*v.* 翻修；翻新
counter〔'kaʊntə 〕*n.* 櫃台；廚房流理台
space〔spes〕*n.* 空間　　arrange〔ə'rendʒ〕*v.* 安排
would like 想要　　definitely〔'dɛfənɪtlɪ〕*adv.* 絕對地；無疑地

check out 看一看　purpose〔ˋpɝpəs〕n. 目標
place〔ples〕v. 放；刊登（廣告）
ad〔æd〕n. 廣告（= advertisement）
information〔ˏɪnfɚˋmeʃən〕n. 資訊
complain〔kəmˋplen〕v. 抱怨

15. (**C**) W : The pizza is so tasty. Aren't you having any?

女：這披薩好好吃。你不吃一些嗎？

M : No, it looks great, but I'm on a diet. Pizza is full of carbohydrates and fat.

男：不了，它看來很好吃，但我在節食。披薩有很多碳水化合物及脂肪。

W : You're on a diet? What for? You're not fat. In fact, if anybody needs to go on a diet, it's me.

女：你在節食嗎？為什麼？你不胖啊。實際上，如果真有人要節食，那個人應該是我。

M : I don't know. You look fine to me.

男：我不太清楚。我覺得妳看起來很好啊。

W : I could stand to lose at least five kilos.

女：我可以再瘦至少五公斤。

Question : What is true about the man?

關於這位男士，何者為真？

(A) He has lost weight recently.　他最近體重減少。

(B) He has gained weight recently.　他最近體重增加。

(C) He is on a diet.　他在節食。

* pizza〔ˋpitsə〕n. 披薩　　tasty〔ˋtestɪ〕adj. 好吃
on a diet 節食　　**be full of** 充滿
carbohydrate〔ˏkɑrboˋhaɪdret〕n. 碳水化合物
fat〔fæt〕n. 脂肪

> *I don't know* 我不清楚；我不敢確定
> stand〔stænd〕*v.* 接受；忍受　　*at least* 至少
> kilo〔'kɪlo〕*n.* 公斤（= *kilogram*）
> *lose weight* 減重　　recently〔'risn̩tlɪ〕*adv.* 最近
> *gain weight* 增重

16. (**A**) M : Where did you go last night? You missed the birthday
cake, and it was delicious.

　　男：妳昨晚去哪了？妳錯過了生日蛋糕，而且這蛋糕很好吃。

W : I wasn't feeling well, so I went home. Sorry I didn't
say goodbye.

　　女：我當時覺得不舒服，所以回家去了。很抱歉我沒有說再見。

M : That's OK. We missed you, though. Are you feeling
better now?

　　男：沒關係。不過我們很想妳。妳現在覺得比較好了嗎？

W : Yes, much better.

　　女：是，好多了。

Question : Where did the man go last night?

　　　　　這位男士昨晚去了哪裡？

(A) To a party. 去一個派對。

(B) To work. 去工作。

(C) Home. 家裡。

* miss〔mɪs〕*v.* 錯過；想念　　well〔wɛl〕*adj.* 健康的
　though〔ðo〕*adv.* 不過
　much〔mʌtʃ〕*adv.*（修飾比較級）更加
　party〔'pɑrtɪ〕*n.* 派對

17. (**B**) M : I'm going to the post office to mail this package. Do
you need anything while I'm out?

男：我正要去郵局寄這個包裹。我外出的時候，妳有需要什麼東西嗎？

W : Yes, would you stop by the dry cleaners and pick up my dress for the party tonight? Here's the claim ticket.

女：有，你可以順道去乾洗店拿我今晚派對的洋裝嗎？領取收據在這。

M : No problem. Anything else?

男：沒問題。還有其他東西嗎？

W : No, thank you.

女：沒有了，謝謝你。

Question : What will the man do at the post office?

　　　　　這個男士在郵局可能會做什麼？

(A) Drop off his laundry. 送他的送洗衣物。

(B) Mail a package. 寄一個包裹。

(C) Accept a delivery. 收件。

* ***post office*** 郵局　　mail〔mel〕*v.* 郵寄
　package〔'pækɪdʒ〕*n.* 包裹　　***stop by*** 順道拜訪
　dry cleaners 乾洗店　　***pick up*** 拿
　dress〔drɛs〕*n.* 洋裝　　claim〔klem〕*n.* 要求
　claim ticket 憑證；領回票　　***drop off*** 送（東西）到
　laundry〔'lɔndrɪ〕*n.* 送洗衣物　　accept〔ək'sɛpt〕*v.* 接受
　delivery〔dɪ'lɪvərɪ〕*n.* 運送；遞送的物品

18. (**A**) M : Beth, would you like to go to the International Flower Show downtown? Some friends and I are planning to go this Saturday. I hear they have a lot of displays from around the world and even a few musical performances are scheduled throughout the day.

男：貝絲，妳想要去市中心的國際花卉展嗎？我跟我一些朋友
計畫這星期六要去。我聽說他們有很多從世界各地來的展
示品，而且那天甚至有排定一些音樂表演。

W : I'd love to, Jim. A lot of people told me they've
enjoyed the show this year. In fact, my neighbor said
it gets really crowded. Why don't we try to get there
early?

女：我想去，吉姆。很多人跟我說他們很喜歡今年的這個展覽。
事實上，我鄰居說那邊真的很擠。我們何不早一點去那邊？

M : Let's take the 8:00 train on Saturday morning. Also,
I'll search the Internet to see if I can find some
discounts for the show. There are usually some
coupons online.

男：我們搭週六早上八點的火車去吧。並且，我會搜尋網路看
是否能找到展覽的折扣。通常網路上都會有一些折價卷。

Question : Why do Beth and Jim want to get to the event
early?　為什麼貝絲與吉姆想要早點去這場活動？

(A) They want to avoid crowds. 他們想要避開人潮。

(B) They will set up a booth. 他們將會擺攤。

(C) Train fares are cheaper in the morning.
火車票早上比較便宜。

* ***would like to V.*** 想要～（ = *would love to* ）
international〔͵ɪntɚˈnæʃən!〕*adj.* 國際的
downtown〔͵daʊnˈtaʊn〕*adv.* 在市中心　　plan〔plæn〕*v.* 計畫
display〔dɪˈsple〕*n.* 展示品；展示
around the world 全世界　　musical〔ˈmjuzɪk!〕*adj.* 音樂的
performance〔pɚˈfɔrməns〕*n.* 表演
schedule〔ˈskɛdʒul〕*v.* 排定
throughout〔θruˈaʊt〕*prep.* 在…期間

enjoy〔ɪnˋdʒɔɪ〕*v.* 享受；喜歡　　***in fact*** 事實上

neighbor〔ˋnebɚ〕*n.* 鄰居　　crowded〔ˋkraʊdɪd〕*adj.* 擁擠的

also〔ˋɔlso〕*adv.* 此外　　search〔sɝtʃ〕*v.* 搜尋

discount〔ˋdɪskaʊnt〕*n.* 折扣　　coupon〔ˋkupɑn〕*n.* 折價券

online〔͵ɑnˋlaɪn〕*adv.* 網路上　　event〔ɪˋvɛnt〕*n.* 大型活動

avoid〔əˋvɔɪd〕*v.* 避免；避開

crowd〔kraʊd〕*n.* 群眾　　***set up*** 建立；架設

booth〔buθ〕*n.* 攤位　　fare〔fɛr〕*n.* 車費

19.（**B**）M：Do you use any social media websites?

男：妳有在使用任何社交媒體網站嗎？

W：I have an account on GoChat, but otherwise, no.

女：我有一個 GoChat 的帳號，但其他的都沒有。

M：Really? What about Facelook? Everybody uses that one.

男：真的嗎？那臉書呢？每個人都在用那一個。

W：No, I'm not interested in Facelook. Isn't that the site where everybody posts pictures of what they had for dinner?

女：沒有，我對臉書沒興趣。那網站不就是讓每個人放上他們晚餐吃什麼的照片嗎？

M：(*laughs*) Yeah. A lot of people are really into that.

男：（笑）對。很多人很愛這樣。

Question：How does the woman feel about the Facelook website? 這位女士覺得臉書這網站怎麼樣？

(A) She loves it. 她喜歡它。

(B) She has no use for it. 她不喜歡它。

(C) She has no opinion of it. 她對臉書沒有意見。

* social〔ˋsoʃəl〕*adj.* 社交的　　media〔ˋmidɪə〕*n.* 媒體

website (ˈwɛbˌsaɪt) *n.* 網站　　account (əˈkaʊnt) *n.* 帳號

chat (tʃæt) *n.* 聊天

otherwise (ˈʌðəˌwaɪz) *adv.* 不然的話；除此之外

What about…? …如何？　　site (saɪt) *n.* 網站

post (post) *v.* 張貼；公布　　laugh (læf) *v.* (出聲) 笑

yeah (jæ) *adv.* 是的 (= *yes*)

into (ˈɪntʊ) *prep.* 對…有興趣　　use (juz) *n.* 使用

have no use for 不喜歡 (= *dislike*)

opinion (əˈpɪnjən) *n.* 意見

20. (**B**) W：What do you usually order for breakfast?

女：你早餐通常點什麼？

M：Just some wheat toast and a cup of fruit.

男：就一些小麥烤吐司及一杯果汁。

W：Wow, that's not really a full meal. You eat like a bird.

女：哇，這真說不上是很豐盛的一餐。你吃得真少。

Question：What does the woman mean?

這位男士意味什麼？

(A) He has a large appetite. 他的食量很大。

(B) He hardly eats anything. 他幾乎沒吃任何東西。

(C) He is overweight. 他體重過重。

* order (ˈɔrdə) *v.* 點 (餐)　　wheat (wit) *n.* 小麥

toast (tost) *n.* 烤吐司

wow (waʊ) *interj.* (表示驚訝、喜悅、痛苦等) 哇

full (fʊl) *adj.* 塞滿的；豐盛的　　meal (mil) *n.* 餐

eat like a bird 吃得很少　　mean (min) *v.* 意思是

large (lɑrdʒ) *adj.* 大的　　appetite (ˈæpəˌtaɪt) *n.* 胃口；食慾

hardly (ˈhɑrdlɪ) *adv.* 幾乎不

overweight (ˌovəˈwet) *adj.* 體重過重的

21. (**C**) Being nervous about starting college is probably the most normal thing any new college student can do. Your anxiety is a sign that you are already interested in doing well. Additionally, rest assured that most of your fears will probably go away after your first few weeks and that, even if they don't, there's always something you can do to change things.

對於開始大學生活感到緊張可能是最正常現象,這是任何大學新生都會的。你的焦慮顯示你很想要把大學讀好。此外,請放心,大部分你的恐懼,可能在剛開始的幾星期後就會消失,而且即使沒有消失,你總是可以做些事情來改變情況。

Question：Who is the speaker most likely talking to?
這位說話者最可能是在對誰說話?

(A) New employees. 新的員工。

(B) High school freshmen. 高中一年級新生。

(C) Incoming college students. <u>將入學的大學生。</u>

* nervous (ˋnɝvəs) *adj.* 緊張的
  college (ˋkɑlɪdʒ) *n.* 學院;大學
  probably (ˋprɑbəblɪ) *adv.* 可能地
  normal (ˋnɔrml̩) *adj.* 正常的
  anxiety (æŋˋzaɪətɪ) *n.* 焦慮   sign (saɪn) *n.* 跡象
  be interested in 對…感興趣   **do well** 表現好
  additionally (əˋdɪʃənl̩ɪ) *adv.* 此外 (= *besides*)
  rest (rɛst) *v.* 休息;放心
  assured (əˋʃʊrd) *adj.* 有把握的;確信的
  rest assured 放心;確信無疑   fear (fɪr) *n.* 恐懼;害怕
  go away 離開;消失   **even if** 即使
  things (θɪŋz) *n. pl.* 情況   likely (ˋlaɪklɪ) *adv.* 可能地
  employee (ɪmˋplɔɪi) *n.* 雇員;員工
  freshman (ˋfrɛʃmən) *n.* 新鮮人;一年級生
  incoming (ˋɪnkʌmɪŋ) *adj.* 即將到達的

TEST 2 詳解

聽力測驗（第 1-21 題，共 21 題）

第一部分：辨識句意（第 1-3 題，共 3 題）

1. (**B**) (A)  (B)  (C)

Jimmy is having lunch by himself. 吉米自己吃午餐。

* have〔hæv〕*v.* 吃　　*by oneself* 獨自地

2. (**C**) (A)  (B)  (C)

Mr. Thomas is a teacher. 湯瑪斯先生是個老師。

3. (**B**) (A)  (B)  (C)

Every Sunday, the Smith family gets together for dinner, where they sit around the table and everyone talks about what they did in the previous week.

每個星期天，史密斯一家人聚在一起吃晚餐，大家圍著桌子坐成一圈，然後每個人談論著他們上一週做了什麼事。

* **get together** 相聚　　previous〔'privɪəs〕adj. 之前的

第二部分：基本問答（第 4-10 題，共 7 題）

4. (**A**) Why did you call the electrician? 你為何打電話給電工？

(A) Because a light fixture is broken.

<u>因為有一個照明裝置壞了。</u>

(B) At 9:30. 在九點半。

(C) Nelson will do it. 尼爾森會做這件事。

* electrician〔ɪ͵lɛk'trɪʃən〕n. 電工　　light〔laɪt〕n. 光；電燈
fixture〔'fɪkstʃɚ〕n. 裝置　　broken〔'brokən〕adj. 壞掉的

5. (**A**) Did you remember to lock the front door when we left?
你有記得在我們離開的時候鎖上前門嗎？

(A) No, I forgot all about it. <u>不，我完全忘了。</u>

(B) Yes, I told them yesterday. 是的，我昨天告訴他們了。

(C) I don't remember his name. 我不記得他的名字。

* remember〔rɪ'mɛmbɚ〕v. 記得　　lock〔lɑk〕v. 鎖上
forget〔fɚ'gɛt〕v. 忘記　　front〔frʌnt〕adj. 前面的

6. (**C**) Are you ready to order, sir? 先生，請問您準備好要點餐了嗎？

(A) Maybe you should start without him.

也許你應該不用管他直接開始。

(B) They are waiting for another table.

他們在等另一張桌子空出來。

(C) Give me another minute. <u>再給我一點時間吧。</u>

* order〔'ɔrdɚ〕v. 點餐　　minute〔'mɪnɪt〕n. 分鐘；片刻

7. (**A**) If you're not busy this weekend, maybe we could hang out.
如果你這個週末不忙的話，也許我們可以出去晃晃。

(A) I'm going out of town this weekend.
我這週末要出城一趟。

(B) The line is always busy. 電話總是忙線中。

(C) I did it yesterday. 我昨天就做了。

* maybe〔'mebi〕*adv.* 或許；可能　　***hang out*** 閒晃；逗留
out of town 出城　　line〔laɪn〕*n.* 電話線；電話

8. (**B**) We're pooling our money together to buy a birthday gift for Tom. Would you like to contribute?
我們要一起集資為湯姆買一個生日禮物。你想要提供一點嗎？

(A) Almost. 幾乎。　　(B) Sure. 當然。

(C) He's over there. 他在那邊。

* pool〔pul〕*v.* 共同出（資）　　***would like to V.*** 想要～
contribute〔kən'trɪbjut〕*v.* 提供；貢獻　　***over there*** 在那裡

9. (**B**) How busy are you this week? 你這個禮拜有多忙啊？

(A) Yes, of course I am. 是的，我當然是。

(B) Very, I have four exams. 非常忙，我有四個考試。

(C) I left a message anyway. 不管怎樣我留言了。

* ***of course*** 當然　　exam〔ɪg'zæm〕*n.* 考試
message〔'mɛsɪdʒ〕*n.* 口信；傳話　　***leave a message*** 留言
anyway〔'ɛnɪ,we〕*adv.* 不管怎樣；無論如何

10. (**B**) Good luck with basketball tryouts tomorrow, Robert. I really hope you make the team. 祝你明天的的籃球選拔賽好運，羅伯特。我真的很希望你能被選入隊伍。

(A) Anytime. 隨時。　　(B) Thanks! 謝謝！

(C) I'm sorry. 我很抱歉。

* ***good luck*** 祝好運　　tryout〔'traɪ,aut〕*n.* 選拔賽
make〔mek〕*v.* 成為…的一員；加入
make the team 被選入隊伍　　anytime〔'ɛnɪ,taɪm〕*adv.* 任何時候

第三部分：言談理解（第 11-21 題，共 11 題）

11. (**B**) W : Since you're going out, would it be possible for you to give me a ride to the library?

女：既然你要出去，你有可能順便載我一程去圖書館嗎？

M : No problem.　Do you mind if we stop and pick up Tony first?　We're going to the game together.

男：沒問題。妳介意我們先停下來接湯尼嗎？我們要一起去看比賽。

W : I don't mind at all.　I'm not in a rush and you're doing me a big favor.

女：我一點都不介意。我並不趕，而且你幫了我一個大忙。

Question : What will the man do?　這位男士將要做什麼？

(A) Give the woman a ride to work.　順路載這個女士去工作。

(B) Give the woman a ride to the library.
　　順路載這個女士去圖書館。

(C) Give the woman a ride to the game.
　　順路載這個女士去比賽。

* since〔sɪns〕*conj.* 既然；因為　　possible〔'pasəbḷ〕*adj.* 可能的
  give sb. a ride 載某人一程　　library〔'laɪˌbrɛrɪ〕*n.* 圖書館
  No problem. 沒問題。　　mind〔maɪnd〕*v.* 介意
  pick up sb. 接某人　　**not…at all** 一點也不…
  in a rush 趕時間　　**do sb. a big favor** 幫某人一個大忙

12. (**A**) W : Dave, I think a customer must've knocked into the orange juice display in aisle 2.　Several bottles fell down and there's juice all over the floor.　It's a real mess.

女：戴夫，我認為有個顧客一定是撞倒了第二條走道陳列的柳橙汁。好幾個瓶子掉下來，而且那裡的地板到處都是果汁。真的是一團糟。

M : Again?　I'll be there in a moment.　I'm just going to get a mop and a bucket from the supply closet.

男：又來了嗎？我會馬上過去。我先去儲物櫃拿拖把和水桶。

W : All right. And after you finishing cleaning up, maybe we should move that display so that people don't keep hitting it with their shopping carts.

女：好的。然後在你清理完以後，也許我們應該把陳列品移開，這樣顧客才不會一直用購物車去撞到。

Question : What is the problem? 有什麼問題？

(A) Some bottles have broken. 有些瓶子破了。

(B) Some prices are marked incorrectly. 有些價格被標錯了。

(C) An employee has not arrived at work.
有一位員工沒來工作。

* customer (ˈkʌstəmə) n. 顧客   *must have + p.p.* 當時一定
  knock into 撞倒   *orange juice* 柳橙汁
  display (dɪˈsple) n. 展示；陳列   aisle (aɪl) n. 走道
  bottle (ˈbatḷ) n. 瓶子   *fell down* 掉落【fall down 的過去式】
  all over 遍及；到處   floor (flor) n. 地板
  mess (mɛs) n. 混亂   *in a moment* 立刻
  mop (map) n. 拖把   bucket (ˈbʌkɪt) n. 水桶
  supply (səˈplaɪ) n. 供應   closet (ˈklazɪt) n. 櫥櫃
  all right 就這樣吧；好的   *clean up* 清理
  cart (kart) n. 手推車   *shopping cart* 購物車
  mark (mark) v. 標示   incorrectly (ˌɪnkəˈrɛktlɪ) adv. 錯誤地
  employee (ɪmˈplɔɪ-i) n. 員工   arrive (əˈraɪv) v. 抵達

13. (**A**) W : Is that Mr. Evans waiting for the bus? We should ask him if he wants a ride.

女：那是埃文斯先生在等公車嗎？我們應該問他想不想搭便車。

M : I don't know him. Do you?

男：我不認識他。妳認識？

W : Of course! He's my next-door neighbor.

女：當然！他是住我隔壁的鄰居。

M : OK, I'll pull over. Roll down the window and call him over.

男：好的，我會靠路邊停車。把車窗搖下來然後叫他過來吧。

Question：Where are the speakers? 說話者在哪裡？

(A) In a car. 在車子裡。　　(B) On a train. 在火車上。

(C) On the bus. 在公車上。

* Evans (ˈɛvənz) *n.* 埃文斯　　***wait for*** 等待
  ride (raɪd) *n.* 搭乘；便車　　next-door *adj.* 鄰家的；隔壁的
  neighbor (ˈnebɚ) *n.* 鄰居　　***pull over*** 靠邊停車
  roll down 搖下　　***call sb. over*** 把某人叫過來

14. (**C**) M : Hi, I was a member of Cosmos Gym back in Vancouver before I moved down here last month. Is it possible to transfer my membership to this one here in Orlando?

男：嗨，我上個月還在溫哥華的時候，也就是我南下搬到這裡以前，是宇宙健身房的會員。請問我有可能將我的會員資格轉移到奧蘭多的這一家嗎？

W : Oh, all the Cosmo Gym locations share the membership database. So updating your information is really easy. Do you have your membership card with you?

女：啊，會員的資料庫是所有宇宙健身房的據點都共享的。所以要更新你的資料很簡單。你有帶會員卡嗎？

M : Here it is. I'm so relieved. I was afraid I had to purchase a whole membership.

男：在這裡。我真的是鬆了一口氣。我很害怕我必須要購買整個會員資格。

W : Well, as a Worldwide Gym member, you are welcome in our gyms wherever they are. In fact, if you give me your new address, I can issue you a new card.

女：嗯，作為一個全球性的健身房會員，歡迎你到任何一家我們的健身房。事實上，如果你把你的新住址給我們的話，我可以發給你一張新卡。

Question：What did the man recently do?
這位男士最近做了什麼事？

(A) He telephoned a local gym. 他打電話給當地的健身房。

(B) He lost his identification badge. 他搞丟了他的識別證。

(C) He moved to a new city. <u>他搬到一個新城市。</u>

* member〔'mɛmbə〕*n.* 會員　　cosmos〔'kɑzməs〕*n.* 宇宙
　gym〔dʒɪm〕*n.* 健身房
　Vancouver〔væn'kuvə〕*n.* 溫哥華【位於加拿大西南部】
　transfer〔transfə〕*v.* 轉移
　membership〔'mɛmbə,ʃɪp〕*n.* 會員資格
　Orlando〔ɔr'lændo〕*n.* 奧蘭多【美國佛羅里達州中部】
　oh〔o〕*interj.*（表示驚訝、恐懼等）啊；哎呀
　location〔lo'keʃən〕*n.* 地點；據點　　share〔ʃɛr〕*v.* 共享
　database〔'detə,bes〕*n.* 資料庫　　update〔ʌp'det〕*v.* 更新
　information〔,ɪnfə'meʃən〕*n.* 情報；資訊
　relieved〔rɪ'livd〕*adj.* 放心的　　afraid〔ə'fred〕*adj.* 害怕的
　have to V. 必須~　　purchase〔'pɝtʃəs〕*v.* 購買
　whole〔hol〕*adj.* 全部的　　well〔wɛl〕*interj.* 嗯　　***in fact*** 事實上
　address〔'ædrɛs, ə'drɛs〕*n.* 地址　　issue〔'ɪʃu〕*v.* 發行
　recently〔'risn̩tlɪ〕*adv.* 最近　　local〔'lokl̩〕*adj.* 當地的
　identification〔aɪ,dɛntəfə'keʃən〕*n.* 身份證明
　badge〔bædʒ〕*n.* 徽章；證章
　identification badge 身份識別卡　　move〔muv〕*v.* 搬家

15. (**C**)　W：So, Andy, what do you think of the play so far?
　　　女：所以，安迪，到目前為止你覺得這場戲如何？
　　　M：Oh, I think it's been fantastic so far. I'm glad that we
　　　　　were able to get tickets at the last minute. This has
　　　　　always been one of my favorite plays and actors are
　　　　　doing an excellent job.
　　　男：噢，我認為到目前為止非常棒。我很開心我們能夠在最後一
　　　　　刻買到票。這一直都是我最喜歡的其中一場戲，而且演員都
　　　　　表現得非常好。
　　　W：I agree. And this is the first time I've been here since
　　　　　the theater's been redone. I'm really impressed. I
　　　　　hardly recognized the place.

女：我同意。而且這是我從戲院重新裝修後第一次來，我真的很
　　感動。我幾乎認不出這個地方。

M : Well, we'd better get back to our seats. The second
act is about to start.

男：嗯，我們最好回到我們的座位上。第二幕即將要開始了。

Question : What will the speakers probably do next?
說話者接下來最可能做什麼？

(A) Purchase tickets. 買票。

(B) Check a schedule. 確認行程。

(C) Return to their seats. <u>回到他們的座位。</u>

* so〔so〕adv. (用作話頭) 所以；確實
  What do you think of…? 你覺得…如何？
  play〔ple〕n. 戲；演劇　　***so far*** 到目前為止
  fantastic〔fæn'tæstɪk〕adj. 很棒的　　glad〔glæd〕adj. 高興的
  be able to V. 能夠～　　get〔gɛt〕v. 拿到；買到
  ticket〔'tɪkɪt〕n. 票；入場券　　***at the last minute*** 在最後一刻
  favorite〔'fevərɪt〕adj. 最喜愛的　　actor〔'æktɚ〕n. 演員
  excellent〔'ɛkslənt〕adj. 優異的　　agree〔ə'gri〕v. 同意
  redone〔ri'dʌn〕v. 重新修理【redo 的過去分詞】
  impressed〔ɪm'prɛst〕adj. 印象深刻的；感動的
  hardly〔'hardlɪ〕adv. 幾乎不　　recognize〔'rɛkəg,naɪz〕v. 認出
  had better… 最好…　　***get back to*** 回到　　seat〔sit〕n. 座位
  act〔ækt〕n. (戲劇的) 幕　　***be about to V.*** 即將～
  purchase〔'pɝtʃəs〕v. 買　　check〔tʃɛk〕v. 檢查；確認
  schedule〔'skɛdʒul〕n. 行程　　return〔rɪ'tɝn〕v. 回到

16. (**C**) W : Excuse me, is this where I get the city bus to the
airport?

女：不好意思，請問我可以在這裡搭到去機場的市區巴士嗎？

M : Yes, this is the right place. The bus is supposed to
run on the hour, but it's always late.

男：對，這裡沒錯。巴士應該要是一小時一班，但它總是遲到。

W : Oh, no. I can't be late today. This is my first day of
work at the airport hotel.

女：噢，不。我今天不能遲到。這是我第一天在機場的旅館上班。

M：Well, if you're worried about the time, you probably should take a taxi instead. Taxis come down the street every few minutes.

男：嗯，如果妳很擔心時間，你可能要改搭計程車。計程車每隔幾分鐘就會來到這街上。

Question：What is the woman concerned about?

這位女士在擔心什麼？

(A) Wearing appropriate clothes. 穿著合適的服裝。

(B) Missing a flight. 錯過班機。

(C) Being late to work. 上班遲到。

* ***excuse me*** 對不起【用於引起注意】　　get〔gɛt〕*v.* 乘坐
airport〔'ɛr,port〕*n.* 機場　　***be supposed to V.*** 應該~
run〔rʌn〕*v.*（交通工具）通行；行駛　　***on the hour*** 在整點
hotel〔ho'tɛl〕*n.* 旅館；飯店　　***be worried about*** 擔心
probably〔'prɑbəblɪ〕*adv.* 可能　　taxi〔'tæksɪ〕*n.* 計程車
instead〔ɪn'stɛd〕*adv.* 代替；改為　　***come down*** 來到附近
concerned〔kən'sɝnd〕*adj.* 擔心的（= *worried*）
appropriate〔ə'propɪɪt〕*adj.* 合適的
clothes〔kloz〕*n. pl.* 衣服　　miss〔mɪs〕*v.* 錯過
flight〔flaɪt〕*n.* 班機　　***be late to work*** 上班遲到

17. (**A**) Looking for something inexpensive and fun to do this weekend? Then join the KDJY Radio crew at the grand opening of Burgess Foster Art Center this Saturday. The new art center, which is located right across from the Hanberry Park, will be hosting a day of free plays and concerts. Plus, comedian Molly Flynn will give a special performance at 8:00 p.m. Unfortunately, tickets for Molly's popular comedy show have already sold out. But if you are one of the first ten listeners to call the station at 555-0154, you'll win a free pair. We're waiting for your call.

你正在尋找這週末有什麼不貴又有趣的事可以做嗎？那麼就加入 KDYJ 廣播組這週六在伯吉斯福斯特藝術中心的盛大開幕吧。這個新的藝術中心，就座落在漢百瑞公園的對面，將會舉行一整天免費的表演和音樂會。除此之外，喜劇演員茉莉·福林將在晚間八點會有一場特別的表演。遺憾的是，茉莉大受歡迎的喜劇門票已經售完。但如果你是前十位撥打 555-0154 到電台的聽眾，將可以獲得兩張免費的票。我們正在等待您的來電。

Question：Who is Molly Flynn? 誰是茉莉·福林？

(A) A comedian. 一位喜劇演員。

(B) A radio host. 一位電台主持人。

(C) An arts critic. 一位藝術評論家。

* **look for** 尋找
  inexpensive〔͵ɪnɪkˈspɛnsɪv〕adj. 不貴的；便宜的
  join〔dʒɔɪn〕v. 加入　　radio〔ˈredɪͺo〕n. 廣播
  crew〔kru〕n. 全體工作人員　　grand〔grænd〕adj. 盛大的
  opening〔ˈopənɪŋ〕n. 開幕　　art〔ɑrt〕n. 藝術
  center〔ˈsɛntɚ〕n. 綜合地區；中心　　**be located** 位於
  across from… 在…對面　　host〔host〕v. 舉行　n. 主持人
  free〔fri〕adj. 免費的　　play〔ple〕n. 戲；演劇
  concert〔ˈkɑnsɝt〕n. 音樂會；演唱會　　plus〔plʌs〕adv. 此外
  comedian〔kəˈmidɪən〕n. 喜劇演員　　give〔gɪv〕v. 給；呈現
  performance〔pɚˈfɔrməns〕n. 表演
  p.m. 午後（= post meridiem）
  unfortunately〔ʌnˈfɔrtʃənɪtlɪ〕adv. 不幸地；遺憾地
  ticket〔ˈtɪkɪt〕n. 票；入場券　　comedy〔ˈkɑmədɪ〕n. 喜劇
  already〔ɔlˈrɛdɪ〕adv. 已經　　**be sold out** 售完
  listener〔ˈlɪsnɚ〕n. 聽眾　　call〔kɔl〕v. 打電話給　n. 打電話
  station〔ˈsteʃən〕n. 電台　　pair〔pɛr〕n. 一對
  wait for 等待　　critic〔ˈkrɪtɪk〕n. 評論家

18. (**B**) Hello, this is Kimberly Hahn from Holden Law Associates. Last Monday, I made a luncheon reservation at your restaurant for some of our attorneys and clients. I requested a private room and selected the food for a

three-course meal. Well, I just learned that two of the guests are vegetarians, which means we have to add an appropriate meatless option to our menu selection. Since our office is just around the corner, I'd like to come over there around 4 o'clock this afternoon to discuss the changes. Please let me know if this will work for you.

哈囉，我是霍頓法律事務所的金柏莉・哈恩。上個星期一，我為我們的幾位律師和客戶預約了你們餐廳的午餐。我當時要求要一個私人包廂和選好了一套三道菜的餐點。嗯，我剛剛得知有兩位客戶是素食者，也就是說我們必須要增加一個適合的、沒有肉的選項到我們選定的菜單中。既然我們的辦公室就在附近，我想要在這個下午四點左右過去一趟討論這些變動。請讓我知道這對你是否方便。

Question : Where does Kimberly Hahn work?
請問金柏莉・韓在哪裡工作？

(A) At a hotel. 在一間飯店。

(B) At a law office. 在一間律師事務所。

(C) At a conference center. 在一個會議中心。

* ***this is*** (用於講電話) 我是　Kimberly ('kɪmbəlɪ) *n.* 金柏莉
Hahn (hɑn) *n.* 哈恩　Holden ('holdən) *n.* 霍頓
law (lɔ) *n.* 法律　associate (ə'soʃɪɪt) *n.* 伙伴；合作人
luncheon ('lʌntʃən) *n.* 午餐
reservation (,rɛzə'veʃən) *n.* 預約　attorney (ə'tɜnɪ) *n.* 律師
client ('klaɪənt) *n.* 客戶　request (rɪ'kwɛst) *v.* 要求；請求
private ('praɪvɪt) *adj.* 私人的　room (rum) *n.* 房間；包廂
select (sə'lɛkt) *v.* 選擇　course (kors) *n.* (菜的) 一道
mean (mil) *n.* 一餐　just (dʒʌst) *adv.* 剛剛；就
learn (lɜn) *v.* 得知　guest (gɛst) *n.* 客人；來賓
vegetarian (,vɛdʒə'tɛrɪən) *n.* 素食者　mean (min) *v.* 意思是
add (æd) *v.* 增加　appropriate (ə'proprɪɪt) *adj.* 合適的
meatless ('mitlɪs) *adj.* 無肉的　option ('ɑpʃən) *n.* 選擇
menu ('mɛnju) *n.* 菜單　selection (sɛ'lɛkʃən) *n.* 選擇
since (sɪns) *conj.* 既然；因為　***around the corner*** 在附近

would like to V. 想要～　　*come over* 過來；順便來訪
discuss〔dɪ'skʌs〕*v.* 討論　　work〔wɜk〕*v.* 行得通
office〔'ɔfɪs〕*n.* 辦公室；(律師) 事務所
conference〔'kɑnfərəns〕*n.* 會議

19. (**C**)　M：Helen, I just found out that our new intern will start
　　　　　　work on September 15. Isn't that when the fashion
　　　　　　shows take place in Milan? We will all be out of town.

　　　　男：海倫，我剛發現我們新的實習生會在九月十五號開始上班。
　　　　　　那不就是米蘭時裝秀舉行的時候嗎？我們將全都出城了。

　　　　W：You're right. You know, it'd be wonderful if we
　　　　　　could have him start at the beginning of September.
　　　　　　Do you think his start date could be changed?

　　　　女：沒錯。你知道嗎，如果我們可以叫他在九月初開始工作就太
　　　　　　完美了。你覺得他開始的日期有可能更改嗎？

　　　　M：Good idea. That way we could begin his training
　　　　　　before we leave.

　　　　男：好主意。那樣的話我們就可以在離開前開始訓練他了。

　　　　Question：Where will Helen be on September 15?
　　　　　　　　　請問海倫九月十五號時會在哪裡？

(A) At a store opening. 在一家店的開幕式。
(B) At a training session. 在一個培訓期間。
(C) At a fashion show. 在一場時裝秀。

* *find out* 發現；得知　　intern〔ɪn'tɜn〕*n.* 實習生
　start work 開工；上班　　fashion〔'fæʃən〕*n.* 時尚
　show〔ʃo〕*n.* 展示；表演　　*take place* 舉行
　Milan〔mɪ'læn〕*n.* 米蘭【義大利北部】　　*out of town* 出城
　You're right. 你說得對；沒錯。
　at the beginning of 在…之初　　date〔det〕*n.* 日期
　Good idea. 好注意。　　*that way* 那樣的話
　training〔'trenɪŋ〕*n.* 訓練　　opening〔'opənɪŋ〕*n.* 開幕
　session〔'sɛʃən〕*n.* 期間

20. (**B**) M : I'm going rock climbing tomorrow morning. Would
        you like to join me?

    男： 我明天早上要去攀岩。妳想要加入我一起去嗎？

    W : I've never been rock climbing before. It sounds
        dangerous. Where?

    女： 我從來沒有攀岩過。這聽起來很危險。在哪裡？

    M : There's a place in Walker Canyon with some fairly
        easy rock faces to scale. I'm just a beginner myself,
        so we won't be doing any difficult climbing.

    男： 在沃克峽谷有個地方，那裡有一些相當輕鬆的岩石表面可以
        攀登。我自己也只是一個初學者，所以我們不會做任何困難
        的攀岩。

    Question : What is true about the woman?

            關於這位女士何者為眞？

    (A) She has never been to Walker Canyon.

        她從沒去過沃克峽谷。

    (B) She has never been rock climbing. 她從來沒有攀岩過。

    (C) She is an expert mountaineer. 她是一個專業的登山者。

    * ***rock climbing*** 攀岩   ***would like to V.*** 想要～
        join〔dʒɔɪn〕*v.* 加入   sound〔saʊnd〕*v.* 聽起來
        dangerous〔'dendʒərəs〕*adj.* 危險的
        canyon〔'kænjən〕*n.* 峽谷   fairly〔'fɛrlɪ〕*adv.* 相當地
        face〔fes〕*n.* 表面   scale〔skel〕*v.* 攀登
        just〔dʒʌst〕*adv.* 只；僅僅   beginner〔bɪ'gɪnə〕*n.* 初學者
        difficult〔'dɪfə,kʌlt〕*adj.* 困難的
        have been to 去過   expert〔'ɛkspət〕*adj.* 專業的；熟練的
        mountaineer〔,maʊntn̩'ɪr〕*n.* 登山者

21. (**C**) Welcome to the Danforth House. I'm glad that you could
        join us today to learn about the life of James Danforth, a
        man considered by many to be one of the most influential
        writers of his time. This building was his home, the place

where he both lived and worked. On our tour, you'll see the actual desk where he worked, the books he read, and even his family portraits hanging on the walls. After we make our way through the house, we'll walk over to the auditorium next door. There we'll have a chance to see a movie about the author's life and career. Now, let's begin here in the dining area.

歡迎來到丹佛斯之家。我很高興您今天能夠加入我們一起學習關於詹姆士・丹佛斯的生平,他是一個被許多人認為在他的時期中最有影響力的一位作家。這棟建築是他的家,也是工作和生活的地方。在我們的導覽中,您會看到他實際工作時的桌子、他讀的書甚至是掛在牆上的家族肖像畫。在我們參觀完房子之後,我們會到隔壁的禮堂。在那裡我們將有機會看一部關於作者生平以及職業生涯的電影。現在,就讓我們從這裡的用餐區開始參觀起。

Question: Who was James Danforth? 誰是詹姆士・丹佛斯?

(A) An architect. 一個建築師。

(B) An actor. 一個演員。

(C) A writer. <u>一個作家。</u>

* Danforth ('dænfɔrθ) n. 丹佛斯　　glad (glæd) adj. 高興的
  learn about 學得;得知有關…的消息
  consider (kən'sɪdə) v. 認為
  influential (ˌɪnflʊ'ɛnʃəl) adj. 有影響力的
  writer ('raɪtə) n. 作家
  time (taɪm) n. (與某人有關的) 時期
  building ('bɪldɪŋ) n. 建築物　　tour (tʊr) n. 導覽;遊覽
  actual ('æktʃʊəl) adj. 實際的　　portait ('portret) n. 肖像畫
  hang (hæŋ) v. 掛　　***make*** one's ***way*** 前進
  through (θru) prep. 通過
  auditorium (ˌɔdə'toriəm) n. 禮堂
  next door 在隔壁　　author ('ɔθə) n. 作者
  career (kə'rɪr) n. 職業生涯　　dining ('daɪnɪŋ) 用餐
  area ('ɛrɪə) n. 區域　　architect ('arkəˌtɛkt) n. 建築師

TEST 3 詳解

聽力測驗（第 1-21 題，共 21 題）

第一部分：辨識句意（第 1-3 題，共 3 題）

1. (**A**) (A)  (B)  (C)

Oscar lives in a two-story house with a large garden in the front yard. 奧斯卡住在一間前院有大花園的兩層樓房裡。

* story〔'storɪ〕*n.* 樓層　　garden〔'gɑrdn̩〕*n.* 花園
large〔lɑrdʒ〕*adj.* 巨大的　　yard〔jɑrd〕*n.* 院子

2. (**C**) (A)  (B)  (C)

Steve left the house without an umbrella.
史蒂夫沒有帶雨傘就出門。

* left〔lɛft〕*v.* 離開【leave 的過去式】
without〔wɪð'aʊt〕*prep.* 沒有

3. (**B**) (A)  (B)  (C)

Some kids are playing near a small pond.

一些小孩正在一個小池塘旁邊玩耍。

* kid〔kɪd〕*n.* 小孩　　pond〔pɑnd〕*n.* 池塘

第二部分：基本問答（第 4-10 題，共 7 題）

4. (**A**) How long did the basketball game last?

這場籃球賽持續了多久？

(A) It didn't end until eleven. 直到十一點才結束。

(B) I'll update the results. 我會更新分數。

(C) There was someone in front of me. 有人在我前面。

* ***basketball game*** 籃球比賽　　last〔læst〕*v.* 持續
end〔ɛnd〕*v.* 結束　　until〔ən'tɪl〕*prep.* 直到
update〔ʌp'det〕*v.* 更新　　result〔rɪ'zʌlts〕*n. pl.* 分數；成績
in front of 在…的前面

5. (**C**) Would you like dessert or coffee? 你想要甜點或咖啡？

(A) He is nice enough. 他人夠好了。

(B) Is she certain? 她確定嗎？

(C) I'll have coffee. 我要喝咖啡。

* ***would like*** 想要　　dessert〔dɪ'zɝt〕*n.* 甜點
enough〔ə'nʌf〕*adv.* 足夠地
certain〔'sɝtn〕*adj.* 確定的（= *sure*）　　have〔hæv〕*v.* 吃；喝

6. (**B**) You have a doctor's appointment on Wednesday, don't you? 你星期三和醫生有個約診，不是嗎？

(A) Sorry, I'm late. 對不起，我遲到了。

(B) Yes, in the afternoon. 是的，在下午。

(C) He was just appointed. 他剛被任命。

* appointment〔ə'pɔɪntmənt〕*n.* 約診
appoint〔ə'pɔɪnt〕*v.* 指派；任命

7. (**B**) What do you want for lunch, Indian or Italian?

你午餐想吃什麼，印度菜或義大利菜？

(A) I've been there twice. 我曾經去那裡兩次。

(B) I'm in the mood for spaghetti. 我想要義大利麵。

(C) Let's watch it together. 我們一起看吧。

* Indian〔'ɪndɪən〕*adj.* 印度的
Italian〔ɪ'tæljən〕*adj.* 義大利的　　twice〔twaɪs〕*adv.* 兩次
in the mood for doing sth. 有心情做某事
spaghetti〔spə'gɛtɪ〕*n.* 義大利麵　　*Let's* ~ 一起 ~ 吧

8. (**C**) Where do you want me to put these groceries?

你想要把這些食品雜貨放在哪裡？

(A) At the wall. 放在牆上。

(B) On the phone. 講電話中。

(C) In the kitchen. 在廚房裡。

* groceries〔'grosərɪz〕*n. pl.* 食品雜貨　　*on the phone* 講電話

9. (**A**) When's the earliest you can meet for breakfast?

你最早可以何時見面吃早餐？

(A) A little before 7:00 a.m. 早上七點前再早一點點。

(B) Since 2002. 自從 2002 年。

(C) Tea and Toast. 茶和土司。

* earliest〔'ɝlɪst〕*adj.* 最早的　　meet〔mit〕*v.* 見面
breakfast〔'brɛkfəst〕*n.* 早餐
a.m. 午前；早上（= *ante meridiem*）　　toast〔tost〕*n.* 土司

10. (**C**) The concert has been postponed. 演唱會延期了。

(A) I still can't find my phone. How can I call him?
我仍然找不到我的電話。我該怎麼打給他？

(B) We had a good time. You should try it sometime.
我們玩得很愉快。你改天也該試試。

(C) Someone should tell Olivia. She was planning to go.
<u>有人應該去告訴奧莉薇亞。她之前有計畫要去。</u>

* concert〔ˈkɑnsɝt〕*n.* 演唱會；音樂會
postpone〔postˈpon〕*v.* 延後　　***have a good time*** 玩得愉快
sometime〔ˈsʌmˌtaɪm〕*adv.* 某天
Olivia〔oˈlɪvɪə〕*n.* 奧莉薇亞　　plan〔plæn〕*v.* 計畫；打算

第三部分：言談理解（第 11-21 題，共 11 題）

11. (**B**)　W : Excuse me, I believe you've given me the wrong meal. I asked the other flight attendant for the chicken, but this isn't chicken.

女：很抱歉，我相信你一定給錯餐了。我和另一位空服員要求雞肉，但這不是雞肉。

M : Oh, that's because I'm giving out the special orders. The passenger list showed that you requested a vegetarian meal when you made your reservation.

男：噢，這是因為我正在發送特殊的點餐。乘客名單上顯示當妳在預訂時，妳要求要素食餐。

W : No, I didn't order anything in advance. I'm sure of that because I just bought my ticket yesterday.

女：不，我沒有事先點任何東西。這點我很確定，因為我昨天才買機票。

M : I apologize for the confusion. I will recheck my list to find out who actually did request the vegetarian meal.

男：我很道歉造成混亂。我會重新確認我的名單去找出實際上是誰上真的要求了素食餐。

Question : What does the woman say she did yesterday?
　　　　　這位女士說她昨天做了什麼？

(A) Picked up her order. 領取她的訂貨。

(B) Purchased a ticket. 購買了機票。

(C) Reserved a room. 預定一個房間。

* **excuse me** 對不起【用於引起注意】
  believe〔bə'liv〕v. 相信；認為　　meal〔mil〕n. 一餐
  flight attendant 空服員　　**ask sb. for sth.** 向某人要求某事
  oh〔o〕interj.（表示驚訝、恐懼等）啊；噢
  give out 發出　　special〔'spɛʃəl〕adj. 特別的
  order〔'ɔrdɚ〕n. 點餐；訂購物　　passenger〔'pæsn̩dʒɚ〕n. 乘客
  list〔lɪst〕n. 列表；名單　　request〔rɪ'kwɛst〕v. 要求
  vegetarian〔͵vɛdʒə'tɛrɪən〕adj. 素食的
  reservation〔͵rɛzɚ'veʃən〕n. 預約；預定
  in advance 事先　　**be sure of** 確信…
  apologize〔ə'pɑlə͵dʒaɪz〕v. 道歉
  confusion〔kən'fjuʒən〕n. 混亂
  recheck〔rɪ'tʃɛk〕v. 重新檢查；再次確認　　**find out** 找出
  actually〔'æktʃʊəlɪ〕adv. 實際上　　**pick up** 獲得；取得
  purchase〔'pɝtʃəs〕v. 購買　　reserve〔rɪ'zɝv〕v. 保留；預定

12. (**B**) W : What do you want to do tonight?

女：你今晚想做什麼？

M : I don't know. There's nothing on television, and it's raining outside.

男：我不知道。電視沒什麼好看的，而且外面正在下雨。

W : How about watching a movie? I've got some new DVDs.

女：那看電影如何？我拿到了一些新的 DVD。

M : No, thanks. I'm in the mood to cozy up on the couch with a good book and a cup of tea.

男：不，謝謝。我想要舒適地靠在沙發上配一本好書和一杯茶。

W : Oh, I just bought some wonderful oolong tea from Taiwan. It's really fresh, too.

女：噢，我剛從台灣買了一些很棒的烏龍茶。它也真的很清新。

Question : Where are the speakers? 說話者在哪裡？

(A) At work. 在工作中。

(B) At home. 在家。

(C) Taking a walk. 正在散步。

* *How about ~ ?* ~如何？　　*in the mood to V.* 想要~
　cozy〔'kozɪ〕 *adj.* 舒適的
　cozy up 感到舒適（= *become more cozy*）
　couch〔kautʃ〕 *n.* 長沙發
　cozy up on the couch 舒適地靠在沙發上
　oolong〔'ulɔŋ〕 *n.* 烏龍茶　　fresh〔frɛʃ〕 *adj.* 清新的
　take a walk 散步

13. (**B**) M : Ms. Kennedy? This is Wally Sparks from Cooper
　　　　　Electrical. We're scheduled to service your central
　　　　　heating system tomorrow afternoon.

男：甘迺迪女士嗎？我是來自庫伯電力的沃利‧斯帕克斯。我們
　　安排明天下午要去維護您的中央暖氣系統。

W : Yes, that's correct. I'll be here to let you in.

女：是的，沒錯。我會在這裡讓你進門。

M : Well, you see, we have a scheduling conflict. As long
　　as it doesn't pose any inconvenience to you, would it
　　be possible for us to come in the morning instead?

男：嗯，您知道的，我們有個行程上的衝突。只要不會對您造成
　　任何不便，我們有可能改成早上過來嗎？

W : I don't think that would be a problem. In fact, that
　　works out better for me.

女：我不認為這會是一個問題。事實上，這樣做對我來說更好。

M : Great. See you tomorrow morning around nine
　　o'clock.

男：太棒了。明早大約九點見。

Question : Why did Wally Sparks call Ms. Kennedy?

爲什麼沃利・斯帕克斯打電話給甘迺迪女士？

(A) To suggest a solution to her problem.

爲了建議她一個問題的解決方案。

(B) To reschedule an appointment. 爲了重新安排一個約見。

(C) To sell her a new product. 爲了賣她一樣新產品。

* Ms〔mɪz〕 *n.* …女士　　Kennedy〔'kɛnədɪ〕 *n.* 甘迺迪
  This is…（用於講電話）我是…
  electrical〔ɪ'lɛktrɪkl̩〕 *adj.* 電力的
  schedule〔'skɛdʒul〕 *v.* 安排　　service〔'sɜvɪs〕 *v.* 維修
  central〔'sɛntrəl〕 *adj.* 中央的　　heating〔'hitɪŋ〕 *n.* 暖氣
  system〔'sɪstəm〕 *n.* 系統　　correct〔kə'rɛkt〕 *adj.* 正確的
  you see 你看；你知道　　scheduling〔'skɛdʒulɪŋ〕 *n.* 行程安排
  conflict〔'kɑnflɪkt〕 *n.* 衝突　　*as long as* 只要
  pose〔poz〕 *v.* 造成　　inconvenience〔ˌɪnkən'vinjəns〕 *n.* 不便
  possible〔'pɑsəbl̩〕 *adj.* 可能的　　instead〔ɪn'stɛd〕 *adv.* 改爲
  problem〔'prɑbləm〕 *n.* 問題　　*in fact* 事實上
  work out 發生；進展　　around〔ə'raʊnd〕 *prep.* 大約
  suggest〔səg'dʒɛst〕 *v.* 建議　　solution〔sə'luʃən〕 *n.* 解決方案
  reschedule〔ˌri'skɛdʒul〕 *v.* 重新安排
  appointment〔ə'pɔɪntmənt〕 *n.* 約見；約定
  product〔'prɑdəkt〕 *n.* 產品

14. (**C**) W : Hi, I'm writing an essay on the history of pharmacies. I know the library has old newspaper articles and photographs. Can I check those out, please?

女：嗨，我正在寫一篇關於藥房歷史的文章。我知道圖書館有舊的報紙文章和照片。請問我可以查看那些嗎？

M : Well, we do have all those newspaper articles in the library, but we keep photographs and other sensitive materials in a secure storage area to prevent damage.

男：嗯，我們圖書館的確有那些報紙文章，但是我們把照片和其他容易被破壞的素材保存在一個安全的儲放區內，以防止損壞。

W : I definitely would like to take a look at those photographs. Is there any way I can do that?

女：我真的想要看看那些照片。有任何方法可以讓我看嗎？

M : Sure, all you need to do is fill out this form. Once it's approved, we'll arrange to have the photographs shipped to us.

男：當然，妳需要做的就是填寫這張表格。一旦它被批准了，我們將會安排讓那些照片運送過來給我們。

Question : Where does the conversation take place?
　　　　 這段對話在哪裡發生？

(A) At a photography studio. 在一個攝影工作室。

(B) At a warehouse. 在一間倉庫。

(C) At a library. <u>在一間圖書館。</u>

* essay (ˈɛse) n. 文章　　on (ɑn) prep. 關於 (= about)
history (ˈhɪstrɪ) n. 歷史　　pharmacy (ˈfɑrməsɪ) n. 藥房
library (ˈlaɪˌbrɛrɪ) n. 圖書館　　newspaper (ˈnuzˌpepɚ) n. 報紙
article (ˈɑrtɪkl̩) n. 文章　　photograph (ˈfotəˌgræf) n. 照片
check sth. **out** 查看某物　　**do** + **V.** 真的～
sensitive (ˈsɛnsətɪv) adj. 敏感的；機密的；需妥善保管的
materials (məˈtɪrɪəlz) n. pl. 材料
secure (sɪˈkjur) adj. 安全的　　storage (ˈstorɪdʒ) n. 儲藏
area (ˈɛrɪə) n. 區域　　prevent (prɪˈvɛnt) v. 預防
damage (ˈdæmɪdʒ) n. 損害
definitely (ˈdɛfənɪtlɪ) adv. 確實地　　**would like to V.** 想要～
all one **need to do is** + **V.** 某人所需要做的就是～
take a look at 看一看　　**fill out** 填寫　　form (form) n. 表格
once (wʌns) conj. 一旦　　approve (əˈpruv) v. 核可；批准
arrange (əˈrendʒ) v. 安排　　ship (ʃɪp) v. 運送
conversation (ˌkɑnvɚˈseʃən) n. 對話

take place 發生　　photography〔fə'tɑgrəfɪ〕*n.* 攝影
studio〔'stjudɪ,o〕*n.* 工作室　　warehouse〔'wɛr,haʊs〕*n.* 倉庫

15. (**A**) Cats are easy pets to care for. Unlike dogs, cats don't need a lot of exercise. The best way to keep your cat happy and healthy is to keep it well-fed. Cats like fresh food and prefer to follow a routine. Don't make big changes to their food or feeding schedule.

貓是很容易照顧的寵物。不像狗，貓不需要很多運動。要使你的貓咪開心和健康，最好的辦法就是使牠在餵飽的狀態。貓喜歡新鮮的食物，並偏好遵循慣例。不要在牠們的食物或是餵食行程表上做出巨大的改變。

Question：Which of the following is NOT needed to keep your cat happy and healthy?

以下哪一點在保持貓咪開心和健康上並不需要？

(A) Daily exercise. <u>日常運動。</u>

(B) Fresh food. 新鮮的食物。

(C) A regular feeding schedule. 一個規律的餵食行程表。

* easy〔'izɪ〕*adj.* 容易的　　pet〔pɛt〕*n.* 寵物　　*care for* 照顧
unlike〔ʌn'laɪk〕*prep.* 與…不同　　*a lot of* 大量的
exercise〔'ɛksə,saɪz〕*n.* 運動　　healthy〔'hɛlθɪ〕*adj.* 健康的
well-fed *adj.* 被餵飽的　　fresh〔frɛʃ〕*adj.* 新鮮的
prefer〔prɪ'fɝ〕*v.* 偏好　　follow〔'fɑlo〕*v.* 跟隨；依循
routine〔ru'tin〕*n.* 慣例；常規　　*make changes to* 改變
feed〔fid〕*v.* 餵

16. (**C**) W：Hi, Tim, you're back. How was your vacation?

女：嗨，提姆，你回來了。你的假期如何？

M：It was great! Bali is a beautiful place and we had so much fun.

男：很棒。巴里島是個漂亮的地方，而且我們玩得很愉快。

W : Did you do any sightseeing or go on a special tour?

女：你有從事任何觀光，或是去特別的觀光遊覽嗎？

M : No, we didn't really do any of those things. We mostly stayed at the resort and enjoyed the sun and surf.

男：沒有，我們並沒有真的去做任何那樣的事。我們幾乎都待在度假勝地享受陽光和海浪。

Question : What are the speakers talking about?

說話者在談論什麼？

(A) Their classes. 他們的課程。

(B) The woman's family. 女士的家庭。

(C) The man's vacation. <u>男士的假期。</u>

＊ vacation〔veˋkeʃən〕n. 假期　　Bali〔ˋbɑlɪ〕n. 巴里島
have fun 玩得愉快　　sightseeing〔ˋsaɪt͵siɪŋ〕n. 觀光
special〔ˋspɛʃəl〕adj. 特別的　　tour〔ˋtʊr〕n. 觀光；旅行
go on a tour 遊覽；觀光　　mostly〔ˋmostlɪ〕adv. 主要地
resort〔rɪˋzɔrt〕n. 休閒勝地　　**the sun** 陽光
surf〔ˋsɝf〕n. 海浪　　class〔klæs〕n. 課程

17. (**A**) M : Hey, I'm Rob Martin. Here to see Walt Jeffers. I have a 10:15 appointment.

男：嘿，我是羅伯・馬汀。來這裡見沃爾特・傑佛斯。我十點十五分有一個約見。

W : Yes, I see, Mr. Martin. If you could just take a seat in one of the chairs over there, Mr. Jeffers will be out to greet you shortly. Can I offer you a cup of tea?

女：是的，我知道了，馬汀先生。您是否可以先在那邊的其中一張椅子坐下，傑佛斯先生很快就會出來迎接您。需要我給您一杯茶嗎？

M : No, thanks.

男：不用，謝謝。

Question：What does the man want? 這位男士想要什麼？

(A) To meet with Walt Jeffers. 與華特・傑佛斯見面。

(B) A cup of tea. 一杯茶。

(C) A chair with soft padding. 一張有軟墊的椅子。

* appointment〔ə'pɔɪntmənt〕 *n.* 約見；約定
  I see. 我知道了。　　*take a seat* 坐下　　greet〔grit〕 *v.* 迎接
  shortly〔'ʃɔrtlɪ〕 *adv.* 不久；很快地　　offer〔'ɔfɚ〕 *v.* 提供
  meet with 和…會面　　soft〔sɔft〕 *adj.* 軟的
  padding〔'pædɪŋ〕 *n.* 襯墊

18. (**C**)　W：Would you mind giving me a ride to the train station?
　　　　I'd really appreciate it.

女：你會介意載我一程到火車站嗎？我會非常感激的。

M：No problem. Don't feel like walking in the rain, huh?

男：沒問題。不想要在雨中走路，是吧？

W：Well, that and I'm running late for school.

女：嗯，還有我上學快遲到了。

Question：What will the man do? 這位男士將會做什麼？

(A) Give the woman a ride to school.
　　載這位女士一程到學校。

(B) Give the woman a ride to the bus station.
　　載這位女士一程到公車站。

(C) Give the woman a ride to the train station.
　　載這位女士一程到火車站。

* mind〔maɪnd〕 *v.* 介意　　*give sb. a ride* 載某人一程
  train station 火車站　　appreciate〔ə'priʃɪˌet〕 *v.* 感激
  No problem. 沒問題。　　*feel like V-ing* 想要~
  in the rain 在雨中；淋雨
  huh〔hʌh〕 *interj.* (表示驚奇、疑問等) 啊；是吧
  be running late 快遲到　　*bus station* 公車站

19. (**B**) M : We're going on a hike in the foothills tomorrow.
Would you like to join us?

男：我們明天要去山麓丘陵遠足。妳想要加入我們嗎？

W : Maybe. How many people are going?

女：也許可以。有多少人要去？

M : There should be about five of us—six if you decide
to join us.

男：我們應該大約有五個人——如果妳決定加入的話六個。

W : I guess it depends on the weather. If it's raining, I
probably won't come.

女：我想這取決於天氣。如果下雨，我可能不會去。

M : If it's raining, we won't be hiking.

男：如果下雨，我們不會去登山。

Question : When will the woman decide if she wants to
go on the hike?

這位女士何時會決定她是否想要去登山？

(A) Later in the day. 當天稍晚。

(B) Tomorrow. 明天。

(C) Next week. 下週。

* hike〔haɪk〕n. 遠足　　**go on a hike** 去遠足
foothills〔'fʊt,hɪlz〕n. pl. 山麓丘陵　　**would like to V.** 想要
join〔dʒɔɪn〕v. 加入　　maybe〔'mebi〕adv. 可能；或許
there + be 有~　　decide〔dɪ'saɪd〕v. 決定
guess〔gɛs〕v. 猜想；認為　　**depend on**… 取決於…
probably〔'prɑbəblɪ〕adv. 可能
later〔'letɚ〕adv. 稍晚；一會兒

20. (**A**) The latest selfie fatality saw a 66-year-old Japanese
tourist die after falling down stairs while attempting to
take a photo at the Taj Mahal. Incidents involving selfies

are now at a toll of twelve this year, overtaking the eight
deaths caused by shark attacks. Some governments are
recognizing this danger and providing safety measures for
people partaking in the craze.

在最新的自拍死亡案件中看到，一位六十六歲的日本遊客在泰姬
瑪哈陵試圖照相時，摔下台階後死亡。涉及自拍的事件在今年已
經有 12 人死亡，超越鯊魚攻擊的死亡人數 8 人。有些政府正意識
到這項危險，並且提供安全措施給參與這項熱潮的民眾。

Question：What does the speaker imply?

這位說話者暗示什麼？

(A) Selfies are more dangerous than sharks.

自拍比鯊魚危險。

(B) Japanese tourists like to take photos.

日本遊客喜歡拍照。

(C) The government is doing nothing about the problem.

政府對於這個問題什麼都沒做。

* latest (ˈletɪst) adj. 最新的
  selfie (ˈsɛlfɪ) v. 自拍【2002 年第一次出現於澳洲網路論壇，2013 年被
  放入牛津網路辭典，並獲選為年度風雲字】
  fatalities (ˈfətælətɪ) n. 死亡
  see (si) v. (地點或時間) 遭受；見證
  Japanese (ˌdʒæpəˈniz) adj. 日本的　　tourist (ˈturɪst) n. 遊客
  fall down 摔落　　stairs (stɛrz) n. pl. 樓梯
  attempt (əˈtɛmpt) v. 嘗試；試圖　　**take a photo** 照相
  Taj Mahal (ˈtɑʒməˈhɑl) n. 泰姬瑪哈陵【印度著名的陵墓】
  incident (ˈɪnsədənt) n. 事件　　involve (ˈɪnvɑlv) v. 牽涉
  toll (tol) n. 傷亡人數　　overtake (ˌovɚˈtek) v. 超過；趕上
  death (dɛθ) n. 死亡　　shark (ʃɑrk) n. 鯊魚
  attack (əˈtæk) n. 攻擊　　government (ˈɡʌvɚmənt) n. 政府
  recognize (ˈrɛkəɡˌnaɪz) v. 認知；意識到
  danger (ˈdændʒɚ) n. 危險　　provide (prəˈvaɪd) v. 提供
  safety (ˈseftɪ) n. 安全　　measures (ˈmɛʒɚz) n. pl. 措施

> *partake in* 參與 (= *take part in*)　　　craze〔krez〕*n.* 熱潮
> imply〔ɪmˋplaɪ〕*v.* 暗示
> dangerous〔ˋdendʒərəs〕*adj.* 危險的
> *do nothing about* 對…沒有行動

21. (**A**)　M：Maria, what happened to your foot?

　　　　女：瑪麗亞，妳的腳怎麼了？

　　　　W：Oh, I fell off my bicycle and twisted my ankle. It's nothing serious.

　　　　女：噢，我從我的腳踏車摔下來，而且扭傷我的腳踝了。不是什麼嚴重的事。

　　　　M：Really? It's bad enough that you need crutches.

　　　　男：真的嗎？妳需要柺杖就已經夠糟了。

　　　　W：Don't worry. I'll be walking again in no time.

　　　　女：別擔心。我很快就能再走路了。

　　　　M：If you need any help, let me know.

　　　　男：如果妳需要任何幫忙，讓我知道。

　　　　Question：How is Maria doing now?　瑪麗亞現在如何？

　　　　(A) She is recovering. 她正在復原。

　　　　(B) She is getting worse. 她正惡化中。

　　　　(C) She is seriously injured. 她受傷很嚴重。

　　　* *What happens to sb.?* 某人怎麼了？
　　　　foot〔fʊt〕*n.* 腳【複數是 feet】　　*fall off* 跌落
　　　　twist〔twɪst〕*v.* 扭傷　　ankle〔ˋæŋkḷ〕*n.* 腳踝
　　　　serious〔ˋsɪrɪəs〕*adj.* 嚴重的　　*bad enough* 夠糟了
　　　　crutch〔krʌtʃ〕*n.* 拐杖　　worry〔ˋwɝɪ〕*v.* 擔心
　　　　in no time 馬上；很快 (= *soon*)
　　　　recover〔rɪˋkʌvɚ〕*v.* 復原
　　　　get worse 變更糟糕；惡化 (= *worsen*)
　　　　seriously〔ˋsɪrɪəslɪ〕*adv.* 嚴重地　　injure〔ˋɪndʒɚ〕*v.* 受傷

TEST 4 詳解

聽力測驗（第 1-21 題，共 21 題）

第一部分：辨識句意（第 1-3 題，共 3 題）

1. (**A**) (A)   (B)   (C)

Lucy and Bill are taking their dog for a walk.
露西和比爾正在遛狗。

* *take…for a walk* 帶…去散步

2. (**C**) (A)   (B)   (C)

It's very windy today, isn't it? 今天風很大，不是嗎？

* windy〔ˋwɪndɪ〕*adj.* 多風的；風大的

3. (**B**) (A)   (B)   (C)

Jeff is watching the film on the computer.

傑夫正在用電腦看電影。

* film〔fɪlm〕*n.* 電影

第二部分：基本問答（第 4-10 題，共 7 題）

4. (**A**) Are you going to the bank? 你正要去銀行嗎？

　　(A) No, I'm going to the supermarket.

　　　　不，我正要去超市。

　　(B) Yes, he has the money. 是的，他有錢。

　　(C) Maybe, if they aren't late.

　　　　也許，如果他們不遲到的話。

　　* bank〔bæŋk〕*n.* 銀行　　supermarket〔'supɚ,mɑrkɪt〕*n.* 超市
　　maybe〔'mebɪ〕*adv.* 或許；可能　　late〔let〕*adj.* 遲到的

5. (**C**) Guess what, Mary? I'll be flying to Seattle for a few days next week. 妳猜看看，瑪莉？我下週要飛去西雅圖幾天。

　　(A) Suit yourself. I've already had dinner.

　　　　隨你便。我已經吃過晚餐了。

　　(B) Not necessarily. I get plenty of exercise.

　　　　不一定。我做了好多運動。

　　(C) That's wonderful. I'll meet you at the airport.

　　　　那太棒了。我會去機場接機。

　　* **Guess what?** 你猜看看？　　fly〔flaɪ〕*v.* 飛；坐飛機
　　Seattle〔si'ætḷ〕*n.* 西雅圖【位於美國華盛頓州的城市】
　　suit〔sut〕*v.* 方便；適合　　**Suit yourself.** 隨你便。
　　already〔ɔl'rɛdɪ〕*adv.* 已經　　have〔hæv〕*v.* 吃
　　necessarily〔'nɛsə,sɛrəlɪ〕*adv.* 必定地；必然地
　　not necessarily 不一定；未必　　**plenty of** 大量的
　　exercise〔'ɛksɚ,saɪz〕*v.* 運動　　**get exercise** 運動
　　wonderful〔'wʌndɚfəl〕*adj.* 極好的
　　meet〔mit〕*v.* 和…見面；迎接　　airport〔'ɛr,port〕*n.* 機場

6. (**B**) I like these shoes but I can't afford them.
我喜歡這雙鞋子，但是我負擔不起。

(A) Try them in a different size. 試穿看看其他尺寸的。

(B) Maybe you could find a cheaper pair.
也許你可以找一雙便宜一點的。

(C) I wear a size nine. 我穿九號的。

* afford (ə'ford) v. 負擔　different ('dɪfrənt) adj. 不同的
size (saɪz) n. 尺寸　cheap (tʃip) adj. 便宜的
pair (pɛr) n. 一雙；一對

7. (**A**) I'm making a pot of tea. Would you like a cup?
我正在泡一壺茶。你想要來一杯嗎？

(A) No, thanks. 不，謝謝。

(B) Go ahead. 去吧。

(C) You're welcome. 不客氣。

* pot (pat) n. 壺　**make tea** 泡茶　**would like** 想要
go ahead 前進；去吧

8. (**A**) Aren't you going to Mount Davidson this Saturday?
你這週六不去戴維森山嗎？

(A) No, my schedule has changed. 不，我的行程改變了。

(B) Several kilometers a day. 一天好幾公里。

(C) Yes, it works. 是的，這是可行的。

* **Mount Davidson** 戴維森山【位於加州】
schedule ('skɛdʒul) n. 行程　change (tʃendʒ) v. 改變
several ('sɛvərəl) adj. 幾個
kilometer ('kɪlə,mitə , kɪ'la,mitə) n. 公里
work (wɜk) v. 行得通

9. (**B**) Where did John leave my laptop?
約翰把我的筆記型電腦放在哪裡？

(A) By 10 o'clock. 到十點前。

(B) On the table. 在桌上。

(C) From New York. 從紐約。

* leave〔ˈliv〕v. 留下；放在　　laptop〔ˈlæpˌtɑp〕n. 筆記型電腦
by〔baɪ〕prep. 在…之前

10. (**C**) Did you read the instructions the teacher passed out?
你讀了老師發的說明了嗎？

(A) It's Ms. Henderson. 這位是韓德森女士。

(B) Yes, they will. 是的，他們會。

(C) Yes, I read them yesterday.
是的，我昨天就讀了。

* instructions〔ɪnˈstrʌkʃənz〕n. pl. 指示；說明
pass out 分配；分發　　Ms.〔mɪz〕n. …女士
Henderson〔ˈhɛndəsən〕n. 韓德森

第三部分：言談理解（第 11-21 題，共 11 題）

11. (**A**) M：Are you hungry? There's some leftover spaghetti in
the fridge.

男：妳餓了嗎？冰箱裡有一些剩下的義大利麵。

W：When did you make it?

女：你何時煮的？

M：Last night.

男：昨晚。

W：Oh, good. Spaghetti is always better on the second
day.

女：噢，很好。義大利麵放隔夜總是更好吃。

Question：What does the man offer the woman?
這位男士提供什麼給這位女士？

(A) Something to eat. 吃的東西。

(B) Somewhere to sit. 坐的地方。

(C) Some place to go. 去的地方。

* hungry〔'hʌŋgrɪ〕*adj.* 飢餓的　　leftover〔'lɛft,ovɚ〕*adj.* 剩餘的
spaghetti〔spə'gɛtɪ〕*n.* 義大利麵
fridge〔frɪdʒ〕*n.* 冰箱 (= *refrigerator*)　　offer〔'ɔfɚ〕*v.* 提供

12. (**C**) W : Your hair looks different, Norman.　Did you get a
haircut recently?

女：你的頭髮看起來不一樣，諾曼。你最近去剪頭髮了嗎？

M : No, but I used some gel to slick it back like this.

男：不，但我用了一些髮膠把頭髮向後梳理光滑。

W : It's a good look for you.

女：這對你來說是個好看的造型。

M : Thanks.　I appreciate the compliment.

男：謝謝。我很感激這個讚美。

Question : What has Norman done to change his
appearance? 諾曼做了什麼去改變他的外表？

(A) He got a haircut. 他剪了頭髮。

(B) He shaved his beard. 他剃了鬍子。

(C) He changed his hair style. 他改變他的髮型。

* look〔lʊk〕*v.* 看起來　*n.* 外表；樣子
different〔'dɪfrənt〕*adj.* 不同的　　Norman〔'nɔrmən〕*n.* 諾曼
haircut〔'hɛr,kʌt〕*n.* 理髮　　recently〔'risn̩tlɪ〕*adv.* 最近
gel〔dʒɛl〕*n.* 髮膠　　slick〔slɪk〕*v.* 使光滑發亮
appreciate〔ə'priʃɪ,et〕*v.* 欣賞
compliment〔'kɑmpləmənt〕*n.* 讚美
appearance〔ə'pɪrəns〕*n.* 外表　　shave〔ʃev〕*v.* 剃
beard〔bɪrd〕*n.* 鬍子　　style〔staɪl〕*n.* 風格；型態

13. (**C**) M : Has it been a year since Scruffy passed away? Gosh, time flies.

男：自從史格菲過世後已經一年了嗎？天哪，時光飛逝。

W : Yes, I miss him so much. Do you remember how he used to curl up in my lap? He'd purr so loud you could hear it on the other side of the room.

女：是的，我很想念牠。你還記得牠是怎樣在我的腿上縮成一團嗎？牠會發出響亮的咕嚕聲，你在房間的另一邊都能聽到。

M : I also remember how he loved to sharpen his claws by scratching on the legs of the coffee table.

男：我也記得牠是多麼喜愛藉由刮咖啡桌腳把爪子磨利。

Question : Who was Scruffy? 誰是史格菲？

(A) Their neighbor. 他們的鄰居。

(B) Their coffee table. 他們的咖啡桌。

(C) Their cat. <u>他們的貓。</u>

* scruffy (ˈskrʌfɪ) *adj.* 邋遢的　　***pass away*** 過世
　gosh (ˈgɑʃ) *interj.* (表示驚訝) 哎呀
　Time flies. 時光飛逝。　　***used to V.*** 過去習慣~
　curl up 卷曲；縮成一團　　lap (læp) *n.* 膝部
　purr (pɝ) *v.* (貓) 發出滿足的咕嚕聲
　sharpen (ˈʃɑrpən) *v.* 使銳利　　claw (klɔ) *n.* 爪子
　scratch (skrætʃ) *v.* 抓　　neighbor (ˈnebɚ) *n.* 鄰居

14. (**C**) Good evening, Mr. Lawton. This is Benson Floyd from Alpha Office Furniture. I'm calling to let you know that your desk has arrived. I'd like to confirm the delivery date you've requested, Tuesday June 17th. Our delivery truck should arrive at your office between 9:00 a.m. and 4:00 p.m. that Tuesday. Our employees will set up the

desk and answer any questions you may have about it.
Please call us at 555-0122 by Monday at the latest if you
need to make other arrangements.

晚安，勞頓先生。我是阿爾發辦公室家具的班森・弗洛伊德。我
來電是爲了讓您知道您的書桌已經到了。我想要和您確認您要求
的送貨日期，六月十七號星期二。我們的送貨車應該會在那個星
期二的早上九點到下午四點之間抵達您的辦公室。我們的員工會
組裝書桌，並且回答任何您的問題。如果您需要任何其他安排，
最晚請於星期一撥打 555-0122 給我們。

Question：Why did Benson Floyd call Mr. Lawton?

爲何班森・弗洛伊德打電話給勞頓先生？

(A) To check a delivery address. 爲了確認送貨地址。

(B) To cancel an order. 爲了取消訂購。

(C) To confirm a delivery date. 爲了確認送貨日期。

* Lawton（'lɔtn̩）n. 勞頓
  This is… （用於講電話）我是…
  Floyd（flɔɪd）n. 弗洛伊德
  alpha（'ælfə）n. 阿爾發；(希臘字母) α
  furniture（'fɜnɪtʃɚ）n. 家具　　desk（dɛsk）n. 書桌
  would like to V. 想要～　　confirm（kən'fɜm）v. 確認
  delivery（dɪ'lɪvərɪ）n. 遞送　　date（det）n. 日期
  request（rɪ'kwɛst）v. 要求　　truck（trʌk）n. 卡車；貨車
  a.m. 午前；上午（= *ante meridiem*）
  p.m. 午後；下午（= *post meridiem*）
  employee（ɪm'plɔɪ-i）n. 員工　　**set up** 組裝
  at the latest 最晚　　arrangement（ə'rendʒmənt）n. 安排
  address（ə'drɛs , 'ædrɛs）n. 地址
  cancel（'kænsl̩）v. 取消　　order（'ɔrdɚ）n. 訂購

15. (**A**)   Hi, Franklin. This is Hillary. I have a problem and I was wondering if you can help me out. I left my science textbook at school. That means I can't study for the exam tomorrow. Do you think I could borrow yours for a few hours? Maybe we could even study together. Please call me back when you hear this. Thanks.

嗨，富蘭克林。我是希拉蕊。我有一個問題，並且想知道你是否可以幫助我。我把我的科學課本留在學校了。這意味著我無法準備明天的考試。你覺得我可以向你借你的課本幾個小時嗎？也許我們甚至可以一起讀書。當你聽到這個訊息，請回我電話。謝謝。

Question：What does Hillary want to borrow from
Franklin? 希拉蕊想跟富蘭克林借什麼？

(A) A chemistry textbook. 一本化學課本。

(B) A calculator. 一台計算機。

(C) A laptop. 一台筆記型電腦。

* Franklin〔'fræŋklɪn〕n. 富蘭克林
Hillary〔'hɪlərɪ〕n. 希拉蕊   wonder〔'wʌndɚ〕v. 想知道
help sb. **out** 幫助某人脫離困境
science〔'saɪəns〕n. 科學   textbook〔'tɛkst,bʊk〕n. 課本
mean〔min〕v. 意思是
exam〔ɪg'zæm〕n. 考試（= examination）
maybe〔'mebi〕adv. 或許   **call back** 回電
chemistry〔'kɛmɪstrɪ〕n. 化學
calculator〔'kælkjə,letɚ〕n. 計算機
laptop〔'læp,tɑp〕n. 筆記型電腦

16. (**A**)   W：Excuse me. I'm new in town. Can you tell me where
the post office is?

女：不好意思。我剛來這個城市。你可以告訴我郵局在哪裡嗎？

M : Sure! But first, welcome to the neighborhood. I'm Jerry. Where are you from?

男：當然。但是首先，歡迎妳來這個地方。我是傑瑞。妳從哪裡來？

W : Thanks, Jerry. My name is Rachel and I'm from Toronto.

女：謝謝，傑瑞。我的名字是瑞秋，而我來自多倫多。

M : Toronto!? Why, I've got a cousin in Toronto. Does the name Rocco Gambini ring a bell?

男：多倫多？！哎呀，我有個表弟在多倫多。洛可‧甘比尼這個名字妳有印象嗎？

W : Hmm, the name sounds familiar. In which part of town does he live?

女：嗯，這個名字聽起來很熟悉。他住在城市哪一區？

M : I think he lives on the north side of the city.

男：我想他住在城市的北邊。

W : That's where I lived. So it's possible I know him.

女：那是我之前住的地方。所以我很可能認識他。

Question : What is true about the woman?

關於這位女士何者為眞？

(A) She recently moved to a new city.

她最近搬去一個新城市。

(B) She works at the post office. 她在郵局上班。

(C) She lives in Toronto. 她現居多倫多。

* ***excuse me*** 對不起【用於引起注意】　　new〔nju〕*adj.* 新來的
　in town 在城裡　　***post office*** 郵局
　sure〔ʃur〕*adv.* 好；當然
　neighborhood〔'nebɚ͵hud〕*n.* 附近；地區

Rachel〔'retʃəl〕*n.* 瑞秋　　Toronto〔tə'rɑnto〕*n.* 多倫多

why〔hwaɪ〕*interj.*（表示驚訝或突然意識到某事）哎呀

ring a bell 聽起來熟悉；有印象

hmm〔hm〕*interj.*（表示不確定、猶豫等）嗯

sound〔saʊnd〕*v.* 聽起來　　familiar〔fə'mɪljɚ〕*adj.* 熟悉的

possible〔'pɑsəbl̩〕*adj.* 可能的　　recently〔'risn̩tlɪ〕*adv.* 最近

move〔muv〕*v.* 搬家　　work〔wɝk〕*v.* 工作；上班

17.（**B**）　W：I have some chocolate chip cookies. Would you like some?

女：我有一些巧克力薄片餅乾。你想要一些嗎？

M：No, I've just finished eating my lunch. I like cookies, though. Thanks for the offer.

男：不，我才剛吃完午餐。雖然我喜歡餅乾。謝謝妳的提供。

W：Well, I'm on a special diet, so I'm not supposed to eat them.

女：嗯，我正在進行一個特殊的節食，所以我不應該吃它們。

M：Why don't you ask Bill? He's always hungry.

男：妳為何不問比爾？他總是很餓。

Question：What is the woman trying to do?

這位女士試著做什麼？

(A) Impress her friend. 讓她的朋友深受感動。

(B) Give away her cookies. 發送她的餅乾。

(C) Enjoy her lunch. 享用她的午餐。

* chocolate〔'tʃɔklɪt〕*n.* 巧克力　　chip〔tʃɪp〕*n.* 薄片

　would like 想要　　though〔ðo〕*adv.* 不過；然而

　offer〔'ɔfɚ〕*n.* 提供　　well〔wɛl〕*interj.* 嗯

　special〔'spɛʃəl〕*adj.* 特別的；特殊的

　diet〔'daɪət〕*n.* 節食　　***be on a diet*** 節食中

　be supposed to V. 應該～

Why don't you ~ ? 何不～？

impress〔ɪm'prɛs〕*v.* 使印象深刻；使感動　　***give away*** 發送

18. (**C**)　M : Attention, everyone.　The library is closing in ten minutes.

男：請注意，各位。圖書關即將於十分鐘後關閉。

W : It is?　But I thought it was open until midnight on the weekdays.

女：是嗎？但我以爲它平日開放到午夜。

M : No, that's only during exam periods.　Then it's open every day until 12 a.m.

男：不，那是只有在考試期間。那時候它每天都開到晚上十二點。

Question : Where are they?　他們在哪裡？

(A) In a high school science lab.　在高中的科學實驗室。

(B) In a popular bookstore.　在一間受歡迎的書店。

(C) In a college library.　在一所大學的圖書館。

* attention〔ə'tɛnʃən〕*interj.* 注意

library〔'laɪ,brɛrɪ〕*n.* 圖書館　　in〔ɪn〕*prep.* 再過

midnight〔'mɪd,naɪt〕*n.* 午夜　　weekday〔'wik,de〕*n.* 平日

during〔'djurɪŋ〕*prep.* 在⋯的期間

exam〔ɪg'zæm〕*n.* 考試（= *examination*）

period〔'pɪrɪəd〕*n.* 期間　　***high school*** 高中

science〔'saɪəns〕*n.* 科學

lab〔læb〕*n.* 實驗室（= *laboratory*）

popular〔'pɑpjələ〕*adj.* 受歡迎的

bookstore〔'buk,stor〕*n.* 書店　　college〔'kɑlɪdʒ〕*n.* 大學

19. (**B**)　W : I've got two tickets to see the Dragons this Saturday.　Do you want to go?

女：我拿到兩張這週六的票去看龍隊，你想去嗎？

M：Would I? I'm a huge fan.

男：我要不要去嗎？我是個超級粉絲。

W：Me, too. I can hardly believe they're in the semifinals this year. Let's hope they win this one, too.

女：我也是。我不敢相信他們在今年進入準決賽。讓我們期望他們這場也贏。

Question：Who or what are the Dragons?

　　　　誰或是什麼是 the Dragons？

(A) A musical group. 一個音樂團體。

(B) A sports team. 一支運動隊伍。

(C) A fan club. 一個粉絲團。

＊ ticket〔'tɪkɪt〕n. 票；門票　　dragon〔'drægən〕n. 龍
the Dragons 龍隊　　　huge〔hjudʒ〕adj. 巨大的
fan〔fæn〕n. 迷；支持者　　hardly〔'hɑrdlɪ〕adv. 幾乎不
believe〔bə'liv〕v. 相信　　semifinal〔ˌsɛmɪ'faɪnḷ〕n. 準決賽
Let's ~　一起~吧　　　musical〔'mjuzɪkḷ〕adj. 音樂的
group〔grup〕n. 團體　　sports〔sports〕adj. 運動的
team〔tim〕n. 團隊　　　club〔klʌb〕n. 社團

20. (**A**) W：Did you hear the news? Jilly Francis is coming to Taipei!

女：你聽到消息了嗎？吉莉‧法蘭西斯要來台北了！

M：Who is Jilly Francis?

男：誰是吉莉‧法蘭西斯？

W：Are you kidding?! She's only the biggest pop star on the planet right now.

女：你在開玩笑嗎？！她是現在地球上唯一最受歡迎的流行明星。

M : Oh, I don't pay attention to pop music, so I have no idea who you're talking about.

男：噢，我沒在關心流行音樂，所以我不知道妳在談論誰。

Question : What is true about the man?

有關這位男士何者為眞？

(A) He doesn't care for pop music. 他不喜歡流行音樂。

(B) He only reads the newspapers. 他只看報紙。

(C) He enjoys telling jokes. 他喜歡講笑話。

* news〔 njuz 〕*n.* 新聞　　Jilly〔'dʒɪlɪ〕*n.* 吉莉
　Francis〔'frænsɪs〕*n.* 法蘭西斯　　***be kidding*** 開玩笑
　big〔 bɪg 〕*adj.* 受歡迎的　　pop〔 pɑp 〕*adj.* 流行的（= *popular*）
　star〔 stɑr 〕*n.* 明星　　planet〔'plænɪt〕*n.* 星球
　the planet 地球　　***right now*** 現在；目前
　oh〔 o 〕*interj.*（表示驚訝、恐懼等）啊；噢
　pay attention to 注意；關心　　***pop music*** 流行音樂
　have no idea 不知道　　***talk about*** 談論
　care for 喜歡　　newspaper〔'nuz,pepɚ〕*n.* 報紙
　tell a joke 講笑話　　enjoy〔 ɪn'dʒɔɪ 〕*v.* 喜愛

21. (**B**)　W : OK, you're done here. Next stop, window 3. Give them your application, take a number, and have a seat.

女：好的，你這裡的都完成了。下一步，窗口三。把你的申請表給他們，領一個號碼牌，然後坐下。

M : Do I have to take a vision test?

男：我需要做視力測驗嗎？

W : Not this time. Once every seven years. Provided you pass the written exam, your new license should arrive in the mail within 10 business days. Have a nice day.

女：這次不用。每七年一次。只要你通過筆試，你新的駕照就會
　　在十個工作天內以寄達。祝你有個美好的一天。

M：Wow, this was a lot easier than I thought it would be.

男：哇，這比我原本想得還要簡單許多。

Question：What is the man probably doing?

　　　　　這位男士可能在做什麼？

(A) Applying for a loan. 申請貸款。

(B) Renewing his driver's license. 更新他的駕照。

(C) Opening a bank account. 開一個銀行帳戶。

* **OK** 好的；沒問題　　done〔dʌn〕adj. 完成的；結束的
stop〔stɑp〕n. 中途停留處
window〔'wɪndo〕n. 窗；(櫃臺) 窗口
application〔͵æplə'keʃən〕n. 申請表
take a number 取號碼牌　　**have a seat** 坐下
have to V. 必須~　　vision〔'vɪʒən〕n. 視力
provided〔prə'vaɪdɪd〕conj. 如果 (= if)
pass〔pæs〕v. 通過
written test 筆試　　license〔'laɪsṇs〕n. 執照
arrive〔ə'raɪv〕v. 到達　　mail〔mel〕n. 郵件；信件
within〔wɪð'ɪn〕prep. 在…之內
business〔'bɪznɪs〕n. 營業；工作
business day 營業日；工作日
Have a nice day. 祝你愉快。
wow〔waʊ〕interj. (表示驚嘆、喜悅等) 哇
a lot (修飾比較級) 非常
probably〔'prɑbəblɪ〕adv. 可能
apply for 申請　　loan〔lon〕n. 貸款
renew〔rɪ'nu〕v. 更新　　**driver's license** 駕照
account〔ə'kaʊnt〕n. 帳戶

TEST 5 詳解

聽力測驗（第 1-21 題，共 21 題）

第一部分：辨識句意（第 1-3 題，共 3 題）

1. (**A**) (A)  (B)  (C)

Kim is learning Chinese calligraphy. 金正在學中文書法。

* Chinese〔tʃaɪˋniz〕 *adj.* 中國的
  calligraphy〔kəˋlɪgrəfɪ〕 *n.* 書法

2. (**C**) (A)  (B)  (C)

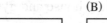

Reggie is pointing at some dolls on a shelf.
雷吉正指著一些架上的洋娃娃。

* Reggie〔ˋrɛdʒɪ〕 *n.* 雷吉　　point〔pɔɪnt〕 *v.* 指
  doll〔bɔl〕 *n.* 洋娃娃　　shelf〔ʃɛlf〕 *n.* 架子

3. (**C**) (A)  (B)  (C)

Henry is playing fetch with his dog.

亨利正在跟他的狗玩撿球遊戲。

* fetch〔fɛtʃ〕*n.* 撿球遊戲

第二部分：基本問答（第 4-10 題，共 7 題）

4.(**A**) This jacket is waterproof, isn't it?

這個夾克是防水的，對嗎？

　(A) I think so. 我覺得是。

　(B) It's half an hour away. 還要半小時。

　(C) I saw it last time. 我上次有看到它。

* jacket〔'dʒækɪt〕*n.* 夾克
  waterproof〔'wɔtɚ'pruf〕*adj.* 防水的
  away〔ə'we〕*adv.*（時間、空間）相距；相隔

5.(**A**) Who is designing the new field house and gymnasium?

是誰在設計新的室內運動場及體育館？

　(A) Bronson Architects. 布朗森建築師事務所。

　(B) At the warehouse. 在倉庫裡。

　(C) A fully equipped model. 一個有完整配備的模型。

* design〔dɪ'saɪn〕*v.* 設計　　field〔fild〕*n.* 球場；運動場
  field house 室內運動場（= *a building for indoor sports*）
  gymnasium〔dʒɪm'nezɪəm〕*n.* 體育館
  architect〔'ɑrkə,tɛkt〕*n.* 建築師
  warehouse〔'wɛr,haʊs〕*n.* 倉庫　　equip〔ɪ'kwɪp〕*v.* 裝備
  model〔'mɑdḷ〕*n.* 模型

6.(**C**) Are you taking more classes this year?

你今年修更多課嗎？

　(A) I heard about that. 我聽過那件事。

　(B) No, different associations. 不，不同的社團。

(C) Yes, I've enrolled in a couple of new courses.
　　對，我已經登記了一些新的課程。

* **take classes** 上課；修課
  association〔ə͵soʃɪ'eʃən〕n. 協會；社團
  enroll〔ɪn'rol〕v. 註冊 < in >　　　**a couple of** 一些；幾個
  course〔kɔrs〕n. 課程

7. (**C**) Why don't we take a taxi to the airport?
　　我們何不搭計程車去機場？

(A) I don't have any. 我一個也沒有。

(B) It might be quicker. 它可能比較快。

(C) Not very far. 不是很遠。

* taxi〔'tæksɪ〕n. 計程車　　airport〔'ɛr͵port〕n. 機場

8. (**C**) Who should I contact about my order?
　　關於我的訂單問題可以連絡誰？

(A) They are numerical order. 他們是照數字順序。

(B) At the Crosby's house. 在克羅斯比的家。

(C) Try calling customer service. 打給客服看看。

* contact〔'kɑntækt〕v. 連絡
  order〔'ɔrdɚ〕n. 訂購（單）；順序
  numerical〔nju'mɛrɪkl̩〕adj. 數字的
  Crosby〔'krozbɪ〕n. 克羅斯比　　**try + V-ing** 試看看～
  customer〔'kʌstəmɚ〕n. 顧客　　service〔'sɝvɪs〕n. 服務

9. (**C**) Don't you want to go to the grand opening of the new
　　shopping mall? 你不想要去這家新購物中心的盛大開幕式嗎？

(A) I have it right here. 我這裡就有。

(B) No, he hasn't quit. 沒有，他還沒辭職。

(C) Sure. I'm looking forward to it. 當然，我很期待。

* grand〔grænd〕*adj.* 盛大的　　opening〔'opənɪŋ〕*n.* 開幕
mall〔mɔl〕*n.* 購物中心；商場　***right here*** 就在這裡
quit〔kwɪt〕*v.* 停止；辭職　　sure〔ʃur〕*adv.* 當然
look forward to 期待

10.（ **C** ）Jacob, are you singing in the talent competition
tomorrow? 雅各，你明天要去才藝比賽唱歌嗎？

(A) Yes, I'll be playing goalie for the team.
對，我會擔任那一隊的守門員。

(B) Sometimes, if it isn't raining.
有時候，如果沒下雨的話。

(C) No, I've come down with a cold and have a bit of a
sore throat. 不，我罹患感冒，喉嚨有點痛。

* Jacob〔'dʒekəb〕*n.* 雅各　　talent〔'tælənt〕*n.* 才能
competition〔͵kɑmpə'tɪʃən〕*n.* 比賽
play〔ple〕*v.* 扮演；擔任　　goalie〔'golɪ〕*n.* 守門員
team〔tim〕*n.* 隊伍　***come down with*** 罹患；因…病倒
cold〔kold〕*n.* 感冒　***a bit of*** 有點；有些
sore〔sɔr〕*adj.* 疼痛的　　throat〔θrot〕*n.* 喉嚨

第三部分：言談理解（第 11-21 題，共 11 題）

11.（ **C** ）W：What are you eating?
女：你在吃什麼？

M：Oh, this is a special Taiwanese treat: sliced melon
served over shaved ice.
男：噢，這是個特別的台灣美食：甜瓜切片佐剉冰。

W：It sounds sweet. Is it tasty?
女：聽起來很甜。好吃嗎？

M：Very. Here, try some.

男：很好吃。這些妳試看看。

Question：What is the man eating?　這位男士在吃什麼？

(A) Lunch.　午餐。

(B) Dinner.　晚餐。

(C) A snack.　甜食。

* oh〔o〕*interj.*（表示驚訝、喜悅等）噢；哎呀
　special〔'spɛʃəl〕*adj.* 特別的
　Taiwanese〔,taɪwɑ'niz〕*adj.* 台灣的
　treat〔trit〕*n.* 美味食物　　sliced〔slaɪst〕*adj.* 切成片的
　melon〔'mɛlən〕*n.* 甜瓜　　serve〔sɝv〕*v.* 供應；上（菜）
　shave〔ʃev〕*v.* 刮；剔　　***shaved ice*** 剉冰
　sound〔saʊnd〕*v.* 聽起來　　tasty〔'testɪ〕*adj.* 好吃的
　snack〔snæk〕*n.* 零食；甜食

12. (**A**) M：You speak German, don't you, Michelle?

男：妳會說德文，不是嗎，蜜雪兒？

W：I do, but not very well these days. If I had more
　　chances to practice, I might be close to fluent.

女：我會，但最近說的不太好。如果我有更多機會練習，我可能
　　會更接近流利的程度。

M：Did you study the language in school or did your
　　parents speak it at home?

男：妳在學校學德語，還是你父母在家說德語？

W：Both.

女：都是。

Question：What does Michelle say about her German
　　　　　skills?　蜜雪兒表示她的德文能力如何？

(A) She's out of practice.　她疏於練習。

(B) She's practically fluent.　她說得夠流利。

(C) She doesn't speak German at all. 她完全不會說德文。

* German〔'dʒɝmən〕 *n.* 德文　　Michelle〔mɪ'ʃɛl〕 *n.* 蜜雪兒
these days 最近　　chance〔tʃæns〕 *n.* 機會
practice〔'præktɪs〕 *v. n.* 練習　　***close to*** 接近
fluent〔'fluənt〕 *adj.* 流利的　　skill〔skɪl〕 *n.* 技能；技巧
out of 不再…；沒有…　　***out of practice*** 疏於練習；荒廢
practically〔'præktɪklɪ〕 *adv.* 幾乎；簡直
not…at all 一點也不…

13. (**A**) W : Should we start the meeting now or wait for Mr.
　　　　　　　 Charles?

　　　女：我們應該現在開始，還是要等查爾斯先生？

　　　M : Let's give him another 10 minutes.　I know traffic
　　　　　 was terrible this morning because of the rain.

　　　男：我們再給他 10 分鐘。我知道今早交通因為下雨很糟糕。

　　　W : Well, we have a lot to get through, so I think we
　　　　　 better begin sooner rather than later.

　　　女：嗯，我們有很多東西要完成，所以我覺得及早開始比較好。

　　　Question : What is implied about Mr. Charles?
　　　　　　　　　　關於查爾斯先生暗示什麼？

　　　(A) He is stuck in traffic. 他遇到塞車。

　　　(B) He is always late. 他總是遲到。

　　　(C) The meeting can't be held without him.
　　　　　 這個會議沒他不能舉行。

* meeting〔'mitɪŋ〕 *n.* 會議　　***wait for*** 等待
Mr.〔'mɪstɚ〕 *n.* …先生　　Charles〔tʃɑrlz〕 *n.* 查爾斯
traffic〔'træfɪk〕 *n.* 交通　　terrible〔'tɛrəbḷ〕 *adj.* 糟糕的
because of 因為　　well〔wɛl〕 *interj.* 嗯
get through 完成 (= *complete*)
sooner rather than later 及早 (= *as soon as possible*)

imply〔ɪm'plaɪ〕v. 暗示

stuck〔stʌk〕adj. 卡住的;動彈不得的　　hold〔hold〕v. 舉辦

14. (**C**)　M : Hi, welcome to Sheppard's Market. How can I help you?

男:嗨,歡迎來到謝博德市場。需要幫忙嗎?

W : I'm not sure if you can. I'm looking for kiwifruit.

女:我不確定你是否可以幫的上忙。我正在找奇異果。

M : Oh, I'm sorry, but we don't carry fresh produce anymore. You should try Colby's Organic over on Yardley Avenue.

男:噢,很抱歉,我們不再賣新鮮農產品了。妳應該去雅德利大道那裡的柯爾比有機食物找看看。

W : Thanks, I'll do that.

女:謝謝,我會的。

Question : What is true about Sheppard's?

關於謝博德超市何者為真?

(A) They don't sell ice cream. 他們沒賣冰淇淋。

(B) They specialize in organic produce.

他們專門賣有機農產品。

(C) They used to carry fruit. <u>他們以前有賣水果。</u>

* Sheppard〔'ʃɛpəd〕n. 謝博德　　market〔'mɑrkɪt〕n. 市場

sure〔ʃur〕adj. 確定的　　***look for*** 尋找

kiwifruit〔'kiwɪ'frut〕n. 奇異果（= *kiwi fruit*）

oh〔o〕interj.（表示驚訝、喜悅等）噢;哎呀

carry〔'kærɪ〕v. 帶;販賣　　fresh〔frɛʃ〕adj. 新鮮的

produce〔'prɑdjus〕n. 農產品　　***not…anymore*** 不再…

Colby〔'kɔlbɪ〕n. 柯爾比　　organic〔ɔr'gænɪk〕adj. 有機的

over〔'ovə〕adv. 在那邊　　Yardley〔'jɑrdlɪ〕n. 雅德利

avenue (ˈævəˌnju) *n.* 大道；大街　　***ice cream*** 冰淇淋
specialize (ˈspɛʃəlaɪz) *v.* 專精 < *in* >　　***used to V.*** 以前~

15. (**C**)　W：Ryan, if you're interested, there's a travel fair at the
　　　　　　　Civic Center this weekend.

女：萊恩，如果你有興趣的話，這個禮拜在市民中心有個旅展。

M：I would love to go, Tamara, but I'll be out of town.

男：我想去，塔瑪拉，但我將會出城去。

W：Oh, really? Where are you going?

女：噢，真的喔？你要去哪裡？

M：Las Vegas.

男：拉斯維加斯。

Question：What do we know about Ryan?

　　　　　關於萊恩，我們知道些什麼？

(A) He will attend a travel fair this weekend.

　　他會參加這禮拜的旅展。

(B) He will visit his family this weekend.

　　他這禮拜會去看他的家人。

(C) He will travel to Las Vegas this weekend.

　　他這週末會去拉斯維加斯。

* Ryan (ˈraɪən) *n.* 萊恩　　interested (ˈɪntrɪstɪd) *adj.* 感興趣的
there + be 有~
travel (ˈtrævl̩) *n.* 旅行；旅遊　*v.* 移動；前進
fair (fɛr) *n.* 展覽　　civic (ˈsɪvɪk) *adj.* 市民的；城市的
center (ˈsɛntɚ) *n.* 中心　　weekend (ˈwikˈɛnd) *n.* 週末
would love to V. 想要~　　***out of town*** 出城
Las Vegas (las ˈvegəs) *n.* 拉斯維加斯
attend (əˈtɛnd) *v.* 參加　　visit (ˈvɪzɪt) *v.* 探訪

16. (**B**) M : Do we need to bring anything for Sally's party
     tonight?

男： 我們今晚要帶任何東西去莎莉的派對嗎？

W : What do you mean? Like snacks or drinks?

女： 你的意思是什麼？像是點心或飲料嗎？

M : Yes. Isn't that the polite thing to do?

男： 對。那樣不是比較有禮貌嗎？

W : I suppose it's a nice gesture. How about we bring a
     bottle of wine? I know Sally loves red wine.

女： 我想這是個表達心意的好方式。我們何不帶一瓶酒？我知道
     莎莉喜歡紅酒。

M : There's a liquor store on the way to her house.

男： 去她家的路上有一間外賣酒店。

Question : What will the speakers most likely do later?

說話者晚點最可能做什麼？

(A) Go grocery shopping. 到雜貨店購物。

(B) Attend a party. 參加派對。

(C) Make dinner. 煮晚餐。

* party〔'partɪ〕n. 派對　　mean〔min〕v. 意思是
  like〔laɪk〕prep. 像是　　snack〔snæk〕n. 點心；零食
  drink〔drɪŋk〕n. 飲料　　polite〔pə'laɪt〕adj. 有禮貌的
  suppose〔sə'poz〕v. 以為　　gesture〔'dʒɛstʃɚ〕n. 姿勢；表示
  How about…? …如何？　　bottle〔'batḷ〕n. 瓶
  wine〔waɪn〕n. 酒　　***red wine*** 紅酒　　liquor〔'lɪkɚ〕n. 酒
  store〔stor〕n. 店；商店　　***liquor store*** 外賣酒店
  on the way to… 在去…的路上
  likely〔'laɪklɪ〕adv. 可能　　later〔'letɚ〕adv. 之後
  grocery〔'grosərɪ〕n. 食品雜貨
  attend〔ə'tɛnd〕v. 參加；出席

17. (**C**) W : How's Dwayne doing?

女：德韋恩現在好嗎？

M : He's recovering. The doctor said he would be released from the hospital as soon as this evening.

男：他正在復原中。醫生說他最快今天傍晚可以出院。

W : Wow, that's amazing if you think about what he went through.

女：哇，那真是太驚人了，如果你想想所經歷過事情。

M : Yes, it's somewhat of a miracle. He was lucky to have survived the crash.

男：對啊，這有點像是個蹟。他很幸運可以在車禍中存活下來。

Question : What happened to Dwayne?

德韋恩發生什麼事？

(A) He was pushed off a ladder. 他被推下樓梯。

(B) He was doused with boiling water. 他被沸水潑到。

(C) He was injured in an auto accident. <u>他在車禍中受傷。</u>

* Dwayne〔dwen〕*n.* 德韋恩
recover〔rɪ'kʌvɚ〕*v.* 復原　　release〔rɪ'lis〕*v.* 釋放
be released from the hospital 出院
wow〔waʊ〕*interj.*（表示驚訝、喜悅等）哇
amazing〔ə'mezɪŋ〕*adj.* 神奇；驚人　**go through** 經歷
somewhat〔'sʌm,hɑt〕*adv.* 有幾分；稍微
somewhat of + **N** 略有；有幾分
miracle〔'mɪrəkl̩〕*n.* 奇蹟
lucky〔'lʌkɪ〕*adj.* 幸運的　　survive〔sə'vaɪv〕*v.* 從…存活
crash〔kræʃ〕*n.* 撞擊；車禍　　ladder〔'lædɚ〕*n.* 梯子
douse〔daʊs〕*v.* 用水潑
boiling〔'bɔɪlɪŋ〕*adj.* 煮沸的；沸騰的
injure〔'ɪndʒɚ〕*v.* 傷害　　auto〔'ɔto〕*n.* 汽車
accident〔'æksədənt〕*n.* 意外

18. (**A**) M : Did you get a new laptop, Darlene?

男：妳買了新的筆電嗎，達琳？

W : I did.　Isn't it neat?　Check it out.

女：買了。它很不錯吧？你看看。

M : Pretty cool.　I like the color.　How much did you pay for it?

男：好酷喔。我喜歡這顏色。妳花了多少錢買它？

W : I paid eighteen thousand.

女：我花了一萬八千元。

Question : What did Darlene buy?　達琳買了什麼？

(A) A computer.　一台電腦。

(B) A television.　一台電視。

(C) A cell phone.　一支手機。

* get〔gɛt〕 *v.* 買　　laptop〔'læp,tɑp〕 *n.* 筆記型電腦
Darlene〔'dɑrlɪn〕 *n.* 達琳　　neat〔nit〕 *adj.* 很不錯的
check it out 看一看　　pretty〔'prɪtɪ〕 *adv.* 相當地
pay〔pe〕 *v.* 支付；花（錢）
cellp phone〔'sɛlfon〕 *n.* 手機（= *cellphone*）

19. (**B**) This food group is a favorite of vegetarians.　While some of these don't always taste that good, all of them are very healthy.　You can enjoy them as a snack or if prepared properly, as a full meal.　These grow from trees, bushes, and sometimes even flowers.　You can find them almost everywhere, but many are grown in warmer climates.

這個食物群是素食者的最愛。雖然其中某些未必那麼好吃，可是它們全部都很健康。你可以享用它們當零食，或是如果料理得宜的話，可作為正餐。這些是從樹上、灌木叢、有時甚至從花裡面長出來的。你幾乎到處都可以找得到它們，但是它們有很多是種植於較溫暖的氣候區。

Question：What is the speaker talking about?

這個對話在幾點發生的？

(A) Candy. 糖果。

(B) Vegetables. 蔬菜。

(C) Meat. 肉類。

* ***food group*** 食物群　　favorite (ˈfevərɪt) *n.* 最喜愛的事物
vegetarian (ˌvɛdʒəˈtɛrɪən) *n.* 素食者
while (hwaɪl) *conj.* 雖然　　***not always*** 並非總是；未必
taste (test) *v.* 嚐起來　　that (ðæt) *adv.* 那麼
healthy (ˈhɛlθɪ) *adj.* 健康的　　snack (snæk) *n.* 零食
prepare (prɪˈpɛr) *v.* 準備；烹調
properly (ˈprɑpəlɪ) *adv.* 適合地
full (fʊl) *adj.* 滿的；豐盛的　　meal (mil) *n.* 一餐
full meal 全餐；正餐　　grow (gro) *v.* 生長；種植
bush (bʊʃ) *n.* 灌木叢　　even (ˈivən) *adv.* 甚至
climate (ˈklaɪmɪt) *n.* 氣候　　candy (ˈkændɪ) *n.* 糖果
vegetables (ˈvɛdʒətəblz) *n. pl.* 蔬菜　　meat (mit) *n.* 肉

20. (**A**) Malcolm Campbell was an English automobile and speedboat racer who set many speed records for motorcycles, airplanes, automobiles, and motorboats. In 1931, he was knighted for his accomplishments. Four years later, driving his famed automobile *Bluebird* at Bonneville Flats, Utah, Campbell set his final land speed record, becoming the first person to drive an automobile faster than 300 miles per hour.

馬爾科姆・坎貝爾是個英國的汽車及快艇的競速選手，他在重型機車、飛機、汽車、汽艇速度方面創下許多的紀錄。在 1931 年，他因他的成就而被封爵。四年後，坎貝爾開著他有名的藍鳥汽車，在猶大州的波利維爾窪地創下了他最後的陸上紀錄，成為第一個汽車開超過每小時三百英哩的人。

Question：What best matches the description of Malcolm
　　　　　Campbell?

哪一個描述最符合馬爾科姆‧坎貝爾？

(A) Daring. 勇敢的。

(B) Troubled. 不安的。

(C) Lazy. 懶惰的。

* Malcolm Campbell（'mɑlkəm 'kæmbəl）n. 馬爾科姆‧坎貝爾
　English（'ɪŋglɪʃ）adj. 英國的
　automobile（'ɔtəmə,bil）n. 汽車
　speedboat（'spid,bot）n. 快艇　　racer（'resɚ）n. 競速選手
　set（sɛt）v. 創（紀錄）
　speed（spid）n. 速度　　record（'rɛkɚd）n. 紀錄
　motorcycle（'motɚ,saɪkl̩）n. 重型機車
　motorboat（'motɚ,bot）n. 汽艇
　knight（naɪt）v. 封（人）爲爵
　accomplishment（ə'kɑmplɪʃmənt）n. 成就
　famed（femd）adj. 有名的；知名的
　Bonneville Flats（'bɑnə,vɪl flæts）n. 波利維爾窪地【美國猶他州
　　西北部，大鹽湖以西一荒蕪平原】
　Utah（'jutɔ）n.（美國）猶他州
　final（'faɪnl̩）adj. 最後的　　mile（maɪl）n. 英里
　per（pɚ）prep. 每…　　match（mætʃ）v. 相配；相符
　description（dɪ'skrɪpʃən）n. 描述
　daring（'derɪŋ）adj. 勇敢的　　troubled（'trʌbl̩d）adj. 不安的
　lazy（'lezɪ）adj. 懶惰的

21. (**C**) To make this snack, first you need a pot and some water.
Put the pot and water over high heat and add your eggs.
Let them cook for 15 minutes and then remove from the
heat. Run the eggs under cold water for two minutes.
Then peel, serve, and enjoy!

要做這個點心的話，首先你需要一個鍋子及一些水。把鍋子與水加熱並放入雞蛋。讓它們煮個 15 分鐘，然後移開熱源。讓那些蛋在冷水下輕輕沖個兩分鐘。然後就去殼、上菜、並好好享用！

Question：What process does the speaker describe?
　　　　這個說話者描述了什麼過程？

(A) Putting a hot dog in a bun.
　　把一支熱狗放進小圓麵包裡。

(B) Eating ice cream from a cone. 吃冰淇淋甜筒。

(C) Boiling eggs in a pot. <u>熱鍋煮蛋。</u>

* snack〔snæk〕*n.* 零食；點心　　pot〔pat〕*n.* 鍋子
　heat〔hit〕*n.* 熱度；熱源　　add〔æd〕*v.* 加
　cook〔kʊk〕*v.*（食物）煮著　　then〔ðɛn〕*adv.* 然後
　remove〔rɪ'muv〕*v.* 移開　　run〔rʌn〕*v.* 輕輕移動
　peel〔pil〕*v.* 去皮；去殼　　serve〔sɝv〕*v.* 供餐；上菜
　process〔'prasɛs〕*n.* 過程
　describe〔dɪ'skraɪb〕*v.* 敘述；描述　　***hot dog*** 熱狗
　bun〔bʌn〕*n.* 小圓麵包
　cone〔kon〕*n.* 圓錐體；（裝冰淇淋的）圓錐餅乾
　boil〔bɔɪl〕*v.* 水煮

TEST 6 詳解

聽力測驗（第 1-21 題，共 21 題）

第一部分：辨識句意（第 1-3 題，共 3 題）

1. (**A**) (A)  (B)  (C)

Tommy is playing baseball. 湯米正在打棒球。

* baseball〔'bes͵bɔl〕*n.* 棒球

2. (**A**) (A)  (B)  (C)

The sun is shining over the mountains.
太陽正在山上照耀著。

* shine〔ʃaɪn〕*v.* 發光；照耀

3. (**B**) (A)  (B)  (C)

The woman is explaining how a recycling program works.

這位女士正在解釋回收計畫是如何運作的。

* explain〔ɪk'splen〕v. 解釋　　recycling〔ˌrɪ'saɪklɪŋ〕n. 回收
program〔'progræm〕n. 計畫　　work〔wɜk〕v. 運作

第二部分：基本問答（第 4-10 題，共 7 題）

4.(**A**) I'm hungry. Is there anywhere to eat around here?

我好餓。這附近有沒有什麼地方可以吃東西。

(A) There's a Burger King on the next block.

下個街區有一家漢堡王。

(B) I had the spaghetti and meatballs.

我吃了義大利麵還有肉丸。

(C) She brought her lunch from home.

她從家裡自己帶午餐。

* hungry〔'hʌŋgrɪ〕adj. 飢餓的
around here 在這附近；這周圍　　***Burger King*** 漢堡王
block〔blɑk〕n. 街區　　spaghetti〔spə'gɛtɪ〕n. 義大利麵
meatball〔'mitbɔl〕n. 肉丸

5.(**C**) The bus comes every fifteen minutes, doesn't it?

這公車每十五分鐘來一班車，對嗎？

(A) No, it runs on weekends. 不是，它週末才行駛。

(B) No, it costs fifty cents. 不是，它要花 15 分錢。

(C) No, it comes every twenty minutes.

不是，它每二十分鐘來一班車。

* run〔rʌn〕v. 運行；行駛　　weekend〔'wik'ɛnd〕n. 週末
cost〔kɔst〕v. 花（錢）　　cent〔sɛnt〕n. 一分錢

6.(**A**) How do you prefer to be called, John, Jonathan, or

Johnny? 你比較喜歡被稱呼為約翰、強納森還是強尼？

(A) John will be fine. 叫我約翰就好。

(B) It came a while ago. 它一陣子前來過。

(C) I'll give you my mobile number.

我會給你我的行動電話號碼。

* prefer〔prɪ'fɝ〕v. 比較喜歡

Jonathan〔'dʒɑnəθən〕n. 強納森

while〔hwaɪl〕n. (一段) 時間

mobile〔'mobḷ〕n. 行動電話；手機 (= mobile phone)

7. (**B**) Who will be leading our group activity?

誰會帶領我們的團體活動？

(A) At the hotel. 在旅館。

(B) Dennis. 丹尼斯。

(C) In June. 在六月。

* lead〔lid〕v. 領導；帶領　　group〔'grup〕n. 團體

activity〔æk'tɪvətɪ〕n. 活動　　hotel〔ho'tɛl〕n. 旅館

8. (**A**) Would you like to stay for dinner? I've made my special

lasagna. 你要留下來吃晚餐嗎？我做了我的特製義大利千層麵。

(A) Sure, I'd love to. 當然，我很樂意。

(B) The feeling is mutual. 這個感覺是共通的。

(C) We had pizza. 我們吃了披薩。

* **would like to V.** 想要～ (= would love to V.)

special〔'spɛʃəl〕adj. 特別的；獨有的

lasagna〔lə'zænjə〕n. 義大利千層麵

mutual〔'mjutʃʊəl〕adj. 共通的；共同的

pizza〔'pitsə〕n. 披薩

9. (**C**) I'm having trouble sleeping at night. 我晚上難以入眠。

(A) Have another piece, won't you? 再吃一塊，好嗎？

(B) Leave it on the bed. 把它放在床上。

(C) Try drinking a glass of warm milk before bedtime.
　　<u>睡前喝一杯溫牛奶試看看。</u>

　* *have trouble* + *V-ing*　做~有困難
　　piece〔pis〕*n.* 一塊；一片　　*try* + *V-ing* 試看看~
　　a glass of 一杯　　bedtime〔'bɛd,taɪm〕*n.* 就寢時間

10. (**C**) Ouch! That hurts! 哎喲！這樣很痛。

　　(A) You're welcome. 不客氣。

　　(B) Thanks. 謝謝。

　　(C) I'm sorry. <u>我很抱歉。</u>

　* ouch〔autʃ〕*interj.*（痛苦或驚訝的叫聲）哎喲
　　hurt〔hɝt〕*v.* 痛

第三部分：言談理解（第 11-21 題，共 11 題）

11. (**A**) W：Steve, you know how we talked about finding ways
　　　　　　to cut costs on office supplies?

　　女：史蒂夫，你知道關於找出減少辦公用品開支的方法，我們是
　　　　怎樣討論的嗎？

　　　　M：Yes, I found an Internet site we could use. Their
　　　　　　prices are 25% lower than what we've been paying.

　　男：我知道，我找到一個我們能用的網站。他們的價格比起我們
　　　　到目前支付的，低了百分之 25。

　　　　W：Well, that's quite a difference, but what about the
　　　　　　shipping costs? Our local supplier has been giving
　　　　　　us free delivery.

　　女：嗯，那真的差很多，但是運費呢？我們當地的供應商一直是
　　　　提供我們免運費。

　　　　M：I didn't take that into consideration.

　　男：我沒有把那個考慮進去。

W : So, it probably won't save us any money in the long run.

女：所以，長遠來看有可能不會幫我們省下任何費用。

Question : What is the woman concerned about?

這位女士在關心的是什麼？

(A) Shipping costs. 運費。

(B) Product quality. 產品品質。

(C) Upcoming deadlines. 即將來臨的期限。

* way〔we〕 *n.* 方式　　cut〔kʌt〕 *v.* 減少
cost〔kɔst〕 *n.* 開支　　office〔'ɔfɪs〕 *n.* 辦公室
supplies〔sə'plaɪz〕 *n. pl.* 供應品　　***office supply*** 辦公用品
Internet〔'ɪntə,nɛt〕 *n.* 網際網路　　site〔saɪt〕 *n.* 地點；網站
price〔praɪs〕 *n.* 價格　　lower〔'loə〕 *adj.* 較低的
well〔wɛl〕 *interj.* 嗯　　quite〔kwaɪt〕 *adv.* 相當地
difference〔'dɪfrəns〕 *n.* 不同；差異
What about~? ~如何？　　shipping〔'ʃɪpɪŋ〕 *n.* 運送
local〔'lokḷ〕 *adj.* 當地的　　supplier〔sə'plaɪə〕 *n.* 供應者
free〔fri〕 *adj.* 免費的　　delivery〔dɪ'lɪvərɪ〕 *n.* 遞送
take…into consideration 把…考慮在內
probably〔'prɑbəblɪ〕 *adv.* 可能　　save〔sev〕 *v.* 節省
in the long run 長遠來看　　***be concerned about*** 關心
product〔'prɑdʌkt〕 *n.* 產品　　quality〔'kwɑlətɪ〕 *n.* 品質
upcoming〔'ʌpkʌmɪŋ〕 *adj.* 即將發生的
deadline〔'dɛd,laɪn〕 *n.* 截止日期；最後期限

12. (**A**) W : Tony, I need you to do something for me.

女：東尼，我需要你幫我做點事。

M : Sure, Ms. Evans. Anything you need.

男：沒問題，埃文斯女士。任何妳需要的事都可以。

W : First, call Jack Hanson and tell him to double our order for next week. Then call Rosa Garcia and tell her to cancel our order for next week.

女：首先，打給傑克・漢森，告訴他我們下週訂單加倍。再來打給羅莎・加西亞，告訴她取消我們下週的訂單。

M：Is that all?

男：就這些嗎？

W：I'll let you know if anything else comes to mind.

女：我如果還有突然想到什麼，會讓你知道。

Question：What is implied about the woman?

關於這位女士，暗示了什麼？

(A) She's Tony's boss. <u>她是東尼的上司。</u>

(B) She's worried about poor sales. 她很擔心銷售不好。

(C) She's busy later in the day. 她那天晚些時候很忙。

* Tony〔ˈtonɪ〕 n. 東尼　　　sure〔ʃʊr〕 adv. 當然；沒問題
  Ms.〔mɪz〕 n. …女士　　　Evans〔ˈɛvəns〕 n. 埃文斯
  first〔fɝst〕 adv. 首先　　　Hanson〔ˈhænsən〕 n. 漢森
  double〔ˈdʌbl̩〕 v. 加倍　　　order〔ˈɔrdɚ〕 n. 訂購（單）
  Garcia〔ɡɑrˈsɪə〕 n. 加西亞　　cancel〔ˈkænsl̩〕 v. 取消
  come to mind 浮現心頭；突然想到　　imply〔ɪmˈplaɪ〕 v. 暗示
  boss〔bɔs〕 n. 老闆；上司　　　**be worried about** 擔心
  poor〔pʊr〕 adj. 可憐的；不如預期的
  sales〔selz〕 n. pl. 銷售額　　　busy〔ˈbɪzɪ〕 adj. 忙碌的
  later〔ˈletɚ〕 adv. 之後；稍晚

13. (**B**) How do you deal with a situation when you overhear someone say something nasty about you? Their cruel words cut deep. What's worse, they probably don't even know you. I'm the type to roll my eyes and walk away, but if you catch me on a bad day, watch out! While it's not polite to eavesdrop on someone's conversation, if they're talking about me, it's a different story.

當你聽到有人惡意中傷你的情況，你會如何處理呢？他們無情的話傷人很深。而且，他們甚至很可能不認識你。我是會翻白眼後就走開的那種人。但是如果你在我心情不好的時候遇到我,就給我小心了!雖然偷聽別人的對話不禮貌,但如果他是在討論我的話,就不是那麼一回事了。

Question : How does the speaker usually react to insults?
這個說話者通常如何回應侮辱?

(A) She repeats them. 她重複侮辱。

(B) She ignores them. 她忽略侮辱。

(C) She appreciates them. 她感激侮辱。

* **deal with** 處理   situation (,sɪtʃu'eʃən) n. 情境;情況
  overhear (,ovə'hɪr) v. 不經意聽到
  nasty ('næstɪ) adj. 惡劣的
  cruel ('kruəl) adj. 殘酷的   words (wɝdz) n. pl. 話語
  cut deep 傷得深   **what's worse** 更糟的是
  type (taɪp) n. …類型的人   roll (rol) v. 使滾動
  roll one's **eyes** 翻白眼   catch (kætʃ) v. 撞見
  a bad day 不愉快的日子
  catch me on a bad day 在我心情不好的時候遇見我
     (= meet me in a bad mood)
  watch out 小心   while (hwaɪl) conj. 雖然
  polite (pə'laɪt) adj. 有禮貌的
  eavesdrop ('ivzdrɑp) v. 偷聽 < on >
  react (rɪ'ækt) v. 反應;回應   insult ('ɪnsʌlt) n. 侮辱
  repeat (rɪ'pit) v. 重複   ignore (ɪg'nor) v. 忽略
  appreciate (ə'priʃɪ,et) v. 感激

14. (**A**) W : John, have you started the internship at Anderson
       Partners yet?
     女:約翰,你開始在安德森夥伴公司實習了嗎?

     M : Next week, Jenny.
     男:下個禮拜,珍妮。

     W : Are you excited?
     女:你感到很興奮嗎?

M : Mostly nervous, but excited, too.

男：主要是很緊張，但也很興奮。

Question : How does John feel about the internship?

關於這個實習約翰覺得如何？

(A) Anxious. 焦慮的。

(B) Careless. 不在意的。

(C) Disappointed and hopeful. 很失望也充滿希望的。

* internship〔ˈɪntən͵ʃɪp〕n. 實習
  Anderson〔ˈændəsən〕n. 安德森　　partner〔ˈpɑrtnɚ〕n. 夥伴
  yet〔jɛt〕adv.【用於疑問句】已經
  mostly〔ˈmostlɪ〕adv. 大部分是；主要是
  nervous〔ˈnɜvəs〕adj. 緊張的　　careless〔ˈkɛrlɪs〕adj. 不在意的
  anxious〔ˈæŋkʃəs〕adj. 焦慮的
  disappointed〔͵dɪsəˈpɔɪntɪd〕adj. 失望的
  hopeful〔ˈhopfəl〕adj. 充滿希望的

15. (**C**) M : Give me the usual, Maggie. Short on the sides,
　　　　　　　longer on the top, and tapered at the neck.

男：老樣子，瑪姬。兩邊剪短，上面留長，削薄到脖子。

W : I see a bit of dandruff, Chad. Have you been using
　　that conditioner I recommended?

女：我看到一些頭皮屑，查德。你有用我推薦的護髮乳嗎？

M : To be honest, yes and no. When I remember, yes, I
　　use it.

男：老實說，有時有，有時沒有。當我記得時，我有用它。

W : I'll give you a hot oil treatment. That should moisten
　　the scalp and eliminate the flaking.

女：我會幫你熱油護理。那個可以滋潤頭皮，除去掉屑的問題。

Question : Where is this conversation taking place?

這個對話發生在何處？

(A) A bakery. 麵包店。

(B) A clothing store. 服飾店。

(C) A hair salon. 美髮沙龍。

* usual ('juʒʊəl) adj. 平常的；一般的
the usual 慣常發生的事；老樣子　　Maggie ('mægɪ) n. 瑪姬
side (saɪd) n. (頭髮的) 側面　　taper ('tepɚ) v. 削薄
a bit of 一點點　　dandruff ('dændrʌf) n. 頭皮屑
Chad (tʃæd) n. 查德　　conditioner (kən'dɪʃənɚ) n. 護髮乳
recommend (ˌrɛkə'mɛnd) v. 推薦　　to be honest 老實說
yes and no 【用於無法給予明確答覆】是又不是
treatment ('tritmənt) n. 療程；修護
moisten ('mɔɪsn̩) v. 滋潤　　scalp (skælp) n. 頭皮
eliminate (ɪ'lɪməˌnet) v. 去除　　flake (flek) v. 掉屑
conversation (ˌkɑnvɚ'seʃən) n. 對話　　take place 發生
bakery ('bekərɪ) n. 麵包店　　clothing ('kloðɪŋ) n. 衣服
salon (sə'lɔn) n. 沙龍；理髮院

16. (**A**) M : Did you hear about Bradley? His doctor said he has
lung cancer.

男：你有沒有沒聽說布萊德利的事？他的醫生說他得了肺癌。

W : I wouldn't doubt it. The guy smokes five packs a day.

女：我不會懷疑這個消息。這傢伙一天抽五包菸。

M : Well, now maybe he'll think about quitting.

男：嗯，現在也許他會考慮戒菸。

Question : What is Bradley's problem?

布萊德利的問題是什麼？

(A) He has a serious illness. 他得了重病。

(B) He has an eating disorder. 他飲食失調。

(C) He has rotten teeth. 他有蛀牙。

* hear about 聽說；耳聞　　Bradley ('brædlɪ) n. 布萊德利
lung (lʌŋ) n. 肺　　cancer ('kænsɚ) n. 癌症

doubt〔daʊt〕v. 懷疑　　smoke〔smok〕v. 抽菸
pack〔pæk〕n. 包　　well〔wɛl〕interj. 嗯
think about 考慮　　quit〔kwɪt〕v. 停止
serious〔'sɪrɪəs〕adj. 嚴重的　　illness〔'ɪlnɪs〕n. 疾病
disorder〔dɪs'ɔrdɚ〕n. 失序；失調　　rotten〔'rɑtn̩〕adj. 壞掉的
rotten teeth 蛀牙 (= _decayed teeth_)

17. (**A**)　M：It's roasting out here today.

　　男：今天外面這裡真是有夠熱的。

　　W：Yeah, like being in an oven.

　　女：對啊,就像在烤箱裡。

　　M：Where's all that rain they're talking about? Goes to show what those weather guys know.

　　男：他們說好的降雨在哪裡?這證明了那些氣象人員所知道的。

　　W：Right. It was supposed to rain all week.

　　女：對啊,應該要下雨下整個禮拜的。

　　Question：What is true about the speakers?

　　　　　　　關於說話者,何者為真?

　　(A) They pay attention to weather forecasts.
　　　　他們有在注意氣象預報。

　　(B) They prefer warm temperatures over rain.
　　　　比起雨天,他們比較喜歡溫暖的天氣。

　　(C) They hope for rain. 他們希望下雨。

　 * roasting〔'rostɪŋ〕adj. 炙熱的；炎熱的　　**_out here_** 外面這裡
　　yeah〔jɛ〕interj. 是 (= _yes_)　　oven〔'ʌvən〕n. 烤箱
　　(it) goes to show that 證明了~；說明了~
　　be supposed to V. 應該要~　　rain〔ren〕v. 下雨
　　pay attention to 注意　　forecast〔'fɔrkæst〕n. 預報
　　weather forecast 天氣預報　　prefer〔prɪ'fɝ〕v. 比較喜歡
　　prefer A over B 喜歡 A 勝過 B (= _prefer A to B_)
　　temperature〔'tɛmpərətʃɚ〕n. 溫度

18. (**C**) How exactly can you build a better brain? Researchers
are still debating the potential power of brain training,
but there is one proven technique that neuroscientists
recognize as a powerful booster of brain health—exercise.
Regular physical activity has been shown to prevent brain
shrinkage as people age and improve mental functioning
both now and throughout life. Exercise can even make
you smarter.

你應該如何發展一個更好的頭腦？雖然研究人員仍然持續在探討
大腦訓練的潛在力量，但有一個經過證實的技巧，並被腦神經科
學家認可爲可以強力促進腦部健康的東西——運動。規律的運動
已經被證實，可以在人老化時，預防腦部萎縮，並且改善心理功
能，不僅是現在，也包含整個生命的過程。運動甚至可以讓你更
聰明。

Question：What is the speaker mainly talking about?
這個說話者主要在談論什麼？

(A) Age and body mass. 年齡及體重。

(B) Diet and nutrition. 飲食及營養。

(C) Health and wellness. 健康保健。

* exactly〔ɪg'zæktlɪ〕*adv.* 正確地
build〔bɪld〕*v.* 建造；發展　　brain〔bren〕*n.* 大腦
researcher〔rɪ'sɜtʃə〕*n.* 研究人員　　debate〔dɪ'bet〕*v.* 辨論
potential〔pə'tɛnʃəl〕*adj.* 能夠發展的；有潛力的
training〔'trenɪŋ〕*n.* 訓練　　proven〔'pruvən〕*adj.* 已經證實的
technique〔tɛk'nik〕*n.* 技術；技巧
neuroscientist〔'njurosaɪəntɪst〕*n.* 神經科學家
recognize〔'rɛkəg,naɪz〕*v.* 認出；承認
booster〔'bustə〕*n.* 促進物；有正面效果的事物
health〔hɛlθ〕*n.* 健康　　exercise〔'ɛksə,saɪz〕*n.* 運動
regular〔'rɛgjələ〕*adj.* 規律的　　physical〔'fɪzɪkl̩〕*adj.* 身體的
activity〔'æktɪvətɪ〕*n.* 活動　　show〔ʃo〕*v.* 證實（= *prove*）

prevent〔 prɪˋvɛnt 〕v. 避免　　shrinkage〔ˋʃrɪŋkɪdʒ 〕n. 萎縮

age〔ˋedʒ 〕v. 老化；變老

mental〔ˋmɛntḷ 〕adj. 精神的；心理的

functioning〔ˋfʌŋkʃənɪŋ 〕n. 功能

throughout〔 θruˋaʊt 〕prep. 在…的期間

mainly〔ˋmenlɪ 〕adv. 主要地　　age〔 edʒ 〕n. 年齡

mass〔 mæs 〕n. 質量；體重（＝weight）

body mass 質量　　diet〔ˋdaɪət 〕n. 節食；飲食

nutrition〔 njuˋtrɪʃən 〕n. 營養

wellness〔ˋwɛlnəs 〕n. 健康（＝health）

19. (**A**) If you have trouble falling asleep at night, you may need more light in the morning. Light exposure plays a key role in telling the body when to go to sleep and when to wake up. A walk outdoors first thing in the morning or light therapy for 30 minutes may help. On the other hand, if you find you're waking up too early in the morning, you may need more light late afternoon and could try taking a walk outdoors or light therapy for 2 to 3 hours in the evening. Home light therapy units are available and may be recommended by your doctor or sleep specialist.

如果你晚上難以入眠，你可能早上需要多一點的日照。日照扮演著重要的角色，在於告訴身體何時該睡覺，以及何時該起床。早晨到外面散步，或是三十分鐘的光療可能有幫助。另一方面，如果你發現早上太早起床，你下午的時候可能需要多一點的陽光，你可以試試看到戶外散步或是傍晚光療 2 到 3 小時。家庭光療裝置可以購買得到，也可能會由你的醫師或睡眠師來建議使用。

Question：What is the speaker mainly talking about?

這個說話者主要在談論什麼？

(A) Sleep. 睡眠。　　　　(B) Exercise. 運動。

(C) Nutrition. 營養。

* *have trouble + V-ing* …有困難 (= *have difficulty + V-ing*)

fall aslepp 睡著；入眠　　light〔laɪt〕*n.* 光線；日光

exposure〔ɪk'spoʒɚ〕*n.* 暴露

play a key role 扮演關鍵的角色　　*wake up* 起床

outdoors〔‚aut'dɔrz〕*adv.* 戶外的

first thing in the morning 早上第一件要做的事

therapy〔'θɛrəpɪ〕*n.* 療程

on the other hand 另外一方面來說

unit〔'junɪt〕*n.* 裝置；機件

available〔ə'veləbl̩〕*adj.* 可取得的；可購買的

recommend〔‚rɛkə'mɛnd〕*v.* 推薦

specialist〔'spɛʃəlɪst〕*n.* 專家　　mainly〔'menlɪ〕*adv.* 主要地

exercise〔'ɛksɚ‚saɪz〕*n.* 運動　　nutrition〔nju'trɪʃən〕*n.* 營養

20. (**B**)　W：Yesterday was Sandy's birthday.　She received many
　　　　　　wonderful gifts.

　　　女：昨天是珊蒂的生日。她收到很多很棒的禮物。

　　　M：What did you get her?

　　　男：妳買什麼給她？

　　　W：A designer handbag.

　　　女：一個名牌手提包？

　　　M：I bet it cost you an arm and a leg.

　　　男：我敢說它花了妳一大筆錢。

　　　Question：What does the man mean?

　　　　　　　　這位男士是什麼意思？

　　　(A) No one remembered his birthday.

　　　　　沒有人記得他的生日。

　　　(B) The handbag was expensive.

　　　　　手提包很貴。

　　　(C) Getting older is hard on everybody.

　　　　　對每個人來說，變老是有害的。

* wonderful〔'wʌndɚfəl〕adj. 很棒的　　gift〔gɪft〕n. 禮物
  get〔gɛt〕v. 買　　designer〔dɪ'zaɪnɚ〕adj. 設計師的；名牌的
  bet〔bɛt〕v. 打賭　　**I bet** 我敢肯定；我敢保證
  cost an arm and a leg 花很多錢（= cost a lot of money）
  mean〔min〕v. 意思是　　expensive〔ɪk'spɛnsɪv〕adj. 昂貴的
  hard〔hɑrd〕adj. 有害的；不利的　　**be hard on** 對…有害

21.(**C**)　W：Will you please stop complaining about the weather,
　　　　　　　Chris? You're driving me crazy.

　　　女：你可不可以停止抱怨天氣，克里斯？你快把我給逼瘋了。

　　　　　M：I can't help it. I'm not used to being indoors so
　　　　　　　much. The rain really brings me down.

　　　男：我就是忍不住。我不習慣待在室內這麼久。這雨會讓我心
　　　　　情很低落。

　　　　　W：It's not raining right now. Why don't you go out and
　　　　　　　get some fresh air? Go take a walk in the park.

　　　女：現在沒有在下雨。你何不出去呼吸新鮮空氣？去公園散步
　　　　　吧。

　　　　Question：What did the woman ask Chris to do?
　　　　　　　　　　這位女士要求克里斯去做什麼？

　(A) Start helping around the house. 開始幫忙做家事。

　(B) Finish playing his game. 結束玩遊戲。

　(C) Stop complaining about the weather. 停止抱怨天氣。

* complain〔kəm'plen〕v. 抱怨＜about＞
  weather〔'wɛðɚ〕n. 天氣　　Chris〔krɪs〕n. 克里斯
  drive sb. crazy 把某人逼瘋；使某人受不了（= really annoy sb.）
  can't help it 情不自禁；忍不住　　**be used to V-ing** 習慣於
  indoors〔ɪn'dɔrz〕adv. 在室內
  bring sb. down 讓某人心情低落；掃某人的興（= disappoint sb.）
  right now 現在；目前　　**get some fresh air** 呼吸新鮮空氣
  go + V. 去～（= go to V. = go and V.）　　**take a walk** 散步
  help around the house 幫忙做家事

TEST 7 詳解

聽力測驗 (第 1-21 題，共 21 題)

第一部分：辨識句意 (第 1-3 題，共 3 題)

1. (**B**) (A)   (B)   (C)

Bobby just crossed the finish line. 巴比剛通過終點線。

* just〔 dʒʌst〕 *adv.* 剛剛　　cross〔 krɔs〕 *v.* 越過
finish〔'fɪnɪʃ〕 *n.* 結束；終結　　line〔 laɪn〕 *n.* 線
finish line 終點線

2. (**C**) (A)   (B)   (C)

Jackson is mopping the floor. 傑克森正在拖地。

* mop〔 mɑp〕 *v.* (用拖把) 拖　　floor〔 flor〕 *n.* 地板

3. (**C**) (A)   (B)   (C)

The man is looking at a work of art.
這位男士正在看一件藝術品。

* work〔wɝk〕*n.* 作品　　art〔ɑrt〕*n.* 藝術
work of art 藝術品

第二部分：基本問答（第 4-10 題，共 7 題）

4. (**A**) When can we place the advertisement?
我們什麼時候可以登廣告？

(A) When Ms. Malloy approves it.
<u>當馬洛伊女士同意的時候。</u>

(B) This is a popular place. 這是一個熱門地點。

(C) In the city newspaper. 在城市報裡面。

* place〔ples〕*v.* 刊登　*n.* 地點
advertisement〔͵ædvɚˈtaɪzmənt〕*n.* 廣告
Ms.〔mɪz〕*n.* …女士　　Malloy〔ˈmælɔɪ〕*n.* 馬洛伊
approve〔əˈpruv〕*v.* 同意；贊成
popular〔ˈpɑpjəlɚ〕*adj.* 受歡迎的
city〔ˈsɪtɪ〕*n.* 城市　　newspaper〔ˈnjuz͵pepɚ〕*n.* 報紙

5. (**C**) Your report should be at least five-pages long.
你的報告應該至少要有五頁長。

(A) Are you sure you wouldn't mind? 你確定你不會介意？

(B) No, I think that's the wrong page.
不，我認為那個是錯誤的頁面。

(C) I've written more than that already.
<u>我已經寫得比那還多了。</u>

* report〔rɪˈport〕*n.* 報告　　*at least* 至少　　page〔pedʒ〕*n.* 頁
long〔lɔŋ〕*adj.* 長度…的　　sure〔ʃur〕*adj.* 確定的
mind〔maɪnd〕*v.* 介意　　wrong〔rɔŋ〕*adj.* 不正確的；錯誤的
already〔ɔlˈrɛdɪ〕*adv.* 已經；早就

6. (**A**) You can use my computer while I'm at lunch.

你可以在我吃午餐的時候，用我的電腦。

(A) Thanks, but mine's working again.

謝謝，但是我的電腦又可以用了。

(B) Yes, I bought mine three years ago.

對，我三年前買了我的電腦。

(C) Usually you meet me at one.

你通常在一點的時候和我碰面。

* use〔juz〕v. 使用　　computer〔kəm'pjutɚ〕n. 電腦
  be at lunch 吃午餐　　mine〔maɪn〕pron. 我的（東西）
  work〔wɝk〕v.（機器）運轉；作用
  bought〔bɔt〕v. 買【buy 的過去式】
  usually〔'juʒʊəlɪ〕adv. 通常　　meet〔mit〕v. 碰面；會面

7. (**A**) How do I get to the fitness center? 我該怎麼去健身中心？

(A) It's right next to the school. 它正好在學校隔壁。

(B) The instructors do. 這些講師這麼做。

(C) For an hour or so. 一個小時左右。

* get〔gɛt〕v. 到達；抵達 < to >　　fitness〔'fɪtnɪs〕n. 健康
  center〔'sɛntɚ〕n. 中心　　**fitness center** 健身中心
  right〔raɪt〕adv. 正好；剛好　　**next to** 在⋯的隔壁
  instructor〔ɪn'strʌktɚ〕n. 講師　　**or so** 大約；左右

8. (**B**) You'll receive your first paycheck next week.

你下禮拜會收到你的第一張薪水支票。

(A) I did that first. 我先做那個。

(B) I'd better open a bank account, then.

那麼我最好要開個銀行戶頭。

(C) She is the cashier. 她是出納員。

* receive〔rɪ'siv〕v. 收到
  first〔fɝst〕adj. 第一的；最初的　adv. 首先；最先

paycheck〔ˋpeˎtʃɛk〕*n.* 薪水支票　　　***had better V.*** 最好～
open〔ˋopən〕*v.* 開立（帳戶）　　　bank〔bæŋk〕*n.* 銀行
account〔əˋkaʊnt〕*n.* 帳戶　　　then〔ðɛn〕*adv.* 那麼
cashier〔kæˋʃɪr〕*n.* 出納員

9. (**A**) Do you speak American? 你說美語嗎？

　　(A) No, I speak English. 不，我說英語。

　　(B) I've been there a few times. 我已經去過那邊幾次了。

　　(C) The food is great. 這個食物很棒。

　　* American〔əˋmɛrɪkən〕*n.* 美語　　time〔taɪm〕*n.* 次

10. (**A**) Don't forget to bring an umbrella with you. It's supposed
　　　to rain this afternoon.

　　　別忘了帶把傘在你身邊。今天下午應該會下雨。

　　(A) Thanks for reminding me. 謝謝你提醒我。

　　(B) That should be fine. 那應該沒有關係。

　　(C) Leave it on the counter. 把它放在櫃台上。

　　* forget〔fɚˋgɛt〕*v.* 忘記　　bring〔brɪŋ〕*v.* 攜帶
　　umbrella〔ʌmˋbrɛlə〕*n.* 雨傘
　　suppose〔səˋpoz〕*v.* 猜想；推測　　***be supposed to V.*** 應該～
　　rain〔ren〕*v.* 下雨　　remind〔rɪˋmaɪd〕*v.* 提醒
　　fine〔faɪn〕*adj.* 令人滿意的；可接受的　　leave〔liv〕*v.* 留下
　　counter〔ˋkaʊntɚ〕*n.* 櫃台

第三部分：言談理解（第 11-21 題，共 11 題）

11. (**C**) M：Do you have any special plans for the long weekend?
　　　男：妳這個週末連假有任何特別的計畫嗎？

　　　W：Not yet. I'm thinking about taking a short trip
　　　　　somewhere.

　　　女：還沒有。我在想去某個地方短程旅行。

M：Hm. I wouldn't want to spend all that time sitting in traffic.

男：嗯。我不想把那所有時間花在塞車上。

Question：What does the man imply? 這位男士暗示什麼？

(A) The woman should go somewhere for the weekend.

　　這位女士週末應該會去某個地方。

(B) He is also taking a trip this weekend.

　　他這個週末也要去旅行。

(C) Many people will be traveling at the weekend.

　　很多人週末的時候會去旅行。

* special〔'spɛʃəl〕adj. 特別的　　plan〔plæn〕n. 計畫
weekend〔'wik'ɛnd〕n. 週末　　**long weekend** 週末連假
not yet 尚未；還沒　　trip〔trɪp〕n. 旅行
somewhere〔'sʌm,hwɛr〕adv. 在某處
hm〔hm〕interj.（表示遲疑、猶豫等）嗯
spend〔spɛnd〕v. 花（時間）　　traffic〔'træfɪk〕n. 交通
sit in traffic 遭遇交通阻塞　　imply〔ɪm'plaɪ〕v. 暗示
travel〔'trævl̩〕v. 旅行

12. (**A**) M：May I help you?

男：有我可以幫忙的嗎？

W：Yes, I need to see a doctor.

女：有，我需要看醫生。

M：What's the problem?

男：有什麼問題呢？

W：I have a terrible pain in my stomach.

女：我的胃痛得很厲害。

Question：Where are they? 他們在哪裡？

(A) In a hospital. 在醫院。　　(B) In a restaurant. 在餐廳。

(C) In a library. 在圖書館。

* help〔hɛlp〕v. 幫助　　need〔nid〕v. 需要
doctor〔'dɑktɚ〕n. 醫生　　**see a doctor** 看醫生
problem〔'prɑbləm〕n. 問題　　terrible〔'tɛrəbḷ〕adj. 劇烈的
pain〔pen〕n. 疼痛　　stomach〔'stʌmək〕n. 胃
hospital〔'hɑspɪtḷ〕n. 醫院　　library〔'laɪ,brɛrɪ〕n. 圖書館

13. (**C**) Green is *in*—and not just as a paint color. The latest, coolest bathroom trend is sure to please the gardeners and plant lovers out there: the green bathroom. Green bathrooms are making the rounds in magazines and design websites, featuring full green walls or small natural touches like a hanging flower pot or a fern on the corner of the counter.

綠色現在正夯——而且不只是指油漆顏色。最新、最酷的浴室趨勢肯定會受到戶外園藝人士，及愛好植物人的喜愛：綠化浴室。綠化的浴室現在不斷在雜誌上及設計師網站上流傳，特色是全綠色的牆或小型天然點綴，像是花盆吊飾，或是在櫃台角落的一叢蕨類植物。

Question： Which of the following would not be found in a green bathroom?

下列哪個不會在綠化的浴室中被找到？

(A) Green paint. 綠色油漆。
(B) Flowers. 花。
(C) Websites. 網站。

* in〔ɪn〕adj. 流行的　　**not just** 不只
paint〔pent〕n. 油漆　　latest〔'letɪst〕adj. 最新的
cool〔kul〕adj. 酷的　　bathroom〔'bæθ,rum〕n. 浴室
trend〔trɛnd〕n. 趨勢　　**be sure to V.** 一定～；勢必～
please〔pliz〕v. 討好；使高興

gardener ('gɑrdṇɚ) n. 園丁;園藝家

plant (plænt) n. 植物   lover ('lʌvɚ) n. 愛好者

make the rounds 流傳   magazine (,mægə'zin) n. 雜誌

design (dɪ'saɪn) n. 設計   website ('wɛb,saɪt) n. 網站

feature ('fitʃɚ) v. 以…為特色   full (fʊl) adj. 充足的;滿的

natural ('nætʃrəl) adj. 天然的   touch (tʌtʃ) n. 修飾;點綴

hanging ('hæŋɪŋ) v. 懸掛的   pot (pɑt) n. 鍋;盆

fern (fɜn) n. 蕨類   corner ('kɔrnɚ) n. 角落

counter ('kaʊntɚ) n. 櫃台

14. (**A**) W : Would you lend me something to write with? I need to fill out this form.

女：你可以借我個寫字的東西嗎？我需要填寫這張表格。

M : Sure. Pencil or pen?

男：當然可以。鉛筆還是原子筆？

W : Either one is fine. Oh, no. Wait. Says it has to be filled out in ink. Do you have a black or blue pen?

女：任何一個都可以。噢，不。等一下。它說要用有墨水的筆來填。你有黑色或藍色原子筆嗎？

M : Yes. Here you go.

男：有。給妳。

W : Thanks. I'll return it as soon as I'm finished.

女：謝謝。我寫完會立刻還。

M : Don't worry about it. I have other pens.

男：不用擔心。我有其他的筆。

Question : What is the woman doing? 這位女士在做什麼？

(A) Filling out a form. 填表。

(B) Applying for a job. 申請工作。

(C) Taking an exam. 考試。

* lend (lɛnd) v. 借   fill (fɪl) v. 裝滿;填滿

fill out 填寫　form〔fɔrm〕*n.* 表格

either〔'iðɚ〕*adj.* 兩者之一的

oh〔o〕*interj.*（表示驚訝、恐懼等）噢；啊

wait〔wet〕*v.* 等候

Says it⋯ 表格上寫著⋯（= *The forms says it⋯*）

ink〔ɪŋk〕*n.* 墨水　　*here you go* 在這裡；給你

return〔rɪ'tɝn〕*v.* 歸還　　*as soon as* 一⋯就

finished〔'fɪnɪʃt〕*adj.*（人）完成的；工作做完的

worry〔'wɝi〕*v.* 擔心 < *about* >

apply〔ə'plaɪ〕*v.* 申請 < *for* >　job〔dʒɑb〕*n.* 工作

exam〔ɪg'zæm〕*n.* 考試（= *examination*）

take an exam 考試

15. (**A**)　M：What are you looking for?

　　　　　男：妳在找什麼？

　　　　　W：My wallet. Have you seen it?

　　　　　女：我的皮夾。你有看到嗎？

　　　　　M：I think I saw it on the kitchen counter this morning.

　　　　　男：我想我今天早上在廚房料理台上有看到。

　　　　　W：That's right! I left it there last night. Thanks.

　　　　　女：沒錯！我昨晚上把它留在那裡了，謝謝。

　　　　　Question：What will the woman most likely do next?

　　　　　　　　　　這位女士接下來最有可能做什麼？

　　　　　(A) Go to the kitchen. 去廚房。

　　　　　(B) Leave for work. 去上班。

　　　　　(C) Make dinner. 做晚餐。

　　* *look for* 尋找　wallet〔'wɑlɪt〕*n.* 皮夾

　　counter〔'kaʊntɚ〕*n.*（廚房的）操作台；工作台

　　That's right. 沒錯。　　likely〔'laɪklɪ〕*adv.* 可能

　　leave〔liv〕*v.* 離開　　*leave for* 前往

　　work〔wɝk〕*n.* 工作

16. (**A**) In young adults, the heart beats between 70 and 200 times per minute. In one year, the heart beats around 100,000 times. In 70 years, your heart will beat more than 2.5 billion times. When at rest, the heart can pump approximately 1.3 gallons of blood per minute. Blood circulates through the entire system of blood vessels in only 20 seconds. In a day, the heart pumps around 2,000 gallons of blood through thousands of miles of blood vessels.

青壯年的心跳每分鐘 70 到 200 次。心臟一年大概跳 10 萬次。你的心臟 70 年下來可以跳超過 25 億次。當休息時,心跳每分鐘可以輸送大概 1.3 加侖的血液。血液只需要 20 秒就可以在整個血管系統循環一次。一天下來,心臟可以在數千英哩的血管中,輸送大概 2000 加侖的血液。

Question: A young adult heart beats how many times per minute? 一位青壯年的心臟每分鐘跳幾次?

(A) Between 70 and 200. 在 70 到 200 次之間。

(B) Around 100,000. 大約 100,000 次。

(C) Less than 1.3. 少於 1.3 次。

* adult〔ə'dʌlt〕n. 成人　*young adult* 年輕成人;青壯年
heart〔hɑrt〕n. 心臟　　beat〔bit〕v.(心臟)跳動
time〔taɪm〕n. 次數　　per〔pɚ〕prep. 每…
around〔ə'raʊnd〕adv. 大概　　billion〔'bɪljən〕n. 十億
rest〔rɛst〕n. 休息　　*at rest* 在休息
pump〔pʌmp〕v.(用幫浦)抽;吸;注入
approximately〔ə'prɑksəmɪtlɪ〕adv. 大約
gallon〔'gælən〕n. 加侖　　blood〔blʌd〕n. 血
circulate〔'sɝkjə,let〕v. 循環　　entire〔ɪn'taɪr〕adj. 全部的
system〔'sɪstəm〕n. 系統　　vessel〔'vɛsl〕n. 血管
mile〔maɪl〕n. 哩;英里【約 1.6 公里】

17. (**C**) M：Are you busy right now?

　　　男：妳現在在忙嗎？

　　　W：No, what do you need?

　　　女：沒有，你需要什麼？

　　　M：I could really use some help carrying these boxes to the car.

　　　男：我可能真的需要有人幫忙我搬這些箱子到那台車去。

　　　W：OK.

　　　女：好。

　　　Question：What does the man ask the woman to do?

　　　　　　　這位男士請這位女士做什麼？

　　　(A) Drive him somewhere. 載他去某處。

　　　(B) Take something to the post office. 拿東西去郵局。

　　　(C) Help him move some boxes. 幫他移動箱子。

　　　* **right now** 現在；目前　　really〔ˋrɪəlɪ〕adv. 真正地
　　　　could use 很想要（= need）　　carry〔ˋkærɪ〕v. 運送；搬運
　　　　box〔bɑks〕n. 箱子　　ask〔æsk〕v. 請求
　　　　drive〔draɪv〕v. 開車載（某人）
　　　　post office 郵局　　move〔muv〕v. 移動

18. (**C**) W：Whose towel is this? Why is it on the floor?

　　　女：這條毛巾是誰的？為什麼它在地上？

　　　M：It's probably Jane's. She was taking a shower.

　　　男：可能是珍的。她剛在洗澡。

　　　W：Well, it's wet. Please hang it up so that it can dry.

　　　女：嗯，它是溼的。請把它掛起來讓它乾。

　　　M：Why me? I didn't leave it on the floor.

　　　男：為什麼是我？我沒有把它放地上。

　　　W：What difference does that make? Just hang it up.

　　　女：有什麼關係？就把它掛起來。

Question：Why is the towel on the floor?

為什麼這條毛巾在地上？

(A) Because it's wet. 因為它是濕的。

(B) The man took a shower. 這位男士洗了澡。

(C) Someone left it there. 有人把它留在那裡。

* towel〔taʊl〕*n.* 毛巾　　floor〔flor〕*n.* 地板
probably〔'prɑbəblɪ〕*adv.* 可能　　shower〔'ʃaʊɚ〕*n.* 淋浴
take a shower 洗澡；淋浴　　well〔wɛl〕*interj.* 嗯
wet〔wɛt〕*adj.* 濕的　　***hang up*** 掛上；掛起
dry〔draɪ〕*v.* 變乾　　difference〔'dɪfrəns〕*n.* 不同；差異
make a difference 有差別；有關係；有影響

19. (**A**) M：Hi, Monica. I'm supposed to give a presentation about our information security services in my computer class tomorrow. I want it to be perfect. Could you listen while I practice it and tell me what you think?

男：嗨，莫妮卡。我明天的電腦課應該要做個關於資訊安全服務的報告。我想要讓這個報告很完美。妳可以聽我練習，然後告訴我妳覺得如何嗎？

W：Of course, I'd be happy to give you some feedback. I'm free right now if that works for you. Where should we go?

女：當然，我很樂意給你一些回饋意見。我現在就有空，如果你也方便的話。我們要去哪裡練？

M：There's no one in the computer lab right now. We could do it there.

男：現在電腦教室沒人。我們可以在那裡練。

Question：What does Monica agree to do?

莫尼卡同意要去做什麼？

(A) Give the man some feedback. 給這男士一點回饋意見。

(B) Take notes at a meeting. 在一個會議中做筆記。

(C) Develop a presentation. 研擬一個報告。

* **be supposed to V**. 應該~

presentation (ˌprɛzən'teʃən) *n.* 報告；介紹

information (ˌɪnfə'meʃən) *n.* 資訊

security (sɪ'kjurətɪ) *n.* 安全   service ('sɝvɪs) *n.* 服務

perfect ('pɝfɪkt) *adj.* 完美的   practice ('præktɪs) *v.* 練習

of course 當然   feedback ('fid,bæk) *n.* 回饋意見

free (fri) *adj.* 有空的   *right now* 現在

work (wɝk) *v.* 有用；行得通

lab (læb) *n.* 實驗室 (= *laboratory*)   agree (ə'gri) *v.* 同意

notes (nots) *n. pl.* 筆記   meeting ('mitɪŋ) *n.* 會議

develop (dɪ'vɛləp) *v.* 發展；制定；研擬

20. (**C**) M : Where should we hold our group meeting? The science lab is already occupied.

男：我們應該在哪裡辦我們的小組會議？科學實驗室已經有人用了。

W : How about right here in the cafeteria?

女：就在這個自助餐廳如何？

M : No, it's too loud and crowded in here. We need to focus on our discussion.

男：不，這裡面太吵又擁擠。我們必須專心討論。

W : We could always sit outside. There's plenty of open space on campus, and besides, it's a nice day.

女：我們可以一直坐在外面。校園內有很多開放空間，而且今天天氣很好。

M : You're right. I'm sure everyone will appreciate the chance to get some fresh air.

男：妳說得對。我很確信大家會珍惜這個呼吸新鮮空氣的機會。

Question : Where will they hold the meeting?
他們會在哪裡舉辦會議？

(A) In the science lab. 在科學實驗室。

(B) In the cafeteria. 在自助餐廳。

(C) Outdoors. 在戶外。

* hold〔hold〕v. 舉行　　group〔grup〕n. 小組
meeting〔'mitɪŋ〕n. 開會　　science〔'saɪəns〕n. 科學
occupy〔'ɑkjə͵paɪ〕v. 佔用；使用　　*How about…?* …如何？
cafeteria〔͵kæfə'tɪrɪə〕n. 自助餐廳　　loud〔laʊd〕adj. 吵雜的
crowded〔'kraʊdɪd〕adj. 擁擠的　　focus〔'fokəs〕v. 專注 *< on >*
discussion〔dɪ'skʌʃən〕n. 討論　　*plenty of* 很多
open〔'opən〕adj. 開放的　　space〔spes〕n. 空間
campus〔'kæmpəs〕n. 校園　　*on campus* 在校園裡
besides〔bɪ'saɪdz〕adv. 此外；而且
nice〔naɪs〕adj.（天氣）宜人的　　*You're right.* 你說的對。
appreciate〔ə'priʃɪ͵et〕v. 感激；重視；珍惜
chance〔tʃæns〕n. 機會　　fresh〔frɛʃ〕adj. 新鮮的
get some fresh air 呼吸新鮮空氣
outdoors〔'aʊt'dorz〕adv. 在戶外

21. (**B**) Global climate change is affecting the world's ecosystem
—and your grocery store offerings—in more ways than
you might realize. As ocean waters get warmer, lobster
populations shift north and supplies run low. With both
daytime and nightly temps continually rising, and pesky
droughts sticking around, many crops are taking a serious
hit. There are many foods that might not survive the heat
at all. And the worst part is that they're likely your
favorites.

全球氣候變遷正在影響世界生態系統——還有你家附近超市的商
品——比你想像的影響還多。當海水越來越溫暖，龍蝦群北遷而供應量減少。隨著日夜溫度持續上升，而討厭的乾旱持續逗留，很多農作物遭受嚴重的損害。有很多作物可能在這種炎熱下完全無法生存。而且最慘的是這些作物可能是你最喜歡吃的。

Question： What does the speaker indicate?

　　　　　　　　說話者指出什麼？

(A) The earth is getting colder. 地球正在變冷。

(B) The oceans are getting warmer. <u>海洋正在暖化。</u>

(C) Food is getting cheaper. 食物正在變便宜。

* global〔ˋglobḷ〕adj. 全球的　　climate〔ˋklaɪmɪt〕n. 氣候
change〔tʃendʒ〕n. 變化；變遷　　affect〔əˋfɛkt〕v. 影響
world〔wɜld〕n. 世界　　ecosystem〔ˋɛkoˏsɪstəm〕n. 生態系統
grocery〔ˋgrosərɪ〕n. 雜貨　　**grocery store** 雜貨店
offering〔ˋɔfərɪŋ〕n. 出售物　　way〔we〕n. 方法；方式
realize〔ˋriəˏlaɪz〕v. 了解　　ocean〔ˋoʃən〕n. 海洋
warm〔wɔrm〕adj. 溫暖的　　lobster〔ˋlɑbstɚ〕n. 龍蝦
population〔ˏpɑpjəˋleʃən〕n. 族群；群體
shift〔ʃɪft〕v. 移動；轉移　　north〔nɔrθ〕adv. 向北
supplies〔səˋplaɪz〕n. pl. 供應；供應量　　run〔rʌn〕v. 變；成
low〔lo〕adj. 低的　　**run low** 快用完；短缺
daytime〔ˋdeˏtaɪm〕adj. 白天的；日間的
nightly〔ˋnaɪtlɪ〕adj. 每夜的；夜間的
temp〔tɛmp〕n. 溫度（= temperature）
continually〔kənˋtɪnjʊəlɪ〕adv. 持續地；不斷地
rise〔raɪz〕v. 上升　　pesky〔ˋpɛskɪ〕adj. 討厭的；麻煩的
drought〔draʊt〕n. 乾旱　　**stick around** 逗留；不離開
crop〔krɑp〕n. 農作物　　serious〔ˋsɪrɪəs〕adj. 嚴重的
hit〔hɪt〕n. 打　　**take a hit** 受到嚴重影響（= be badly affected）
survive〔səˋvaɪv〕v. 存活；生還　　heat〔hit〕n. 熱
not at all 一點也不　　favorite〔ˋfevrɪt〕n. 最喜愛的事物
speaker〔ˋspikɚ〕n. 說話者　　indicate〔ˋɪndəˏket〕v. 指出
earth〔ɝθ〕n. 地球

TEST 8 詳解

聽力測驗 (第 1-21 題，共 21 題)

第一部分：辨識句意 (第 1-3 題，共 3 題)

1. (**B**) (A)　　　　　　(B)　　　　　　(C)

They are cleaning the beach. 他們正在淨灘。

* clean〔klin〕v. 清理　　beach〔bitʃ〕n. 海灘

2. (**A**) (A)　　　　　　(B)　　　　　　(C)

 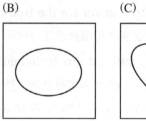 

This is a star. 這是一個星型。

* star〔stɑr〕n. 星；星狀物

3. (**B**) (A)　　　　　　(B)　　　　　　(C)

The painting costs 50,000 NT. 這幅畫要價新台幣五萬元。

* painting (ˈpentɪŋ) *n.* 畫　　cost (kɔst) *v.* 值⋯價錢
NT 新台幣 (= *New Taiwan* = *NT$* = *NTD*)

第二部分：基本問答（第 4-10 題，共 7 題）

4. (**B**) Can you have my order ready by tomorrow morning?

你可以在明天早上把我點的餐準備好嗎？

(A) Thanks. See you then. 謝謝。到時候見。

(B) We'll do our best. 我們會竭盡全力。

(C) It's the second door on the right.

在右手邊的第二扇門。

* order (ˈɔrdɚ) *n.* 點餐　　ready (ˈrɛdɪ) *adj.* 預備好的
do one's best 竭盡全力　　right (raɪt) *n.* 右側；右方

5. (**A**) I'd like to register for the free computer training class.

我想要登記免費的電腦訓練課程。

(A) OK. Fill out this form and return it to me.

好的。填寫這張表格然後交回來給我。

(B) Not yet. He'll be here in a minute.

還沒有。他很快就會來這裡。

(C) Sometimes. I'm not sure. 有時候。我不確定。

* *would like to V.* 想要～　　register (ˈrɛdʒɪstɚ) *v.* 登記；註冊
free (fri) *adj.* 免費的　　computer (kəmˈpjutɚ) *n.* 電腦
training (ˈtrenɪŋ) *n.* 訓練　　class (klæs) *n.* 課
fill out 填寫　　form (fɔrm) *n.* 表格
return (rɪˈtɝn) *v.* 交還　　*not yet* 尚未；還沒
minute (ˈmɪnɪt) *n.* 分鐘　　*in a minute* 立刻
sure (ʃʊr) *adj.* 確定的

6. (**A**) I was wondering if I might ask a favor?

我想知道我是否可以請你幫個忙？

(A) Sure. What can I do for you?

當然。我可以爲你做什麼？

(B) Not at all. It was on my way. 一點也不。我在路上。

(C) That's OK. I wasn't hungry. 沒關係。我不餓。

* wonder〔'wʌndɚ〕v. 想知道　　ask〔æsk〕v. 請求；要求
favor〔'fevɚ〕n. 幫忙　　sure〔ʃur〕adv. 當然
not at all 一點也不　　hungry〔'hʌŋgrɪ〕adj. 飢餓的

7. (**C**) How many vacation days do you have left?

你還剩下幾天休假？

(A) Yes. Next Friday. 是的。下週五。

(B) I don't know yet. Sometime in July.

我還不知道。七月的某個時候。

(C) None. I've used them up already.

沒有。我已經把它們用光了。

* vacation〔ve'keʃən〕n. 休假
left〔lɛft〕v. 剩下【leave 的過去式】
know〔no〕v. 知道　　use〔juz〕v. 使用
use up 用完；耗盡　　already〔ɔl'rɛdɪ〕adv. 已經

8. (**C**) What does your father do for a living?

你父親是從事什麼謀生？

(A) Not very often. 不是很常。

(B) That's my brother. 那位是我的兄弟。

(C) He's a doctor. 他是一位醫生。

* living〔'lɪvɪŋ〕n. 生計；生活　　doctor〔'dɑktɚ〕n. 醫生

9. (**B**) Why are you still in bed? It's going on noon!

你爲什麼還在床上？已經要接近中午了！

(A) Thanks, I'll do that. 謝謝，我會那麼做的。

(B) I don't feel well. <u>我覺得不太舒服。</u>

(C) Open the window. 把窗戶打開。

* ***be going on*** 接近；快到　　noon〔nun〕*n.* 中午
feel〔fil〕*v.* 感覺到　　well〔wɛl〕*adj.* 健康的；安好的
window〔'wɪndo〕*n.* 窗戶

10. (**B**) Would you like to subscribe to our newsletter?

你想要訂閱我們的時事通訊嗎？

(A) On the black card. 在黑卡上。

(B) I signed up last week. <u>我上個禮拜訂了。</u>

(C) The calendar of community events.
社區活動的行事曆。

* suscribe〔səb'skraɪb〕*v.* 訂閱＜*to*＞
newsletter〔'njuz'lɛtə〕*n.* 時事通訊
black card 黑卡【美國運通發行的邀請式信用卡】
sign up 註冊；報名　　calendar〔'kæləndə〕*n.* 行事曆
community〔kə'mjunətɪ〕*n.* 社區　　event〔ɪ'vɛnt〕*n.* 事件

第三部分：言談理解（第 11-21 題，共 11 題）

11. (**A**) W：It's a beautiful day for the Saturday market, isn't it?
And it looks like you've got some nice strawberries
for sale today. Are these from your farm?

女：這對週六的市場來說眞是美好的一天，不是嗎？而且看來今
天你有一些很不錯的草莓可以賣。這些都是從你的農場來的
嗎？

M : Yes, all the fruit you see here was grown right on my farm. It's picked just before we bring it to the market so it's always fresh.

男：是的，你看到的所有水果都是在我的農場種的。這都是在我們帶來市場前才採收的，所以總是很新鮮。

Question : Where are the speakers? 說話者在哪裡？

(A) At an outdoor market. 在一個戶外市場。

(B) At an art studio. 在一間藝術工作室。

(C) On a farm. 在一個農場。

beautiful ('bjutəfəl) *adj.* 很好的；很棒的
market ('mɑrkɪt) *n.* 市集；市場   *look like* 看來；好像
nice (naɪs) *adj.* 好的   strawberry ('strɔ,bɛrɪ) *n.* 草莓
sale (sel) *n.* 銷售；出售   *for sale* 出售的
farm (fɑrm) *n.* 農場   fruit (frut) *n.* 水果
grow (gro) *v.* 種植；栽培   right (raɪt) *adv.* 正好；剛好
pick (pɪk) *v.* 摘；採   bring (brɪŋ) *v.* 帶來
fresh (frɛʃ) *adj.* 新鮮的   outdoor ('aut,dor) *adj.* 戶外的
art (ɑrt) *n.* 藝術   studio ('stjudɪ,o) *n.* 工作室

12. (**C**) M : You've put in a lot of hours lately, Shelly. Why don't you take the rest of the weekend off?

男：妳最近已經投入很多時間，雪莉。為什麼剩下的週末妳不好好休假呢？

W : I can't, Mr. Jackson. I have to finish these reports.

女：我不能，傑克森先生。我必須完成這些報告。

M : Don't worry about the reports, Shelly. We don't need them until the middle of next week.

男：別擔心那些報告，雪莉。我們一直到下禮拜三以前都不需要它們。

W : Thanks, Mr. Jackson. I guess I really could use a
　　break.

女：謝謝，傑克森先生。我想我真的需要休息一下。

Question : What kind of boss is Mr. Jackson?

　　　　　傑克森先生是怎樣的老闆？

(A) Mean. 卑鄙的。

(B) Funny. 滑稽的。

(C) Caring. 貼心的。

* **put in** 投入；花費（時間）　　hours〔aurz〕*n. pl.* 長時間
　lately〔'letlɪ〕*adv.* 最近　　rest〔rɛst〕*n.* 剩餘
　take off 休假　　finish〔'fɪnɪʃ〕*v.* 完成
　report〔rɪ'port〕*n.* 報告
　worry〔'wɝi〕*v.* 擔心；憂慮＜*about*＞
　until〔ən'tɪl〕*prep.* 直到　　middle〔'mɪdḷ〕*n.* 中間
　guess〔gɛs〕*v.* 猜想　　use〔juz〕*v.* 利用
　could use 需要（＝*need*）　　break〔brek〕*n.* 休假；休息
　boss〔bɔs〕*n.* 老闆　　mean〔min〕*adj.* 卑鄙的
　funny〔'fʌnɪ〕*adj.* 滑稽的　　caring〔'kɛrɪŋ〕*adj.* 貼心的

13. (**B**) M : Could you make me a cup of coffee?

　　　　　男：妳可以幫我泡一杯咖啡嗎？

　　　　W : Sure. How do you take it?

　　　　　女：當然。你想要怎麼喝？

　　　　M : Cream and sugar, if you don't mind.

　　　　　男：加奶精和糖，如果妳不介意的話。

　　　　W : No problem.

　　　　　女：沒問題。

　　　　Question : What do we know about the man?

　　　　　　　　　關於這位男士，我們知道什麼？

(A) He prefers tea. 他偏好茶。

(B) He drinks coffee. 他喝咖啡。

(C) He enjoys sweets. 他很喜歡甜食。

* make〔mek〕v. 做；製作　　cup〔kʌp〕n. 一杯的量
coffee〔'kɔfɪ〕n. 咖啡　　take〔tek〕v. 吃；喝
cream〔krim〕n. 奶精　　sugar〔'ʃugɚ〕n. 糖
mind〔maɪnd〕v. 介意　　problem〔'prɑbləm〕n. 問題
prefer〔prɪ'fɝ〕v. 比較喜歡　　tea〔ti〕n. 茶
drink〔drɪŋk〕v. 喝；飲　　enjoy〔ɪn'dʒɔɪ〕v. 享受；享用
sweets〔swits〕n. pl. 甜食

14. (**B**)　M : How much is a round-trip ticket to London?

男：去倫敦的來回機票要多少錢？

W : That depends.

女：這要看情況。

M : On what?

男：看什麼情況？

W : When you buy the ticket and when you plan to travel.

女：你什麼時候買票和你計畫什麼時候去旅行。

Question : What does the man want to know?

這位男士想知道什麼？

(A) The schedule of flights to London.

飛往倫敦的航班時間表。

(B) The price of a ticket to and from London.

來回倫敦的機票價錢。

(C) The dates when the woman will be in London.

這位女士會在倫敦的日期。

* round-trip〔'raʊnd,trɪp〕adj. 來回的；雙程的
ticket〔'tɪkɪt〕n. 機票　　London〔'lʌndən〕n. 倫敦

depend〔dɪ'pɛnd〕v. 視…而定 < on >
plan〔plæn〕v. 計畫　　travel〔'trævḷ〕v. 旅行
schedule〔'skɛdʒul〕n. 時間表
flight〔flaɪt〕n. 班機；航班　　price〔praɪs〕n. 價錢
to and from 來回　　date〔det〕n. 日期

15. (**A**) Getting fruit from the tree to the table is complicated. A citrus fruit is a living organism which must be protected from injury, decay and water loss on its journey across the country or across the ocean. Fruit are carefully picked by hand and put into bins which hold about 900 pounds. The bins are hauled by truck to a packing house, where the fruit is washed to clean away field dirt and dust.

從樹上把水果送到桌上的過程是很複雜的。一顆柑橘類水果是一個活的有機體，在跨國或越洋的旅程中必須被保護好，以免碰傷、腐爛和流失水分。水果被小心翼翼地用手摘取，並且放進可以容納 900 磅的大箱子。箱子被卡車拖進一個包裝間，在那裡水果被清洗，將田裡的污垢和灰塵去除。

Question：How is fruit usually brought to the packing house? 水果通常是如何被帶去包裝間的？

(A) By truck. 用卡車。

(B) By hand. 用手。

(C) By ship. 用船。

* complicated〔'kɑmplə,ketɪd〕adj. 複雜的
citrus〔'sɪtrəs〕adj. 柑橘屬的　　living〔'lɪvɪŋ〕adj. 活的
organism〔'ɔrgən,ɪzəm〕n. 有機體
protect〔prə'tɛkt〕v. 保護
protect…from ~ 保護…免於~
injury〔'ɪndʒərɪ〕n. 傷害；損害　　decay〔dɪ'ke〕n. 腐爛

loss〔lɔs〕*n.* 減少　　journey〔'dʒɜnɪ〕*n.* 旅程

across〔ə'krɔs〕*prep.* 橫越　　country〔'kʌntrɪ〕*n.* 國家

ocean〔'oʃən〕*n.* 海洋　　carefully〔'kɛrfəlɪ〕*adv.* 小心地

pick〔pɪk〕*v.* 採；摘　　put〔pʊt〕*v.* 放置

bin〔bɪn〕*n.* 大箱子　　hold〔hold〕*v.* 容納

pound〔paʊnd〕*n.* 磅　　haul〔hɔl〕*v.* 拖；拉

truck〔trʌk〕*n.* 卡車；貨車

packing〔'pækɪŋ〕*n.* 包裝

house〔haʊs〕*n.* (特殊用途的) 建築物

wash〔waʃ〕*v.* 洗滌　　clean〔klin〕*v.* 清理

field〔fild〕*n.* 田地　　dirt〔dɜt〕*n.* 泥土

dust〔dʌst〕*n.* 塵土　　ship〔ʃɪp〕*n.* 船

16. (**B**) M：Where did you get these delicious oranges?

男：妳從哪裡買到這些好吃的橘子？

W：At the produce market on 46th Avenue.

女：在第四十六大道上的農產品市場。

M：Are oranges in season right now?

男：現在橘子盛產嗎？

W：Because they're grown in many parts of the world, oranges are always in season.

女：因爲世界上很多地方都有種，所以橘子一直處於盛產。

Question：Where did the woman get the oranges?

這位女士從哪裡買到橘子？

(A) From a tree in her backyard. 從她後院的一棵樹上。

(B) From a local market. 從一個當地的市場。

(C) From a supermarket. 從一個超級市場。

* get〔gɛt〕*v.* 買　　delicious〔dɪ'lɪʃəs〕*adj.* 美味的

produce〔'pradjus〕*n.* 農產品　　market〔'markɪt〕*n.* 市場

avenue〔'ævə,nju〕*n.* 大道　　season〔'sizn̩〕*n.* 季節

in season　當季的；盛產的　　grow〔gro〕v. 種植
parts〔parts〕n. pl. 地方　　backyard〔'bækjard〕n. 後院
local〔'lokḷ〕adj. 當地的；本地的
supermarket〔'supɚ,markɪt〕n. 超市

17. (**C**)　W : Hey, where have you been?

女：嘿，你去哪裡了？

M : I've been training for a marathon. I've been running day and night, sometimes up to 20 miles a day.

男：我一直在為了一場馬拉松訓練。我日夜不停的持續跑步，有時候一天達到二十哩。

W : Wow. Sounds like you have to be pretty dedicated.

女：哇。聽起來你必須要非常投入。

Question : What has the man been doing?

這位男士一直在做什麼？

(A) Studying for an exam.　為了考試讀書。

(B) Hiding from the woman.　躲避這位女士。

(C) Training for an athletic event.　為了競賽項目訓練。

* train〔tren〕v. 訓練
 marathon〔'mærə,θɑn〕n. 馬拉松
 run〔rʌn〕v. 跑步　　day and night　日以繼夜
 up to　高達　　mile〔maɪl〕n. 哩；英里
 sound〔saʊnd〕v. 聽起來　　have to V. 必須～
 pretty〔'prɪtɪ〕adv. 相當；非常
 dedicated〔'dɛdə,ketɪd〕adj. 專注的；投入的
 exam〔ɪg'zæm〕n. 考試（= examination）
 hide〔haɪd〕v. 躲避；藏匿　　hide from sb.　躲避某人
 athletic〔æθ'lɛtɪk〕adj. （運動）競賽的；體育的
 event〔ɪ'vɛnt〕n. 事件；（運動）項目

18. (**B**) The Chinese Ghost Festival is a month long event which takes place every year, during the seventh month of the Chinese calendar, which is around August in the western calendar. Religious events related to the Chinese Ghost Festival are held at various temples in cities throughout Taiwan during the entire month.

中元節是個每年舉行長達一個月的活動，在中國農曆的第七個月，大約在西曆的八月。在這整個月期間，全台灣各個城市的許多寺廟都會舉行和中元節相關的宗教活動。

Question : In which month does the Ghost Festival take place? 中元節是在哪一個月份舉行？

(A) Sixth. 第六個。

(B) Seventh. 第七個。

(C) Eighth. 第八個。

* ghost〔gost〕*n.* 鬼　　festival〔'fɛstəv!〕*n.* 節日；節慶
the Chinese Ghost Festival 中元節
long〔lɔŋ〕*adj.* 長度…的　　***take place*** 舉行
calendar〔'kæləndɚ〕*n.* 日曆；月曆
Chinese calendar 中國農曆
around〔ə'raund〕*prep.* 大約　　western〔'wɛstən〕*adj.* 西洋的
religious〔rɪ'lɪdʒəs〕*adj.* 宗教的　　***related to*** 與…有關
hold〔hold〕*v.* 舉行　　various〔'vɛrɪəs〕*adj.* 各式各樣的
temple〔'tɛmp!〕*n.* 寺廟　　city〔'sɪtɪ〕*n.* 城市
throughout〔θru'aut〕*prep.* 遍及
entire〔ɪn'taɪr〕*adj.* 全體的；全部的

19. (**A**) M : Is it supposed to rain this afternoon? I'm planning to go on a hike.

男：今天下午會下雨嗎？我正在計畫要去遠足。

W : There's a chance of a thunderstorm this afternoon.
You'd better take an umbrella, just in case.

女： 今天有可能會有午後雷陣雨。你最好帶一支傘，以防萬一。

M : I really don't want to carry an umbrella throughout
the hike. I don't have one that will fit in my
backpack.

男： 我眞的不想要整個遠足都帶著一支雨傘。我沒有一支可以放
進我後背包的傘。

W : In that case, a light raincoat might be a good choice.

女： 那樣的話，一件輕便雨衣可能是一個好選擇。

Question : What will happen this afternoon?

今天下午會發生什麼事？

(A) The man will go on a hike. <u>這位男士會去遠足。</u>

(B) The man will carry an umbrella.

這位男士會帶一支傘。

(C) It will rain. 會下雨。

* suppose〔 sə'poz 〕v. 認爲
  be supposed to V. 據說~　　rain〔 ren 〕v. 下雨
  afternoon〔ˌæftə'nun 〕n. 下午
  plan〔 plæn 〕v. 計畫　　hike〔 haɪk 〕n. 遠足
  go on a hike 去遠足　　chance〔 tʃæns 〕n. 機會
  thunderstorm〔'θʌndəˌstɔrm 〕n. 雷雨
  had better V. 最好~　　umbrella〔 ʌm'brɛlə 〕n. 雨傘
  case〔 kes 〕n. 情形；場合　　**in case** 以防萬一
  carry〔'kærɪ 〕v. 攜帶
  throughout〔 θru'aʊt 〕prep. 在…的期間
  fit〔 fɪt 〕v. 適合；符合　　backpack〔'bækˌpæk 〕n. 後背包
  in that case 那樣的話　　light〔 laɪt 〕adj. 輕的
  raincoat〔'renˌkot 〕n. 雨衣　　choice〔 tʃɔɪs 〕n. 選擇

20. (**B**) W : How long have you been a smoker?

女：你抽煙多久了？

M : I started in high school.

男：我從高中開始。

W : It's a really bad habit, you know. Smoking kills thousands of people every year.

女：這真的是一個壞習慣，你知道的。每年有好幾千人因為吸煙而死亡。

M : I know. I'm trying to cut back. Quitting is very difficult.

男：我知道。我正在試著減量。戒掉是非常困難的。

W : Have you tried seeking medical treatment? They have special programs to help people quit.

女：你有嘗試尋求醫療嗎？他們有特殊的計畫幫助人們戒煙。

M : Nah, I don't have the time or patience for that.

男：不，我沒有時間和耐心做那個。

Question : What do we know about the man?

關於這位男士，我們知道什麼？

(A) He is trying to quit smoking. 他正在試著戒煙。

(B) He started smoking in high school.

他從高中開始抽煙。

(C) He has many bad habits. 他有很多壞習慣。

* smoker〔'smokɚ〕 *n.* 吸煙者　　start〔stɑrt〕*v.* 開始
high school 高中　　habit〔'hæbɪt〕*n.* 習慣
know〔no〕*v.* 知道　　 ***thousands of*** 好幾千的
try〔traɪ〕*v.* 嘗試　　 ***cut back*** 減少
quit〔kwɪt〕*v.* 停止；戒　　seek〔sik〕*v.* 尋找
medical〔'mɛdɪkl̩〕*adj.* 醫學的
treatment〔'tritmənt〕*n.* 治療

special〔'spɛʃəl〕*adj.* 特別的
program〔'prog*r*æm〕*n.* 計畫
patience〔'peʃəns〕*n.* 耐心　　smoke〔smok〕*v.* 吸煙

21. (**B**) I broke my leg last month and spent a few days in the hospital. My friend Oscar came to visit me. He brought his guitar and sang a song to cheer me up. Nobody else came to see me. My brother is away at college, and both of my parents work full-time jobs.

我上個月摔斷我的腿並且在醫院住了好幾天。我的朋友奧斯卡來探望我。他帶了他的吉他然後唱一首歌來鼓勵我。沒有其他人來看我。我的哥哥在外地上大學，而我的雙親都有全職的工作。

Question : Why was the speaker in the hospital?

　　　　　　為什麼說話者之前在醫院？

(A) He had a serious illness. 他生了一場重病。

(B) He suffered an injury. 他受了傷。

(C) He was taking some tests. 他在接受檢查。

* break〔brek〕*v.* 折斷　　spend〔spɛnd〕*v.* 度過（時間）
hospital〔'hɑspɪtḷ〕*n.* 醫院　　visit〔'vɪzɪt〕*v.* 拜訪
guitar〔gɪ'tɑr〕*n.* 吉他　　cheer〔tʃɪr〕*v.* 振作；鼓勵
cheer sb. up 鼓舞某人　　college〔'kɑlɪdʒ〕*n.* 學院；大學
full-time〔'fʊl'taɪm〕*adj.* 全職的　　job〔dʒɑb〕*n.* 工作
serious〔'sɪrɪəs〕*adj.* 嚴重的　　illness〔'ɪlnɪs〕*n.* 疾病
suffer〔'sʌfɚ〕*v.* 承受；遭受　　injury〔'ɪndʒərɪ〕*n.* 受傷
test〔tɛst〕*n.* 測驗；檢查

TEST 9 詳解

聽力測驗（第 1-21 題，共 21 題）

第一部分：辨識句意（第 1-3 題，共 3 題）

1.(**A**) (A)　　　　　　(B)　　　　　　(C)

It's Jackie's birthday! 這是傑奇的生日！

* birthday (ˈbɝθ͵de) *n.* 生日

2.(**B**) (A)　　　　　　(B)　　　　　　(C)

Steve is helping an elderly woman cross the busy intersection. 史帝夫正幫助一位老婦人穿越熱鬧的十字路口。

* elderly (ˈɛldɚlɪ) *adj.* 有年紀的　　cross (krɔs) *v.* 越過
intersection (͵ɪntɚˈsɛkʃən) *n.* 十字路口 (= *crossroads*)

3.(**A**) (A)　　　　　　(B)　　　　　　(C)

Bob heard someone shouting his name.

鮑伯聽到有人在大喊他的名字。

* hear〔hɪr〕v. 聽見　　shout〔ʃaʊt〕v. 大聲喊叫；吼叫

第二部分：基本問答（第 4-10 題，共 7 題）

4. (**A**) Tomorrow is my mom's birthday and I still haven't bought her a gift.

明天是我媽媽的生日，而且我還沒有買給她的禮物。

　(A) You'd better do it now.　It's getting late.　All the stores will be closing soon.

　　你最好現在買。已經越來越晚了。所有的店很快就會關門。

　(B) I've heard her say that before.　You should ask.　It would be good to know.

　　我之前曾經聽她說過。你應該問問。知道了會比較好。

　(C) They aren't coming today.　Maybe tomorrow.　We'll know later.

　　他們今天不會來。也許是明天。我們稍晚會知道。

* gift〔gɪft〕n. 禮物　　***had better V.*** 最好～
　late〔let〕adj. 晚的　　store〔stor〕n. 商店
　close〔kloz〕v. 停止營業；打烊
　soon〔sun〕adv. 不久；馬上　　hear〔hɪr〕v. 聽聞；聽說
　ask〔æsk〕v. 詢問　　maybe〔'mebi〕adv. 或許；可能

5. (**B**) Where did you put the catalog?　你把目錄放在哪裡？

　(A) On Thursday.　星期四。

　(B) Isn't it on the desk?　它不是在書桌上嗎？

　(C) I'll check page 12.　我會檢查第十二頁。

* put〔pʊt〕v. 放置　　catalog〔'kætḷˌɔg〕n. 目錄

desk〔dɛsk〕*n.* 書桌   check〔tʃɛk〕*v.* 檢查

page〔pedʒ〕*n.* 頁

6. (**C**) What size shoe do you wear? 你穿什麼尺寸的鞋子？

    (A) I prefer brown. 我偏好棕色。

    (B) I use a medium brush. 我用中等大小的刷子。

    (C) I wear a size five. <u>我穿五號。</u>

    * size〔saɪz〕*n.* 尺寸   shoes〔ʃuz〕*n. pl.* 鞋子
    wear〔wɛr〕*v.* 穿   prefer〔prɪˈfɝ〕*v.* 比較喜歡
    brown〔braʊn〕*n.* 棕色   use〔juz〕*v.* 使用
    medium〔ˈmidɪəm〕*adj.* 中等的；中號的
    brush〔brʌʃ〕*n.* 刷子

7. (**A**) Does anyone have any questions? 有任何人有問題嗎？

    (A) Yes, I do. <u>是的。我有。</u>

    (B) Yes, I am. 是的。我是。

    (C) Yes, I was. 是的。我以前是。

    * anyone〔ˈɛnɪˌwʌn〕*pron.* 任何人
    question〔ˈkwɛstʃən〕*n.* 問題

8. (**C**) What did you do yesterday? 你昨天做了什麼？

    (A) They saw her at Taipei 101. 他們在台北 101 看到她。

    (B) He was busy in Muzha. 他有事情在木柵忙。

    (C) I went for a hike on Yangmingshan.
        <u>我去陽明山遠足。</u>

    * *go for* 去做；從事   hike〔haɪk〕*n.* 健行；遠足

9. (**C**) How long have you worked here? 你在這裡工作多久？

    (A) Five miles. 五英里。

(B) Six foot two. 六英呎兩吋。

(C) Seven years. 七年。

* work〔wɜk〕*v.* 工作　　mile〔maɪl〕*n.* 英里【1.6公里】
  foot〔fʊt〕*n.* 英尺【30.48公分】

10. (**B**) Why did you decide to move to the Da'an District?
　　你為什麼決定要搬去大安區？

(A) Yes, very decisive. 是的，非常重大。

(B) It's closer to my office. 離我辦公室比較近。

(C) January of last year. 去年一月。

* decide〔dɪ'saɪd〕*v.* 決定　　move〔muv〕*v.* 搬家
  district〔'dɪstrɪkt〕*n.* 區
  decisive〔dɪ'saɪsɪv〕*adj.* 決定性的；重大的
  close〔klos〕*adj.* 接近的　　*close to* 接近（= *near*）
  office〔'ɔfɪs〕*n.* 辦公室
  January〔'dʒænjʊˌɛrɪ〕*n.* 一月

第三部分：言談理解（第 11-21 題，共 11 題）

11. (**B**) W : You're new here, aren't you?
　　女：你是新來的，不是嗎？

M : Yes.　It's my first day.　My name is Mark.
男：是的。這是我第一天來。我的名字是馬克。

W : Nice to meet you, Mark.　I'm Amy.
女：很高興認識你，馬克。我是艾美。

M : Are you a junior or…?
男：妳是大三還是…？

W : Actually, I'm only a sophomore.
女：事實上，我才大二。

M : Me, too! Maybe we'll be in some of the same classes.

男：我也是！也許我們會在某些課同班。

W : Maybe.

女：也許。

M : OK, Amy. I'll see you around.

男：好的，艾美。回頭見。

W : I'm sure you will.

女：我確定你會的。

Question : Who is Mark? 誰是馬克？

(A) An old friend. 一個老朋友。

(B) A new student. 一個新學生。

(C) A popular teacher. 一個受歡迎的老師。

* new〔nju〕*adj.* 新進的；新來的
meet〔mit〕*v.* 認識；初次會面
junior〔'dʒunjɚ〕*n.* 大學三年級生
actually〔'æktʃʊəlɪ〕*adv.* 實際上；事實上
sophomore〔'sɑfm̩,or〕*n.* 大學二年級生
some〔səm〕*adj.* 一些的　　same〔sem〕*adj.* 相同的
see you around 回頭見；再見　　sure〔ʃʊr〕*adj.* 確定的
popular〔'pɑpjəlɚ〕*adj.* 受歡迎的

12. (**C**) M : Here's Jack's book bag. His lunch is ready to go. There's money on the counter for his field trip to the museum.

男：這是傑克的書包。他的午餐已經準備好了。長桌上的錢是要讓他去博物館校外教學的。

W : Did you sign the permission slip for the field trip?

女：妳有簽校外教學同意書的回條了嗎？

M : I did, and Jack took it to school yesterday. I didn't ask if he remembered to turn it in.

男：我有，然後傑克昨天拿去學校了。我忘記問他是否有記得交出去。

W : I'll ask him when he comes out of the bathroom.

女：他從浴室出來時我會問他。

M : OK, I've gotta run now or I'll be late for work.

男：好的，我現在得走了不然我工作會遲到。

Question : Who are the speakers? 說話者是誰？

(A) Jack's friends. 傑克的朋友。

(B) Jack's teachers. 傑克的老師。

(C) Jack's parents. 傑克的家長。

* ready (ˈrɛdɪ) adj. 準備好的　counter (ˈkaʊntɚ) n. 長桌
field trip 校外教學　museum (mjuˈziəm) n. 博物館
sign (saɪn) v. 簽名　permission (pɚˈmɪʃən) n. 同意書
slip (slɪp) n. 紙條　ask (æsk) v. 問
remember (rɪˈmɛmbɚ) v. 記得　**turn in** 交出；遞交
come out of 從…出來　bathroom (ˈbæθˌrum) n. 浴室
have gotta V. 必須~；得~ (= have got to V.)

13. (**B**) W : Greg, what are you doing?

女：葛列格，你在做什麼？

M : Nothing, Mom. Just watching TV.

男：沒什麼，媽。只是在看電視。

W : How many times have I told you to take off your shoes before you come in the house? Now there's mud all over my carpet!

女：我跟你說過多少次，在你進來房子以前要把鞋子脫掉？現在我的地毯上都是泥巴！

M : Sorry, Mom. I forgot.

男：對不起，媽。我忘記了。

W : Now take off those shoes and go to your room.
    You're grounded for the rest of the day.

女：現在把你的鞋子脫掉然後去你的房間。你今天剩下來的時間
    都被禁足了。

M : But Mom!

男：但是媽！

W : No "buts." Go.

女：沒有「但是」。去。

Question : Why is the woman upset?

          為什麼這位女士生氣？

(A) Greg is eating too close to dinner time.

    葛瑞格在太靠近晚餐時間的時候吃東西。

(B) Greg didn't take off his shoes. 葛瑞格沒有脫鞋子。

(C) Greg came home late. 葛瑞格晚回家。

* time〔taɪm〕n. 次數　　***take off*** 脫下
  there + be 有～　　mud〔mʌd〕n. 泥巴
  all over 遍及　　carpet〔'kɑrpɪt〕n. 地毯
  forgot〔fə'ɡɑt〕v. 忘記【forget 的過去式】
  ground〔ɡraʊnd〕v. 禁足　　rest〔rɛst〕n. 剩餘
  upset〔ʌp'sɛt〕adj. 生氣的　　***close to*** 接近

14. (**A**) M : I want to return this shirt. I don't have the receipt,
                  but I bought it here.

          男：我想要退回這件襯衫。我沒有收據，但我是在這裡買的。

          W : All right. Did you remove the tags?

          女：好的。你把標籤拆掉了嗎？

          M : Yes, but I didn't wear it.

男：是的，但是我沒穿過。

W : Unless you can show me the receipt and the original tags, I can't take back the shirt. It's store policy.

女：除非你可以給我看收據和原本的標籤，不然我不能把襯衫收回來。這是店裡的規定。

M : That's a terrible policy. I want to speak with your manager.

男：這是個糟糕的規定。我想要跟你們的經理談。

W : I am the manager.

女：我就是經理。

Question : What does the man want? 這位男士想要什麼？

(A) A refund. 退款。

(B) A discount. 折扣。

(C) A guarantee. 保證書。

＊ return〔rɪˋtɝn〕v. 退回　　receipt〔rɪˋsit〕n. 收據
all right 好的；可以　　remove〔rɪˋmuv〕v. 去除
tag〔tæg〕n. 標籤　　unless〔ənˋlɛs〕conj. 除非
show〔ʃo〕v. 出示
original〔əˋrɪdʒənl〕adj. 原本的；本來的　　**take back** 收回
policy〔ˋpɑləsɪ〕n. 政策；規定　　terrible〔ˋtɛrəbl〕adj. 糟糕的
speak with 和…談話；和…商量
manager〔ˋmænɪdʒɚ〕n. 經理　　refund〔ˋriˌfʌnd〕n. 退款
discount〔ˋdɪskaʊnt〕n. 折扣
guarantee〔ˌgærənˋti〕n. 保證書

15. (**C**) W : Would you mind? I'm trying to take a nap.

女：你介意嗎？我正試著要小睡片刻。

M : What? Is the TV too loud?

男：什麼？電視太大聲了嗎？

W : Yes. I can hear it all the way in my bedroom.

女：是的。我在我的房間從頭到尾都聽得很清楚。

M : Close your door.

男：把妳的門關上。

W : I did, and I can still hear it. Would you please just turn it down? Why do you need to have the thing blasting so loud?

女：我關了，然後我還是聽得見。可以請你就把它關小聲嗎？爲什麼你需要有個東西發出這麼大的聲音？

M : That's how I like it.

男：我就是喜歡這樣。

W : Well, if you don't turn it down, I'm going to tell Dad.

女：好吧，如果你不關小聲，我要去跟爸爸說。

Question : Who are the speakers?

說話者是誰？

(A) Teacher and student. 老師和學生。

(B) Doctor and patient. 醫生和病人。

(C) Brother and sister. 哥哥和妹妹。

* mind〔maɪnd〕*v.* 介意　　nap〔næp〕*n.* 打盹；小睡
loud〔laʊd〕*adj.*（聲音）大的　　*all the way* 從頭到尾；完全地
turn down 關小聲　　blast〔blæst〕*v.* 發出巨響
well〔wɛl〕*interj.* 嗯　　doctor〔'dɑktɚ〕*n.* 醫生
patient〔'peʃənt〕*n.* 病人

16. (**C**) W : You look tired, Josh.

女：你看起來很累，喬許。

M : I was up very late last night.

男：我昨天熬夜到非常晚。

W : What were you doing?

女：你在做什麼？

M : I couldn't fall asleep, so I practiced my guitar.

男：我睡不著，所以我在練習彈吉他。

Question : Why was Josh up late last night?

為什麼吉姆昨晚熬夜？

(A) He was doing homework. 他在做作業。

(B) He was out with friends. 他跟朋友出去。

(C) He was unable to fall asleep. 他睡不著。

* look〔lʊk〕v. 看起來　tired〔taɪrd〕adj. 累的
be up late 熬夜（= *stay up late*）　asleep〔ə'slip〕adj. 睡著的
fall asleep 入睡　practice〔'præktɪs〕v. 練習
guitar〔gɪ'tɑr〕n. 吉他　unable〔ʌn'ebḷ〕adj. 不能…的

17. (**A**) M : Well, someone certainly enjoyed herself at the party last night.

男：嗯，某人昨晚一定在派對上玩得很愉快。

W : What do you mean?

女：你是什麼意思？

M : Here, you left your purse in my car last night.

男：這裡，妳昨晚把皮夾留在我的車子裡了。

W : Did you drive me home?

女：你昨晚有載我回家嗎？

Question : What probably happened to the woman last night? 這位女士昨晚最可能發生了什麼事？

(A) She had too much to drink. 她喝了太多酒。

(B) She spent too much money. 她花了太多錢。

(C) She took too much time getting ready.

她花了太多時間準備。

* certainly〔'sɜtṇlɪ〕*adv.* 一定;必定 *enjoy oneself* 玩得愉快
  mean〔min〕*v.* 意思是   purse〔pɜs〕*n.* 錢包
  drive〔draɪv〕*v.* (開車) 載   probably〔'prɑbəblɪ〕*adv.* 可能
  drink〔drɪŋk〕*v.* 喝;喝酒
  have too much to drink 喝太多酒 (= *drink too much*)
  get ready 準備好

18. (**A**) Are dogs really better than cats? I am a "dog person." I
have always loved dogs and cannot imagine life without
at least one dog to follow me around, hog the bed and
smother me with wet kisses. This being said, I am a lover
of all animals and I am also a cat owner who adores her
sweet kitties. It is certainly hard for me to imagine life
without the soft purrs, kneading and gentle head butting.
狗眞的比貓更好嗎?我是個「愛狗人士」。我一直都很愛狗,而
且無法想像沒有至少一隻狗跟在我周圍、霸佔床鋪,而且用濕濕
的吻舔得我快窒息的生活。話雖如此,我是所有動物的愛好者,
而且我也是一隻貓的主人,非常熱愛牠可愛的小貓們。對我來
說,要想像沒有柔軟呼嚕聲、揉捏、以及溫柔的頭對頭靠在一起
的生活的確是很困難的。

Question:What is implied by the speaker?
說話者暗示什麼?

(A) She owns a dog. 她有一隻狗。

(B) She doesn't own a dog. 她沒有狗。

(C) She isn't a people person. 她不是個善於社交的人。

* *dog person* 愛狗人士   imagine〔ɪ'mædʒɪn〕*v.* 想像
  without〔wɪ'ðaʊt〕*prep.* 沒有   *at least* 至少
  follow〔'fɑlo〕*v.* 跟著   around〔ə'raʊnd〕*adv.* 在周圍
  hog〔hɑg〕*v.* 霸佔   smother〔smʌðɚ〕*v.* 使窒息

wet〔wɛt〕*adj.* 濕的　　kiss〔kɪs〕*n.* 親吻

This being said. 話雖如此。　　lover〔'lʌvɚ〕*n.* 愛好者

animal〔'ænəml̩〕*n.* 動物　　owner〔'onɚ〕*n.* 所有者；主人

adore〔ə'dor〕*v.* 喜愛　　sweet〔swit〕*adj.* 可愛的

kitty〔'kɪtɪ〕*n.* 小貓　　certainly〔'sɝtn̩lɪ〕*adv.* 一定；必定

hard〔hɑrd〕*adj.* 困難的　　soft〔sɔft〕*adj.* 柔軟的

purr〔pɝ〕*n.* 呼嚕聲　　knead〔nid〕*v.* 揉捏

gentle〔'dʒɛntl̩〕*adj.* 溫柔的　　butt〔bʌt〕*v.* 以頭碰撞

imply〔ɪm'plaɪ〕*v.* 暗示　　***people person*** 善於社交的人

19. (**C**)　W : If you're headed to the supermarket, there are a few
things I need you to pick up, if you don't mind.

女：如果你要去超市的話，有些東西我需要你幫我買，如果你不
介意的話。

M : Make a list. But don't go crazy. I don't want to do a
week's worth of grocery shopping.

男：列一張清單。但是不要太失控。我不想要弄得跟一週一次的
日用品採購一樣

W : Relax. It's just a few items, like dish soap and toilet
paper.

女：放輕鬆。只是幾樣東西而已，像是洗碗精和衛生紙。

M : That I can handle.

男：那我可以負荷。

W : Great. Are you leaving now? Hang on a minute and
let me write up a quick list for you.

女：太棒了，你現在要出發了嗎？等一下，讓我寫一張簡單的清
單給你。

Question : What will the woman probably do next?

這位女士接下來最可能做什麼事？

(A) Wash the dishes. 洗碗。

(B) Go to the supermarket. 去超市。

(C) Make a list. 列一張清單。

* *be headed to* 前往　supermarket〔'supɚ,mɑrkɪt〕*n.* 超市

　a few 一些　*pick up* 採購；買

　list〔lɪst〕*n.* 清單　*go crazy* 發瘋；失控

　worth〔wɝθ〕*n.* 價值；相當於⋯的份量

　a week's worth of sth. 可維持一星期份量的某物

　grocery shopping 日用品採購　relax〔rɪ'læks〕*v.* 放鬆

　item〔'aɪtəm〕*n.* 物品　*dish soap* 洗碗精

　toilet paper 衛生紙　handle〔'hændl̩〕*v.* 處理；負荷

　leave〔liv〕*v.* 離開　*hang on* 等一下

　write up 把⋯整理成文；詳細寫出

　quick〔kwɪk〕*adj.* 快速的

20. (**A**)　M：We've been waiting 15 minutes already, and the
　　　　　　movie starts in five. I wonder what's keeping Ralph?

男：我們已經等了十五分鐘了，而且電影五分鐘後就要開始了。
　　我在想到底是什麼耽擱了拉爾夫？

W：He's probably stuck in traffic. It is rush hour, you
　　know.

女：他很可能被塞車困住。這是尖峰時段，你知道的。

M：You're right. I forgot about that.

男：你是對的。我忘了這一點。

Question：Where is Ralph right now?

　　　　　羅夫現在在哪裡？

(A) Most likely stuck in traffic. 最可能被塞車困住。

(B) Probably walking home. 可能正在走路回家。

(C) Possibly watching a movie. 可能正在看電影。

* wait〔wet〕v. 等待 already〔ɔl'rɛdɪ〕adv. 已經
in〔ɪn〕prep. 再過~ keep〔kip〕v. 使停留；耽誤
Ralph〔rælf〕n. 拉爾夫 probably〔'prɑbəblɪ〕adv. 可能
traffic〔'træfɪk〕n. 交通 **be stuck in traffic** 遇到塞車
rush〔strʌɪk〕adj. 急忙的
rush hour 尖峰時間；交通擁擠時間
You're right. 你說得對。 **right now** 現在；目前
likely〔'laɪklɪ〕adv. 可能

21. (**B**) W : Thank you for calling Applebee's. How can I help you?

女：感謝您來電愛普比。請問我能爲您做什麼呢？

M : I'd like to reserve a table for eight o'clock on Friday night.

男：我想要預訂星期五晚上八點的位子。

W : Your name and phone number, please?

女：請問您的姓名以及電話號碼是？

Question : What is the man doing?

這位男士正在做什麼？

(A) Booking a hotel room. 訂飯店房間。

(B) Making a reservation at a restaurant. 預約餐廳訂位。

(C) Cancelling a subscription. 取消訂閱。

* call〔kɔl〕v. 打電話給 **would like to V**. 想要~
reserve〔rɪ'zɝv〕v. 保留；預訂 table〔'tebḷ〕n. 餐桌
book〔bʊk〕v. 預訂 hotel〔ho'tɛl〕n. 大飯店；旅館
reservation〔ˌrɛzə'veʃən〕n. 預約；預訂
make a reservation 預約；預訂
restaurant〔'rɛstərənt〕n. 餐廳 cancel〔'kænsḷ〕v. 取消
subscription〔səb'skrɪpʃən〕n. 訂閱

TEST 10 詳解

聽力測驗（第 1-21 題，共 21 題）

第一部分：辨識句意（第 1-3 題，共 3 題）

1. (**B**) (A)   (B)   (C)

Joe gave Mary 500 dollars. 喬給了瑪莉五百元。

  * gave〔gev〕v. 給【give 的過去式】   dollar〔'dɑlɚ〕n. 元

2. (**A**) (A)   (B)   (C)

All the students are seated in class, but the teacher is absent. 所有的學生都坐在教室裡，但是老師卻不在。

  * ***be seated*** 坐（= *sit*）   absent〔'æbsn̩t〕*adj.* 缺席的；不在的

3. (**B**) (A)   (B)   (C)

On the math exam, Judy scored 85; Max scored 70; and Hank scored 45. 在數學考試中，茱蒂得到八十五分，馬克斯得到七十分，漢克得到四十五分。

* math〔mæθ〕*n.* 數學（= *mathematics*）
  exam〔ɪɡˋzæm〕*n.* 考試　　score〔skor〕*v.* 得分

第二部分：基本問答（第 4-10 題，共 7 題）

4. (**C**) Excuse me, is this the bus or the train station?
   不好意思，請問這是公車站還是火車站？
   (A) You need to take the train. 你需要搭火車。
   (B) Taxis aren't allowed here. 這裡是不允許計程車進入的。
   (C) Actually, it's both. 事實上，它兩個都是。

   * ***excuse me*** 不好意思【用於引起注意】　　station〔ˋsteʃən〕*n.* 車站
     need〔nid〕*v.* 需要　　train〔tren〕*n.* 火車
     taxi〔ˋtæksɪ〕*n.* 計程車　　allow〔əˋlaʊ〕*v.* 允許
     actually〔ˋæktʃʊəlɪ〕*adv.* 事實上

5. (**C**) Did you get enough to eat? 你拿的份量夠吃嗎？
   (A) No, I'm tired. 不，我很累。
   (B) Maybe I'm hungry. 也許我餓了。
   (C) Yes, I'm full. 是的，我很飽。

   * enough〔əˋnʌf〕*adj.* 足夠的　　tired〔taɪrd〕*adj.* 疲倦的
     hungry〔ˋhʌŋɡrɪ〕*adj.* 飢餓的　　full〔fʊl〕*adj.* 滿的；飽的

6. (**B**) What is the chair made of? 這張椅子是用什麼做成的？
   (A) Yes, I can make one. 是的，我可以做一張。
   (B) It's made of wood. 它是木頭製的。
   (C) It makes a good table. 這真是一張好桌子。

   * ***be made of*** 由…製成　　wood〔wʊd〕*n.* 木材
     make〔mek〕*v.* 成為；是

7. (**A**) How long have you known Richard? 你認識理查多久了？

    (A) We just met. 我們才剛碰面。

    (B) I'll be there tomorrow. 我明天會在那裡。

    (C) Six o'clock. 六點整。

    * know〔no〕v. 認識　　met〔mɛt〕v. 和～見面【meet 的過去式】

8. (**C**) What's so funny? 什麼事這麼有趣？

    (A) Rocky told a sad story. 羅奇說了一個傷心的故事。

    (B) Mr. Wilson lost his job. 威爾森先生失業了。

    (C) Jules made a joke. 朱爾斯開了個玩笑。

    * funny〔'fʌnɪ〕adj. 滑稽的　　story〔'storɪ〕n. 故事
    lost〔lɔst〕v. 失去【lose 的過去式】　　job〔dʒab〕n. 工作
    joke〔dʒok〕n. 笑話；玩笑　　***make a joke*** 開玩笑

9. (**C**) Do you know the name of that pretty girl over there?
你認識在那邊的漂亮女生的名字嗎？

    (A) It's four o'clock. 現在是四點鐘。

    (B) This is an iPhone. 這是一台 iPhone。

    (C) I think it's Sarah. 我認為那是莎拉。

    * know〔no〕v. 認識　　pretty〔'prɪtɪ〕adj. 漂亮的
    over there 在那邊　　think〔θɪŋk〕v. 認為

10. (**B**) Where is the nearest MRT station? 最近的捷運站在哪裡？

    (A) The Blue Line goes to Nangang. The Brown Line
goes to Wangfang Hospital.
藍線是去南港。棕線是去萬芳醫院。

    (B) Turn right at the next intersection. You can't miss it.
在下一個十字路口右轉。你不會錯過它的。

    (C) Take the stairs to the second floor. He's waiting for
you there. 走樓梯到二樓。他在那裡等你。

* near〔nɪr〕*adj.* 近的；接近的
  MRT 捷運（= *mass rapid transit*）
  line〔laɪn〕*n.*（交通）路線　　hospital〔'hɑspɪt!〕*n.* 醫院
  turn〔tɜn〕*v.* 轉向；轉彎　　right〔raɪt〕*adv.* 向右地；右側地
  intersection〔,ɪntə'sɛkʃən〕*n.* 十字路口
  miss〔mɪs〕*v.* 錯過　　stairs〔stɛrs〕*n. pl.* 樓梯；階梯
  take the stairs 走樓梯　　floor〔flor〕*n.* 樓層
  wait〔wet〕*v.* 等候；等待

第三部分：言談理解（第 11-21 題，共 11 題）

11.（**A**）W : Hi, George. What can I do for you?

女：嗨喬治。我可以爲你做什麼呢？

M : Hi, Vivian. It's about the noise. We don't mind if you have people over, but you need to keep it down after 10:00 p.m.

男：嗨，薇薇安。是有關噪音。我們不介意妳有客人來，但是妳們必須要在十點之後控制音量。

W : I'm sorry about that. I didn't realize we were being so loud last night.

女：我對於這一點感到很抱歉。我沒意識到我們昨晚這麼大聲。

M : It wasn't just last night. It's been every night for the last two weeks.

男：不只是昨天晚上。這兩個禮拜以來每天晚上都是。

W : Oh, you see, my brother has been staying with me. He's going back to school tonight, so things will be much quieter from now on.

女：噢，你也看到了，我弟弟這段時間一直和我住在一起。他今晚就要回學校了，所以從現在開始會變得安靜很多。

Question : Why did George visit Vivian?

爲什麼喬治去拜訪薇薇安？

(A) To complain about the noise. 去抱怨噪音。

(B) To ask her advice. 去詢問她的意見。

(C) To thank her for a favor. 去感謝她的幫忙。

noise〔nɔɪz〕*n.* 噪音　　mind〔maɪnd〕*v.* 介意
have sb. over 邀請某人到家裡作客　　***keep down*** 降低（音量）
realize〔'rɪə‚laɪz〕*v.* 意識到　　loud〔laʊd〕*adj.* 大聲的
stay〔ste〕*v.* 客居；作客　　things〔θɪŋz〕*n. pl.* 事態；情況
quiet〔'kwaɪət〕*adj.* 安靜的　　***from now on*** 從現在開始
visit〔'vɪzɪt〕*v.* 拜訪　　complain〔kəm'plen〕*v.* 抱怨
advice〔əd'vaɪs〕*n.* 忠告；勸告　　favor〔'fevɚ〕*n.* 幫忙

12. (**C**) M：Taylor, it's time to go.

男：泰勒，該走了。

W：But I'm not ready, Dad. I can't find my cell phone.

女：但是我還沒準備好，爸。我找不到我的手機。

M：Hurry up. I don't want to be late. Where did you last
see the phone?

男：快點。我不想要遲到。妳最後一次看到手機是在哪裡？

W：I thought I left it on my desk, but it's not there.

女：我覺得我把它放在我的書桌上，但是它不在那裡。

Question：What is Taylor doing? 泰勒正在做什麼？

(A) Getting ready for bed. 準備好上床睡覺。

(B) Surfing the Internet. 上網。

(C) Looking for her cell phone. 尋找她的手機。

* ***it's time to + V.*** 該是做…的時候　　***cell phone*** 手機
find〔faɪnd〕*v.* 找到；尋獲　　hurry〔'hɝɪ〕*v.* 趕快；急忙
want〔wɑnt〕*v.* 想要　　late〔let〕*adj.* 遲到的
think〔θɪŋk〕*v.* 想；認為　　leave〔liv〕*v.* 遺留
get ready 準備好　　bed〔bɛd〕*n.* 就寢時間
surf〔sɝf〕*v.* 上（網）　　Internet〔'ɪntɚ‚nɛt〕*n.* 網際網路
look for 尋找

13. (**B**)　W：How much is your chicken?

女：你的雞肉賣多少錢？

M：Five ninety-nine a pound.

男：一磅五塊錢九十九分。

W：Oh, that's too much. When did chicken get so expensive?

女：噢，那好貴。雞肉什麼時候變得這麼貴了？

M：There's been a shortage on the market because of the bird flu crisis. Millions of chickens had to be destroyed. Sorry. But I have ground pork on sale for three ninety-nine a pound.

男：因為禽流感造成雞肉這陣子在市場上短缺。好幾百萬隻雞必須被撲殺。抱歉。但我有正在特價的豬絞肉一磅三塊錢九十九分。

Question：Who is the man? 這位男士是誰？

(A) An artist. 一位藝術家。

(B) A butcher. 一位肉販。

(C) A farmer. 一位農夫。

* chicken (ˈtʃɪkɪn) n. 雞肉　　pound (paʊnd) n. 磅
  get (gɛt) v. 變得　　expensive (ɪkˈspɛnsɪv) adj. 昂貴的
  shortage (ˈʃɔrtɪdʒ) n. 短缺；不足
  market (ˈmarkɪt) n. 市場　　flu (flu) n. 感冒
  bird flu 禽流感　　crisis (ˈkraɪsɪs) n. 危機
  million (ˈmɪljən) n. 百萬　　**millions of** 幾百萬的
  have to V. 必須~　　destroy (dɪˈstrɔɪ) v. 消滅；殺死
  ground (graʊnd) adj. 磨碎的【grind 的過去分詞】
  pork (pork) n. 豬肉　　sale (sel) n. 銷售
  on sale 特價；廉價出售
  artist (ˈartɪst) n. 藝術家　　butcher (ˈbʊtʃɚ) n. 肉販
  farmer (ˈfarmɚ) n. 農夫

14. (**C**) M : I heard Greyson's dog got hit by a car last week.

男：我聽說格雷森的狗上禮拜被車子撞到了。

W : Yes. The dog was injured pretty badly, so the vet had to put him down.

女：是的。那隻狗被傷得非常嚴重，所以獸醫不得不放棄。

M : That's awful. I'll bet Greyson is taking it pretty hard.

男：太糟糕了。我敢打賭格雷森的心情一定相當沈重。

W : He is, but that's to be expected.

女：他是，但這也是可以被預料的。

M : We should be extra nice to him.

男：我們應該加倍地對他好。

W : I don't think that's really necessary. Just don't bring up the subject when you see him.

女：我不認為這真的很必要。只要當你看到他時不要提起這個話題就好。

Question : How is Greyson feeling right now?

　　　　格雷森現在感覺如何？

(A) Angry. 生氣的。　　　(B) Happy. 開心的。

(C) Heartbroken. 極度悲痛的。

* Greyson〔'gresən〕*n.* 格雷森　　hit〔hɪt〕*v.* 撞擊
injure〔'ɪndʒɚ〕*v.* 受傷　　pretty〔'prɪtɪ〕*adv.* 相當；頗
badly〔'bædlɪ〕*adv.* 嚴重地
vet〔vɛt〕*n.* 獸醫（= *veterinarian*）　　***have to V.*** 必須～
put down　（無痛地）殺死　　awful〔'ɔful〕*adj.* 糟糕的
bet〔bɛt〕*v.* 打賭　　***I'll bet*** 我敢肯定；我敢確定
take sth. ***hard*** 對某事感到悲傷　　expect〔ɪk'spɛkt〕*v.* 預期
extra〔'ɛkstrə〕*adv.* 額外地；特別地
necessary〔'nɛsə,sɛrɪ〕*adj.* 必要的　　***bring up*** 提起
subject〔'sʌbdʒɪkt〕*n.* 主題
heartbroken〔'hɑrt,brokən〕*adj.* 極度悲傷的

15. (**C**) W : Good to have you back, Chester. Everybody really missed you.

女：真高興你回來，契斯特。每個人真的都很想念你。

M : I'm happy to be back, Tiffany.

男：我很開心回來，蒂芬妮。

W : So how'd it go? You know—the surgery?

女：所以結果如何？你知道的──手術？

M : Fine, fine. The doctors said they removed the tumor, and I'm good as new.

男：很好，很好。醫生說他們移除了腫瘤，而且我完好如初。

W : I hope you don't mind, but there are some flowers on your desk.

女：希望你不會介意，但你的桌上有一些花。

M : What a thoughtful gesture, Tiffany. Thanks.

男：這是多麼體貼的舉動啊，蒂芬妮。謝謝。

Question : What do we know about the man?

關於這位男士我們知道什麼？

(A) He is a florist. 他是一位花商。

(B) He is a doctor. 他是一位醫師。

(C) His name is Chester. <u>他的名字叫做契斯特。</u>

* miss〔mɪs〕*v.* 想念　　go〔go〕*v.* 進展
surgery〔'sɝdʒərɪ〕*n.* 手術　　remove〔rɪ'muv〕*v.* 移除
tumor〔'tumɚ〕*n.* 腫瘤
(*as*) *good as new* 完好如初；健康良好 (= *as healthy as normal*)
thoughtful〔'θɔtfəl〕*adj.* 體貼的　　gesture〔'dʒɛstʃɚ〕*n.* 表示
florist〔'florɪst〕*n.* 花商

16. (**A**) M : Do you know why I pulled you over?

男：妳知道我為什麼要妳靠邊停車嗎？

W : I have a pretty good idea.

女：我有一個相當棒的點子。

M : Now, I'm going to let you off with just a warning this time. Do me a favor and watch your speed from now on, OK? Don't be in such a rush to get where you're going. Speeding is the number one cause of traffic accidents.

男：現在，我只是要警告妳，然後這一次我就會原諒妳。幫我個忙，從現在起好好注意妳的速度，好嗎？不要這麼急著趕去妳要去的地方。超速駕駛是造成交通事故的頭號原因。

W : Thank you, officer. I'll slow down, I promise.

女：謝謝你，長官。我會減速，我保證。

Question : Why did the woman get pulled over?

　　　　爲什麼這位女士靠邊停車？

(A) She was speeding. 她剛剛超速駕駛。

(B) She had a broken headlight. 她有一個車頭燈破了。

(C) She ignored a stop sign. 她忽視一個停車的號誌。

* **pull** *sb.* **over** 讓某人把車停靠路邊　　idea〔aɪ'diə〕*n.* 主意
  let off 饒過；原諒　　warning〔'wɔrnɪŋ〕*n.* 警告
  time〔taɪm〕*n.* 次　　**do** *sb.* **a favor** 幫某人一個忙
  watch〔watʃ〕*v.* 注意　　speed〔spid〕*n.* 速度　*v.* 超速行駛
  in a rush 急忙地；匆忙地　　get〔gɛt〕*v.* 到達
  cause〔kɔz〕*n.* 原因　　traffic〔'træfɪk〕*n.* 交通
  accident〔'æksədənt〕*n.* 事故　　officer〔'ɔfəsɚ〕*n.* 長官；警官
  slow down 放慢；減速
  promise〔'pramɪs〕*v.* 保證
  headlight〔'hɛd,laɪt〕*n.* (車) 前燈；車頭燈
  ignore〔ɪg'nor〕*v.* 忽視　　sign〔saɪn〕*n.* 號誌

17. (**A**) M : Hi, Alicia, could you organize a one-hour meeting for all the employees here at the clinic? I want to show them the new software for scheduling patients' appointments.

男：嗨，艾莉西亞，妳可以幫這間診所有的員工，安排一個一小時的會議嗎？我想要讓他們看看新的安排病人門診時間的軟體。

W : Sure, I'll set something up for early next week. I didn't realize we were getting new software. Why are we changing software?

女：當然，我會把一些事情在下禮拜初就安排好。我沒有意識到我們有新的軟體。我們為什麼要換軟體？

M : Well, the biggest advantage is that we'll be able to track how long each appointment takes. So it will help us to manage our time better and schedule appointments more accurately.

男：嗯，最大的好處是我們將能夠追蹤每一個門診花了多少時間。所以這可以幫助我們更有效地管理時間以及更準確的安排門診。

W : Well, I'm sure our patients will appreciate that. I'll let you know as soon as I get the meeting set up.

女：嗯，我確定我們的病人會欣賞這個作法的。我一把會議安排好就會盡快讓你知道。

Question : What does the man ask the woman to do?

這位男士要求這位女士做什麼？

(A) Set up a meeting. 安排一個會議。

(B) Cancel his appointment. 取消他的門診。

(C) Install some software. 安裝某個軟體。

* organize〔'ɔrgən,aɪz〕v. 安排　　meeting〔'mitɪŋ〕n. 會議
employee〔ɪm'plɔɪ-i〕n. 受雇者　　clinic〔'klɪnɪk〕n. 診所
software〔'sɔft,wɛr〕n. 軟體　　schedule〔'skɛdʒul〕v. 安排
patient〔'peʃənt〕n. 病人
appointment〔ə'pɔɪntmənt〕n. 門診
set up 設置；安排　　change〔tʃendʒ〕v. 更換
advantage〔əd'væntɪdʒ〕n. 好處　　*be able to V.* 能夠～
track〔træk〕v. 追蹤　　take〔tek〕v. 花（時間）
manage〔'mænɪdʒ〕v. 管理
accurately〔'ækjərɪtlɪ〕adv. 精確地
appreciate〔ə'priʃɪ,et〕v. 欣賞　　*as soon as* 一…就～
cancel〔'kænsḷ〕v. 取消　　install〔ɪn'stɔl〕v. 安裝

18. (**C**) M : Do you ever buy things on the Internet?

　　男：妳曾經在網路上買過東西嗎？

W : Sometimes. I pay some of my bills online.

　　女：偶爾。有些帳單我是在網路上付的。

M : You do? Aren't you worried about privacy and
　　security?

　　男：是嗎？妳不擔心隱私權和安全性嗎？

W : Not at all. I feel very safe online.

　　女：一點也不。我在網路上感覺很安全。

M : I don't. I would never give out any of my personal
　　information on the Internet.

　　男：我不覺得。我絕對不會在網路上送出任何我的個人資料。

Question : What is implied about the man?

　　　　　　關於男士，暗示什麼？

(A) He does not own a computer. 他沒有電腦。

(B) He does a lot of shopping on the Internet.

　　　他在路上大量購物。

(C) He doesn't pay his bills online.

　　他不在網路上付帳單。

* sometimes〔ˋsʌmˏtaɪmz〕adv. 偶爾　　pay〔pe〕v. 支付
bill〔bɪl〕n. 帳單　　online〔ɑnˋlaɪn〕adv. 在網路上
worry about 擔心　　privacy〔ˋpraɪvəsɪ〕n. 隱私
security〔sɪˋkjʊrətɪ〕n. 安全性　　***not at all*** 一點也不
give out 送出　　personal〔ˋpɝsn̩ḷ〕adj. 個人的
information〔ˏɪnfɚˋmeʃən〕n. 資訊

19. (**A**)　W : Julia says she graduated from Harvard, but I don't
　　　　　believe her.

　　女：茱莉亞說她從哈佛畢業，但是我不相信她。

　　M : Why? What does it say on her resume?

　　男：為什麼？她的履歷表上是怎麼寫的？

　　W : It says she has a BA in Art History from Harvard.

　　女：上面寫她有哈佛藝術史的學士學位。

　　M : Well, there you go. What more proof do you need?

　　男：嗯，那就是這樣。妳還需要什麼證據？

　　W : There is something about her that isn't genuine. And
　　　　besides, you can put anything you want on a resume.
　　　　It's up to the employer to check the facts.

　　女：有一些關於她的事情不是真的。而且，你可以在履歷上放任
　　　　何你想放的東西。這完全是由雇主決定要不要去查證事實。

　　M : So what do you want to do? We need to hire
　　　　somebody soon.

　　男：所以妳想要做什麼？我們需要快點雇用一個人。

　　Question : Where did Julia say she went to college?

　　　　　　　茱莉亞說她是去哪讀大學的？

(A) Harvard. 哈佛大學。

(B) Oxford. 牛津大學。

(C) She didn't say. 她沒說。

* graduate ('grædʒʊ,et) v. 畢業
  Harvard ('hɑrvəd) n. 哈佛大學　　resume ('rɛzʊ,me) n. 履歷表
  BA 學士學位 (= *Bachelor of Arts*)　　***Art History*** 藝術史
  There you go. 就這樣了；沒關係，讓它去吧。【表示無法改變現
  　狀，只能接受】　　proof (pruf) n. 證據
  genuine ('dʒɛnjʊɪn) adj. 真的　　besides (bɪ'saɪdz) adv. 此外
  up to sb. 由某人決定　　employer (ɪm'plɔɪə) n. 雇主
  check (tʃɛk) v. 檢查　　fact (fækts) n. pl. 事實；申述的事
  hire (haɪr) v. 雇用　　soon (sun) adv. 盡快
  college ('kɑlɪdʒ) n. 大學　　Oxford ('ɑksfəd) n. 牛津大學

20. (**B**) M : Irene, it's getting late. Turn off the computer and get
　　　　　ready for bed.

男：艾琳，時間不早了。把電腦關掉然後準備睡覺了。

W : But Dad, I'm just about to reach the next level in the
　　game.

女：但是爸，我才剛要到遊戲的下一級而已。

M : OK, I'll give you 10 minutes. And then shut it down
　　for the night.

男：好吧，我會給你十分鐘。然後就要把它關掉去睡覺。

Question : What will happen in 10 minutes?
　　　　　在十分鐘後會發生什麼事？

(A) The movie will start. 電影會開始。

(B) The girl will turn off her computer.
　　這位女孩會把電腦關掉。

(C) The man will make dinner. 這位男士會煮晚餐。

* Irene〔ɑɪ'rin〕n. 艾琳　　　***get late*** 晚了；不早了
turn off 關掉（開關）　　***get ready*** 準備好
be about to V. 正要~　　　reach〔ritʃ〕v. 到達
level〔'lɛvl̩〕n. 水平；關卡　　***shut down*** 關掉
for the night（當天）晚上　　in〔ɪn〕prep. 再過~

21.（**A**）Humans depend on fresh water for survival. While it is
possible to remove salt from ocean water, it is expensive,
and the cost of transporting water inland is not cheap.
Rain keeps rivers and lakes filled. Forms of life that
depend on rivers would not have survived without rain.
人類仰賴新鮮的淡水生存。雖然從海水中將鹽分去除是可行的，
卻很昂貴，而且將水運到內陸的價格也不便宜。雨水保持河川和
湖泊的充裕。沒有雨水的話，各種仰賴河流的生物將無法生存。

Question：What is true about ocean water?
　　　　　　　關於海水何者為真？

(A) It contains salt. 它包含了鹽分。

(B) It's more expensive than fresh water. 它比淡水更貴。

(C) It would not survive without rain.
　　　沒有雨水它就無法生存。

* human〔'hjumən〕n. 人類　　　***depend on*** 仰賴；依靠
fresh〔frɛʃ〕adj. 新鮮的　　　***fresh water*** 淡水
survival〔sə'vaɪvl̩〕n. 生存　　while〔hwaɪl〕conj. 雖然
remove〔rɪ'muv〕v. 去除　　salt〔sɔlt〕n. 鹽
ocean〔'oʃən〕n. 海洋　　expensive〔ɪk'spɛnsɪv〕adj. 昂貴的
cost〔kɔst〕n. 成本；費用　　transport〔træns'port〕v. 運輸
inland〔'ɪnlənd〕adv. 向內陸　　cheap〔tʃip〕adj. 便宜的
river〔'rɪvə〕n. 河流　　lake〔lek〕n. 湖泊
fill〔fɪl〕v. 裝滿；填滿　　form〔fɔrm〕n. 形式
survive〔sə'vaɪv〕v. 生存　　contain〔kən'ten〕v. 包含

TEST 11 詳解

聽力測驗（第 1-21 題，共 21 題）

第一部分：辨識句意（第 1-3 題，共 3 題）

1. (**A**) (A)   (B)   (C)

They are standing in line to have sushi.

他們正在排隊要吃壽司。

* stand〔stænd〕v. 處於某種狀態   *in line* 排隊
    sushi〔'suʃi〕n. 壽司

2. (**C**) (A)   (B)   (C)

This is a kitchen. 這是廚房。

3. (**C**) (A)   (B)   (C)

Betty is studying now, but later she will play soccer.

貝蒂現在正在讀書，但待會她會去踢足球。

* study 〔'stʌdɪ〕 *v.* 讀書　　later 〔'letɚ〕 *adv.* 待會；過一陣子
soccer 〔'sɑkɚ〕 *n.* 足球

第二部分：基本問答（第 4-10 題，共 7 題）

4. (**A**) Are you going to the concert tomorrow night?

你明天晚上要去聽演唱會嗎？

(A) No, my dad says I have to stay home.

沒有，我爸說我必須待在家裡。

(B) No, they weren't playing the kind of music I like.

沒有，他們當時沒有彈奏我喜歡的音樂。

(C) No, it doesn't happen all the time.

不，它不是經常發生的。

* concert 〔'kɑnsɝt〕 *n.* 音樂會；演唱會　　***have to V.*** 必須~
stay 〔ste〕 *v.* 停留；留下　　***all the time*** 一直；經常

5. (**C**) Who were you talking to?　你剛在跟誰說話？

(A) That's what I said.　那是我所說的。

(B) They talk too much.　他們講了太多了。

(C) I was talking to my sister.　我剛在跟我妹妹說話。

6. (**C**) What an exciting game, don't you think?

真是場刺激的比賽，你不覺得嗎？

(A) It had me on the tip of my tongue.

它讓我想講卻記不起來。

(B) It had me at the end of my rope.

它讓我忍無可忍。

(C) It had me on the edge of my seat.　它讓我全神貫注。

* exciting〔ɪk'saɪtɪŋ〕*adj.* 令人興奮的　　think〔θɪŋk〕*v.* 認為
tip〔tɪp〕*n.* 提示；尖端
on the tip of *one's* ***tongue*** 到舌邊；知道卻想不起來
rope〔rop〕*n.* 繩
at the end of *one's* ***rope*** 忍無可忍；智窮力竭
(= *having no patience or energy left to cope with sth.*)
edge〔ɛdʒ〕*n.* 邊緣
on the edge of *one's* ***seat*** 全神貫注
(= *very excited and giving one's full attention to sth.*)

7. (**C**) Do you have enough money to pay for both of our tickets?
你有錢足夠付我們兩人的票嗎？

(A) I am. 我是。

(B) I was. 我當時是。

(C) I do. <u>我有。</u>

* enough〔ə'nʌf〕*adj.* 足夠的；充足的　　pay〔pe〕*v.* 支付
both〔boθ〕*n.* 兩者　　ticket〔'tɪkɪt〕*n.* 票

8. (**B**) Do you see that boy over there? I've got a crush on him.
你有看到那裡的男孩嗎？我迷上他了。

(A) You should get more exercise. 你應該多運動了。

(B) That's my brother! <u>那是我的哥哥！</u>

(C) I should introduce myself. 我應該自我介紹。

* crush〔krʌʃ〕*n.* 迷戀
get a crush on *sb.* 愛上某人；迷上某人 (= *have a crush on sb.*)
exercise〔'ɛksə͵saɪz〕*n.* 運動　　introduce〔͵ɪntrə'djus〕*v.* 介紹

9. (**A**) Do you have any plans this morning?
你今天早上有沒有任何計畫？

(A) Yes, I'm going to see the doctor.
<u>有，我要去看醫生。</u>

(B) No, I was home all night. 沒有，我整個晚上都在家。

(C) Maybe, I didn't ask him. 或許，我沒有問他。

* plan〔plæn〕*n.* 計畫；打算　　***see a doctor*** 看醫生

　maybe〔'mebɪ〕*adv.* 大概；或許　　ask〔æsk〕*v.* 問；詢問

10. (**B**) Mark said he will help me write my final essay.
馬克說他會幫助我寫我的期末報告。

(A) I can't handle them. 我無法處理它們。

(B) That's very nice of him. 他人真好。

(C) The exam is tomorrow. 考試是在明天。

* final〔'faɪnl̩〕*adj.* 最後的；期末的　　essay〔'ɛse〕*n.* 文章；報告

　exam〔ɪg'zæm〕*n.* 考試　　handle〔'hændl̩〕*v.* 處理

第三部分：言談理解（第 11-21 題，共 11 題）

11. (**C**) W：Do you have time to meet this morning?

女：你今天早上有時間見面嗎？

M：I'm afraid not. I'm booked until late afternoon.

男：恐怕沒有。我到下午前都約滿了。

W：What time would work for you?

女：你什麼時間方便？

M：Well… I've got a massage at five, and dinner reservations at six. So how about we do it tomorrow?

男：嗯…。我五點有按摩，晚餐預約在六點。所以我們明天來做這件事如何？

W：Sounds good. How about first thing in the morning?

女：聽來不錯。那就是明早的第一件事如何？

M：I'll be in at nine.

男：我九點會在。

Question : What does the woman want to do?

女士想要做什麼？

(A) Get a massage. 按摩。

(B) Make dinner reservations. 預約晚餐。

(C) Schedule a meeting with the man.

跟這位男士安排見面。

meet〔mit〕v. 見面　　afraid〔ə'fred〕*adj.* 恐怕

book〔bʊk〕v. 預定（人）　　until〔ən'tɪl〕*prep.* 到…為止

work〔wɜk〕v. 行得通　　massage〔mə'sɑʒ〕n. 按摩

reservation〔ˌrɛzə'veʃən〕n. 預約

how about…? …如何？；…怎樣？

sound〔saʊnd〕v. 聽起來

first thing in the morning 早上第一件事

schedule〔'skɛdʒul〕v. 安排　　***make a reservation*** 預約

meeting〔'mitɪŋ〕n. 見面；會議

12.(**B**) M：Hi, Ms. Walker.

男：嗨，沃克女士。

W：Hi, Bobby. What brings you to my door?

女：你好，鮑比。什麼事讓你到我家們口來？

M：I'm here to apologize. I'm the one who knocked over your mailbox yesterday. I'm here to pay for the damage.

男：我是來這裡道歉的。我是昨天撞到你家信箱的人。我來這是支付你的損失。

W：Oh, that's OK, Bobby. I've already had it repaired. Besides, you're just a young boy, and these accidents happen from time to time. I'm proud of you for admitting what happened though.

女：噢，那沒關係，鮑比。我已經請人修好它了。此外，你只是個小孩，而且這類的意外偶爾會發生。然而我為你承認所發生的事感到驕傲。

Question：What just happened?
剛剛發生什麼事？

(A) Bobby broke the window. 鮑比打破了窗戶。

(B) Bobby admitted to causing some damage.
<u>鮑比承認造成一些損失。</u>

(C) Bobby paid for the damage. 鮑比賠償了損失。

* Ms.〔mɪz〕*n.* …女士　　bring〔brɪŋ〕*v.* 把…帶到
apologize〔əˈpɑləˌdʒaɪz〕*v.* 道歉　　***knock over*** 撞倒
mailbox〔ˈmelˌbɑks〕*n.* 信箱　　***pay for*** 為…付錢；賠償
damage〔ˈdæmɪdʒ〕*n.* 損害　　repair〔rɪˈpɛr〕*v.* 修理
besides〔bɪˈsaɪdz〕*adv.* 此外
accident〔ˈæksədənt〕*n.* 意外
from time to time 偶爾　　***be proud of*** 為…感到驕傲
admit〔ədˈmɪt〕*v.* 承認　　though〔ðo〕*adv.* 然而
admit to V-ing 承認～　　cause〔kɔz〕*v.* 造成

13. (**C**) W : It looks like someone is inside the house. Didn't you turn off all the lights before we left?

女：看起來有人在房子裡。我們出去之前你沒有關掉所有燈嗎？

M : I did. Uh-oh. It looks like the front door is open, too.

男：我有。噢，不。看起來前門也是開著的。

W : I'm scared!

女：我很害怕。

M : Calm down. I'll call the police. You go next door and stay with the Swansons until they get here.

男：冷靜下了。我會報警。你去隔壁然後和史汪森一家人待在一起直到警方到這裡。

Question：What might have happened?

什麼事可能已經發生了？

(A) They are at the wrong house. 他們在錯誤的房子。

(B) They forgot their keys. 他們忘了鑰匙。

(C) A burglar broke into their house.

一個竊賊闖入他們家。

* look〔luk〕*v.* 看起來　　inside〔'ɪn'saɪd〕*prep.* 在…裡面

  turn off 關掉　　light〔laɪt〕*n.* 燈

  left〔lɛft〕*v.* 離開【leave 的過去式】

  uh-oh〔'ʌ͵o〕*interj.*（表示做錯事或遇到麻煩）哎唷

  front〔frʌnt〕*adj.* 前面的　　scared〔skɛrd〕*adj.* 害怕的

  calm down 冷靜下來　　police〔pə'lis〕*n.* 警方

  call the police 報警　　***next door*** 在隔壁

  stay with 與…暫住　　Swanson〔'swɑnsn〕*n.* 史汪森

  the Swansons 史汪森一家人

  might have + p.p. 當時可能～

  forgot〔fə'gɑt〕*v.* 忘記【forget 的過去式】

  burglar〔'bɝglɚ〕*n.* 竊賊　　***break into*** 闖入

14. (**C**) M：According to the map, this highway doesn't go to Central City.

男：根據地圖，這條公路沒有通往中央市。

W：So we're headed in the wrong direction?

女：所以我們開往錯誤的方向了嗎？

M：Looks like it. Get off at the next exit and I'll ask for directions.

男：看來是。在下一個交流道出去，然後我來問路。

W：OK. I saw signs for a gas station a few miles back.
　　It wouldn't hurt to stop and get some gas.

女：好。我幾哩之前有看到一個加油站標示。停下來加點油也
　　無妨。

M：Yeah, I need to hit the restroom, too.

男：好的，我也需要去洗手間。

Question：What are the speakers doing?

　　　　　說話者在做什麼？

(A) Riding a bus. 搭公車。

(B) Flying a plane. 開飛機。

(C) Driving a car. <u>開車。</u>

＊ ***according to*** 根據；按照　　highway〔'haɪ,we〕*n.* 公路；幹道
　　central〔'sɛntrəl〕*adj.* 中央的　　***be headed*** 前往
　　direction〔də'rɛkʃən〕*n.* 方向　　***get off*** 離開
　　exit〔'ɛksɪt〕*n.* 出口　　***ask for directions*** 問路
　　sign〔saɪn〕*n.* 路標；記號
　　gas〔gæs〕*n.* 汽油　　station〔'steʃən〕*n.* 站
　　mile〔maɪl〕*n.* 哩；英里　　***it wouldn't hurt to*** … 做…也無妨
　　yeah〔jæ〕*interj.* 是的（= *yes*）
　　hit〔hɪt〕*v.* 去；到　　restroom〔'rɛst,rum〕*n.* 洗手間
　　plane〔plen〕*n.* 飛機　　ride〔raɪd〕*v.* 搭乘
　　fly〔flaɪ〕*v.* 駕駛（飛機）

15. (**C**) W：Have you told your parents about the test, Eric?

　　　　　女：你有跟你爸媽說考試的事了嗎，艾瑞克？

　　　　　M：Not yet. They're going to be angry. I'm waiting for
　　　　　　　the right moment.

　　　　　男：還沒。他們將會很生氣。我正等待適當的時候。

　　　　　W：When might that be?

女：那會是什麼時候？

M：When they are in a good mood.

男：當他們心情好時。

Question：How did Eric most likely do on the test?

下划線 艾瑞克的考試結果可能是什麼？

(A) He got a B-plus. 他得到了乙上。

(B) He only missed one question. 他只錯了一題。

(C) He failed. <u>他不及格。</u>

* ***be going to V***. 即將～；將要～   angry〔'æŋgrɪ〕*adj.* 生氣的
  wait for 等待   moment〔'momənt〕*n.* 時刻
  mood〔mud〕*n.* 心情；情緒   ***in a good mood*** 心情好
  most likely （很）可能   plus〔plʌs〕*adj.* 比…略好一些的
  B-plus 乙上   miss〔mɪs〕*v.* 未擊中；讓…溜掉
  fail〔fel〕*v.* 失敗；不及格

16. (**B**) M：Hey, I'm Chen-li's cousin, Ai-wei, from Taiwan.

男：嘿，我是成禮的表哥，艾偉，來自台灣。

W：Nice to meet you, Ai-wei. I'm Jenny from South
　　Korea.

女：很高興認識你，艾偉。我是從南韓來的珍妮。

M：Say, you look familiar. Have we met before?

男：哎，妳看來很面熟。我們之前有見過嗎？

W：I don't think so. Have you ever been to South Korea?

女：我不認為我們見過。你有去過南韓嗎？

M：No, but I feel like I've seen you before.

男：沒有，但我覺得我曾經見過妳。

Question：Which of the following statements is TRUE?

下划線 下列哪一個敘述為真？

(A) Chen-li is from South Korean. 成禮是從南韓來的。

(B) Ai-wei is Chen-li's cousin. 艾偉是成禮的表哥。

(C) Jenny is from Taiwan. 珍妮是從台灣來的。

* cousin〔'kʌzn̩〕*n.* 表（堂）兄弟姐妹
  Korea〔kə'riə〕*n.* 韓國　***South Korea*** 南韓
  say〔se〕*interj.* （用於表示驚訝或引起注意）哎；我說
  look〔lʊk〕*v.* 看起來　familiar〔fə'mɪljə〕*adj.* 熟悉的
  have been to 去過　statement〔'stetmənt〕*n.* 陳述

17. (**B**) W : Quincy isn't answering his phone. What should we do?

女：昆西不接電話。我們該怎麼辦？

M : He's always late. I think we should start without him.

男：他總是遲到。我想我們沒有他也應該先開始了。

W : Should we order something for him?

女：我們應該幫他點些什麼東西嗎？

M : No, we have no idea what he wants. Let him decide when—if he gets here.

男：不，我們不知道他想要什麼。讓他決定，當——如果他會來到這裡的話。

Question : What do we know about Quincy?

關於昆西，我們知道什麼？

(A) He's stuck in traffic. 他遇到塞車。

(B) He's late. 他遲到了。

(C) He's paying for dinner. 他正在付晚餐錢。

* Quincy〔'kwɪnsɪ〕*n.* 昆西
  answer〔'ænsə〕*v.* 回答；接（電話）
  order〔'ɔrdə〕*v.* 點菜　***have no idea*** 不知道
  decide〔dɪ'saɪd〕*v.* 決定

stuck〔stʌk〕*adj.* 卡住的；困住的　　traffic〔'træfɪk〕*n.* 交通

be stuck in traffic 遇到塞車

18. (**B**) M：What's bugging you today, Gloria?

男：今天什麼事情讓妳困擾，葛洛莉亞？

W：I don't know.

女：我不知道。

M：Is it something I said?

男：是我說了什麼嗎？

W：No, I just woke up on the wrong side of the bed this morning, Bob.

女：不，我只是今天早上有起床氣，鮑伯。

M：Let me know if there's anything I can do to cheer you up.

男：如果我能做什麼可以讓妳開心的事，請讓我知道。

Question：What's wrong with Gloria?

葛洛莉亞怎麼了？

(A) She is under the weather. 她不舒服。

(B) She is in a bad mood. <u>她心情不好。</u>

(C) She is worried about her test results.

她在擔心她的考試成績。

* bug〔bʌg〕*v.* 使煩惱　　***wake up*** 醒來

wake up on the wrong side of bed 有起床氣；沒理由地心情不好

（*=feel slightly angry or annoyed for no particular reason*）

cheer〔tʃɪr〕*v.* 使高興

cheer sb. up 使某人振奮；使某人高興

under the weather 不舒服

be in a bad mood 心情不好

results〔rɪ'zʌlts〕*n. pl.* 成績；分數

19. (**A**)　W：Be careful, Ralph.

女：小心點，羅夫。

M：I'm fine, Jane.　Just keep holding the ladder.

男：我沒事，珍。繼續抓緊梯子。

W：My arms are getting tired.

女：我的手臂開始累了。

M：Two more minutes, OK?　Hang in there.　I'm almost done.

男：再兩分鐘，好嗎？撐下去。我快好了。

W：I really think you should have called someone to come out and take care of this, Ralph.　You're not a carpenter.

女：我真的覺得你當時應該打電話請人出來處理這個，羅夫。你不是木匠。

M：Just pipe down, Jane.

男：閉嘴啦，珍。

Question：What might the man be doing?

男士可能在做什麼？

(A)　Fixing a leaky roof.　修漏水的屋頂。

(B)　Digging a hole.　挖一個洞。

(C)　Changing a flat tire.　換爆胎。

* **be careful** 當心；注意　　Ralph〔rælf〕n. 羅夫
hold〔hold〕v. 握住；撐著　　ladder〔'lædə〕n. 梯子
arm〔ɑrm〕n. 手臂　　get〔gɛt〕v. 變得
tired〔taɪrd〕adj. 疲倦的　　**hang in there** 堅持下去
done〔dʌn〕adj. 完成的　　**come out** 出來；出現
take care of 照顧；處理　　carpenter〔'kɑrpəntə〕n. 木匠
pipe down 【口】安靜；閉嘴　　fix〔fɪks〕v. 修理
leaky〔'likɪ〕adj. 漏水的　　roof〔ruf〕n. 屋頂

dig〔dɪg〕v. 挖　　hole〔hol〕n. 洞
flat〔flæt〕adj. 沒有氣的；平的　　tire〔taɪr〕n. 輪胎

20. (**C**) Dave has a job interview this afternoon. He recently applied for his first job, so it is a really big deal. The interview is in an hour, but Dave is nervous. He's not sure if the bus will get him there on time, so he has decided to call a taxi instead. He believes it is better to be safe than sorry.

戴夫今天下午有個工作面試。他最近應徵了他的第一份工作，所以這是一件大事。這面試再一小時後開始，但是戴夫很緊張。他不確定公車是否可以準時載他到那裡，所以他決定要改叫計程車。他相信事前小心總比事後後悔好。

Question：How does Dave feel right now?

　　　　戴夫現在覺得如何？

(A) Shy. 很害羞。

(B) Confident. 有自信。

(C) Uneasy. <u>不安。</u>

* interview〔'ɪntəvju〕n. 面試　　apply〔ə'plaɪ〕v. 申請
　a big deal 一件重要的事
　in〔ɪn〕prep. 再過~；（某段時間）之後
　nervous〔'nɝvəs〕adj. 緊張的　　sure〔ʃur〕adj. 確定的
　get〔gɛt〕v. 使移動　　***on time*** 準時
　taxi〔'tæksɪ〕n. 計程車　　instead〔ɪn'stɛd〕adv. 改做；替代
　believe〔bɪ'liv〕v. 相信
　better safe than sorry 事前小心總比事後後悔好；安全至上
　shy〔ʃaɪ〕adj. 害羞的
　confident〔'kɑnfədənt〕adj. 有自信的
　uneasy〔ʌn'izɪ〕adj. 不安的；不自在的

21. (**C**) This holiday takes place in the fall at the end of October. Many children look forward to this holiday, since it gives them a chance to dress up in costumes. Also, they go around the neighborhood and ask for candy. Although this holiday only lasts one day, it's something that children look forward to all year.

這個節日是在十月底的秋天。很多小孩很期待這個節日，因為這個節日給他們一個變裝的機會。而且，他們在社區附近走來走去要糖果。儘管這個節日只持續一天，它卻是小孩們整年都在期待的日子。

Question：What holiday is the speaker describing?

說話者在描述什麼節日？

(A) Easter. 復活節。

(B) Christmas. 聖誕節。

(C) Halloween. 萬聖節。

* holiday（ˈhɑlə͵de）*n.* 節日；假日　　*take place* 發生
  fall（fɔl）*n.* 秋天　　*at the end of* 在…結束時
  October（ɑkˈtobɚ）*n.* 十月　　children（ˈtʃɪldrən）*n. pl.* 小孩
  look forward to 期待　　since（tʃæns）*conj.* 因為；由於
  chance（tʃæns）*n.* 機會　　*dress up* 變裝
  costume（ˈkɑstjum）*n.* 戲服；服裝　　also（ˈɔlso）*adv.* 而且
  go around 四處走動　　neighborhood（ˈnebɚ͵hud）*n.* 附近
  ask for 要某事物　　candy（ˈkændɪ）*n.* 糖果
  last（læst）*v.* 持續　　*all year* 一整年
  describe（dɪˈskraɪb）*v.* 描述
  Easter（ˈistɚ）*n.* 復活節【三月二十二日至四月二十五日間的某個
    星期日】
  Christmas（ˈkrɪsmɑs）*n.* 聖誕節【十二月二十五日】
  Halloween（͵hæloˈin）*n.* 萬聖節【十月三十一日】

TEST 12 詳解

聽力測驗 (第 1-21 題，共 21 題)

第一部分：辨識句意 (第 1-3 題，共 3 題)

1. (**B**) (A)   (B)   (C)

Gina is chasing after her cat. 吉娜正在追她的貓。

  * chase〔tʃes〕*v.* 追逐；追趕 < *after* >

2. (**A**) (A)   (B)   (C)

There are two white lambs and two brown pigs.

有兩隻小羊和兩隻咖啡色的豬。

  * **There + be** 有~   lamb〔læm〕*n.* 羔羊；小羊

3. (**C**) (A)   (B)   (C)

Roger is trying to explain his grade report to his parents, and they aren't happy about it. 羅傑正在試著向他父母解釋他的成績單，而他的父母對此很不開心。

* ***try to V***. 試著~   explain〔ɪk'splen〕*v.* 解釋
grade〔gred〕*n.* 成績   report〔rɪ'pɔrt〕*n.* 報告
grade report 成績單   ***be happy about*** 對…感到高興

第二部分：基本問答（第 4-10 題，共 7 題）

4. (**A**) Who was on the phone? 誰在講電話？

    (A) Grandma. 奶奶。

    (B) Six degrees. 六度。

    (C) I couldn't wait that long. 我無法等那麼久。

    * ***on the phone*** 講電話   degree〔dɪ'gri〕*n.* 度

5. (**C**) What do you hope to achieve by using the new software?
你希望藉由新軟體達到什麼效果？

    (A) I looked for her but she wasn't there.
       我找她，但她不在那裡。

    (B) I wanted to see him in person. 我想親自去看他。

    (C) I hope to improve our scheduling.
       我希望改善我們的時間安排。

    * achieve〔ə'tʃiv〕*v.* 達到；贏得   software〔'sɔftwer〕*n.* 軟體
    look for 尋找；期待   ***in person*** 親自
    improve〔ɪm'pruv〕*v.* 改善；增進
    scheduling〔'skɛdʒulɪŋ〕*n.* 時間安排

6. (**A**) Henry will leave for Hong Kong in the morning.
亨利早上要前往香港。

    (A) I hope he has a safe trip. 我希望他一路平安。

    (B) I'll see you in the morning. 我早上將會跟你見面。

(C) I've been there several times. 我已經去了那裡幾次了。

* ***leave for*** （離開某地）前往　　***Hong Kong*** 香港
　safe〔sef〕*adj.* 安全的　　trip〔trɪp〕*n.* 旅行
　several〔'sɛvərəl〕*adj.* 幾個的　　time〔taɪm〕*n.* 次數

7. (**A**) Where did you buy your new laptop?
　你的新筆電是在哪邊買的？
　(A) At a computer store. 在一家電腦店。
　(B) At a local library. 在一間當地的圖書館。
　(C) At a medical clinic. 在一間醫療診所。

　* laptop〔'læp,tɑp〕*n.* 筆電　　local〔'lokḷ〕*adj.* 當地的
　　library〔'laɪ,brɛrɪ〕*n.* 圖書館　　medical〔'mɛdɪkḷ〕*adj.* 醫療的
　　clinic〔'klɪnɪk〕*n.* 診所

8. (**C**) What were you doing at the shopping mall?
　你在那家購物中心做什麼？
　(A) Updating a website. 更新一個網站。
　(B) Organizing a meeting. 籌辦一場會議。
　(C) Returning a product. 歸還一件商品。

　* mall〔mɔl〕*n.* 購物中心　　***shopping mall*** 購物中心
　　update〔ʌp'det〕*v.* 更新　　website〔'wɛb,saɪt〕*n.* 網站
　　organize〔'ɔrgən,aɪz〕*v.* 組織；籌辦
　　meeting〔'mitɪŋ〕*n.* 會議　　return〔rɪ'tɝn〕*n.* 歸還
　　product〔'prɑdʌkt〕*n.* 商品；產品

9. (**B**) Are you feeling better today, Rex?
　你今天感覺好多了嗎，雷克斯？
　(A) No, I'm sorry. 不，我很抱歉。
　(B) Yes, thank you. 對啊，謝謝你。
　(C) OK, no problem. 好，沒問題。

10. (**A**) Oliver, I will be working late tonight. Will you be OK for dinner? 奧利佛，我今天將會工作到很晚。你晚餐可以自理嗎？

   (A) Yes, I can take care of myself.

      <u>可以，我可以自己照顧自己。</u>

   (B) Sometimes, if you're going to be late.

      有時候，如果你將要遲到的話。

   (C) Sure, if you want me to wait.

      當然，如果你要我等的話。

   * ***take care of*** 照顧；留意

      sometimes〔'sʌm,taɪmz〕*adv.* 有時候   late〔let〕*adj.* 遲到的

      wait〔wet〕*v.* 等待

第三部分：言談理解（第 11-21 題，共 11 題）

11. (**B**) Daisy, I liked your idea of expanding our product line to include frozen yogurt. But since we currently only make regular yogurt, it would be a very large investment for our small company. I'm not sure if it will be profitable. I'd like you to do some market research to see how big the demand is for frozen yogurt in this region. That way you will have an idea whether it would be worthwhile. When you have the data, let me know. Thanks.

黛西，我喜歡妳將我們產品線擴展到包含冷凍優格的想法。但由於我們目前只做一般的優格，這對我們小公司而言將會是一筆大投資。我不確定它會不會獲利。我想要妳做些市場調查來看看，這個區域對冷凍優格的需求有多大。這樣一來妳就會知道它是否值得。當妳有這些資料後，讓我知道。謝謝。

Question：What does the man ask Daisy to do?

      這位男士要求黛西去做什麼事？

   (A) Change work schedules. 改變工作計畫。

(B) Conduct market research. 進行市場調查。

(C) Post a job description. 張貼一份職務說明。

expand〔ɪk'spænd〕v. 擴展　***product line*** 產品線；產品系列
include〔ɪn'klud〕v. 包含　frozen〔'frozn̩〕adj. 冷凍的
yogurt〔'jogɚt〕n. 優格　since〔tʃæns〕conj. 因為；由於
currently〔'kɝəntlɪ〕adv. 目前　regular〔'rɛgjəlɚ〕adj. 一般的
large〔lɑrdʒ〕adj. 大的　investment〔ɪn'vɛstmənt〕n. 投資
company〔'kʌmpənɪ〕n. 公司　sure〔ʃur〕adj. 確定的
profitable〔'prɑfɪtəbl̩〕adj. 能獲利的
market〔'mɑrkɪt〕n. 市場　research〔'risɝtʃ〕n. 研究；調查
demand〔dɪ'mænd〕n. 需求　region〔'ridʒən〕n. 區域
that way 那樣的話　worthwhile〔,wɝθ'waɪl〕adj. 值得的
data〔'detə〕n. pl. 資料；數據　ask〔æsk〕v. 要求
schedule〔'skɛdʒul〕n. 時間表　conduct〔kən'dʌkt〕v. 執行
post〔post〕v. 張貼　description〔dɪ'skɪpʃən〕n. 描述
job description 工作說明；職務說明

12. (**B**) M : How long will you be in Singapore?

男：妳會在新加坡多久？

W : I'm leaving tomorrow.

女：我明天就要走了。

M : Oh, that's too bad. I was hoping we would have more time to hang out. I wanted to show you around town.

男：喔，真是太遺憾了。我原本希望我們可以有更多時間在一起閒逛。我想帶妳到城裡到處看看。

W : Maybe next time.

女：也許下一次吧。

M : OK, well, get home safe. See you.

男：好，嗯，平安回家。再見。

Question : What will the woman do tomorrow?

明天女士會做什麼？

(A) Return to Singapore. 回來新加坡。

(B) Leave Singapore. 離開新加坡。

(C) Go sightseeing in Singapore. 在新加坡觀光。

* ***how long*** 有多久　　Singapore〔'sɪngə‚pɔr〕*n.* 新加坡
That's too bad. 真遺憾。　　***hang out*** 閒逛；逗留
show sb. around 帶某人到處參觀　　maybe〔'mebɪ〕*adv.* 或許
well〔wɛl〕*interj.* 嗯　　safe〔sef〕*adj.* 安全的
see you 再見　　return〔rɪ'tɜn〕*v.* 回來
leave〔liv〕*v.* 離開　　sightsee〔'saɪt‚si〕*v.* 觀光
go sightseeing 去觀光

13. (**C**) M：Do you live in Taipei City?

男：你住在台北市嗎？

W：No, I live in Banqiao, which is considered New Taipei City.

女：不，我住在板橋，是屬於新北市。

M：How do you like it there?

男：你喜歡那裡嗎？

W：It's OK.

女：還可以。

Question：Does the woman like living in Banqiao?

女士喜歡住在板橋嗎？

(A) Yes, she loves it. 是，她喜歡板橋。

(B) No, she hates it. 不，她討厭板橋。

(C) She is indifferent about it. 她對板橋沒什麼感覺。

* consider〔kən'sɪdɚ〕*v.* 視為　　***like it there*** 喜歡那裡
indifferent〔ɪn'dɪfrənt〕*adj.* 冷漠的；沒興趣的

14. (**C**) M：I'll need to see some ID before I can let you into the club.

男：我要看妳的身分證件才能讓你進夜店。

W : I forgot my driver's license at home.

女：我把我的駕照忘在家裡。

M : I'm sorry.　You must be 18 to enter the club, and you must be able to prove it.　Sorry, it's the law.

男：我很抱歉。你必須18歲才能進入夜店，而且妳必須證明。抱歉，這是規定。

W : Please!　I'm 25, honest.

女：拜託！我25歲了，沒騙你。

Question : What do we know about the woman?

關於女士，我們知道什麼？

(A) She isn't old enough to drink.

她年紀沒有大到可以喝酒。

(B) She doesn't know how to dance.　她不知道如何跳舞。

(C) She is trying to enter a club.　她正在試著進入夜店。

* ID　*n.* 身分證件（＝ *identification* ）　　club〔klʌb〕*n.* 夜店
driver〔'draɪvə〕*n.* 駕駛　　license〔'laɪsn̩s〕*n.* 證照；執照
driver's license 駕照　　enter〔'ɛntə〕*v.* 進入
be able to V. 能夠~　　prove〔pruv〕*v.* 證明
law〔lɔ〕*n.* 法律　　honest〔'ɑnɪst〕*adj.* 誠實的
enough〔ə'nʌf〕*adj.* 足夠的；充足的
drink〔drɪŋk〕*v.* 喝；喝酒

15. (**B**) M : What are you doing after class?

男：妳放學後要做什麼？

W : Nothing.　I'll go home, study, and rest.　Why?

女：沒什麼。我會回家、讀書，然後休息。爲什麼這樣問？

M : I was thinking about going to the shopping mall.

男：我剛在想說要去購物中心。

W : Are you looking for anything in particular?

女：你有特別要找什麼東西嗎？

M : No. I'm just bored.

男：沒有。我只是感到無聊。

Question : Why does the man want to go to the shopping mall? 男士為何想去購物中心？

(A) He has a part-time job in the food court.

他們百貨美食廣場有兼職工作。

(B) He is bored. 他感到無聊。

(C) He needs a new pair of shoes. 他需要一雙新鞋。

* ***after class*** 放學後   rest〔rɛst〕*v.* 休息
think about 考慮   ***shopping mall*** 購物中心
look for 尋找；期待   ***in particular*** 尤其；特別；特地
bored〔bɔrd〕*adj.* 無聊的
part-time job 兼職工作   ***food court*** 百貨美食廣場

16. (**B**) W : Can I go outside and play now, Dad?

女：我現在可以出去玩了嗎，爸？

M : Have you finished your homework?

男：妳完成你的功課了嗎？

W : Yes, and I cleaned my room, too.

女：有，而且我也打掃好我的房間了。

M : OK. Be safe. Don't stray too far, and be home in time for dinner.

男：好，注意安全。不要跑太遠，要趕在晚餐的時間回家。

Question : What does the girl want to do?

女孩想要做什麼？

(A) Finish her homework. 完成她的功課。

(B) Go outside. 去外面。

(C) Have dinner. 吃晚餐。

* outside〔'aʊt'saɪd〕*adv.* 在外面   finish〔'fɪnɪʃ〕*v.* 完成
clean〔klin〕*v.* 清潔   safe〔sef〕*adj.* 安全的

stray〔stre〕 *v.* 流浪　　***in time*** 及時；準時
have〔hɛv〕 *v.* 吃；有

17.（ **A** ） M：Betty, how do you avoid getting sick?

　　　男：貝蒂，妳是如何避免生病的？

　　　W：I guess I have some pretty healthy habits, Vince.
　　　　　I eat right, sleep right, and wash my hands as often as
　　　　　possible.

　　　女：我想我有一些很健康的習慣，文斯。我吃好，睡好，而且儘
　　　　　可能常洗手。

　　　M：I should do that. Maybe I wouldn't get sick three
　　　　　times a year.

　　　男：我應該那麼做。或許我就不會一年生三次病。

　　　Question：What is one of Betty's healthy habits?

　　　　　　　　貝蒂的健康習慣其中有一個是什麼？

　　　(A) She frequently washes her hands. 她經常洗手。

　　　(B) She seldom smokes cigarettes. 她很少抽菸。

　　　(C) She always wakes up early. 她總是早起。

　　　* avoid〔ə'vɔɪd〕 *v.* 避開；躲開　　***get sick*** 生病
　　　　guess〔gɛs〕 *v.* 想；認為　　pretty〔'prɪtɪ〕 *adv.* 相當地
　　　　healthy〔'hɛlθɪ〕 *adj.* 健康的　　habit〔'hæbɪt〕 *n.* 習慣
　　　　habit〔'hæbɪt〕 *n.* 習慣　　right〔raɪt〕 *adv.* 正確地；妥當地
　　　　as ~ as possible 儘可能；愈…愈好
　　　　maybe〔'mebɪ〕 *adv.* 或許；可能　　time〔taɪm〕 *n.* 次數
　　　　frequently〔'frikwəntlɪ〕 *adv.* 經常地
　　　　seldom〔'sɛldəm〕 *adv.* 不常　　smoke〔smok〕 *v.* 抽（菸）
　　　　cigarette〔ˌsɪgə'rɛt〕 *n.* 香菸　　***wake up*** 起床（= *get up*）
　　　　early〔'ɝlɪ〕 *adv.* 早地

18.（ **A** ） W：The air pollution is really bad today. I can barely
　　　　　breathe and my eyes are burning.

女：今天的空氣污染眞是嚴重。我幾乎不能呼吸而且我的眼睛
感到刺痛。

M：Really? I hadn't noticed.

男：眞的嗎？我沒注意到。

W：You haven't? The air is so bad we can't even see the
Sears Tower from here.

女：你沒有？空氣糟到我們甚至不能從這看到希爾斯大廈。

M：I don't know. I never think about it.

男：我不知道。我從來沒有想過。

W：Don't you ever read the news? The government has
been trying to clean up the air for years.

女：你都沒有看新聞嗎？政府已經試著去清淨空氣很多年了。

M：No, I don't pay attention to the news.

男：沒有，我沒有注意到這則新聞。

Question：What is the woman complaining about?

這位女士正在抱怨什麼？

(A) Air pollution. 空氣污染。

(B) Water pollution. 水污染。

(C) Noise pollution. 噪音污染。

* pollution〔pə'luʃən〕n. 污染　　bad〔bæd〕adj. 嚴重的；厲害的
barely〔'bɛrlɪ〕adv. 幾乎不　　breathe〔'briz〕v. 呼吸
burning〔bɜn〕v. 灼痛；感到刺痛　　notice〔'notɪs〕v. 注意
even〔'ivən〕adv.〔加強語氣〕甚至；連
Sears Tower 希爾斯大廈【位於美國伊利諾州芝加哥的一幢摩天大樓，
又譯爲威利斯大廈，The Willis Tower】
news〔njuz〕n. 新聞　　government〔'gʌvənmənt〕n. 政府
clear up 清理　　**pay attention to** 注意
complain〔kəm'plen〕v. 抱怨；控訴　　noise〔'nɔɪz〕n. 噪音

19. (**B**) W：I hope you don't mind, but Steve will be joining us
for dinner tonight.

女：我希望你不介意，但是史帝夫今晚將會跟我們一起用餐。

M：Of course, I don't mind. What a nice surprise! It's been so long since we've had him over.

男：當然不介意。這眞是很棒的驚喜！他來我們家作客已經這麼久了。

W：Yes, well, he's been busy promoting his latest book.

女：對啊，嗯，他一直在忙著推銷他最新書籍。

Question：How does the man feel about Steve coming for dinner? 男士對於史帝夫來用餐的感覺如何？

(A) Sad. 難過的。

(B) Happy. 快樂的。

(C) Busy. 忙錄的。

* mind 〔 maɪnd 〕 *v.* 在意　　join 〔 dʒɔɪn 〕 *v.* 加入
  of course 當然　　surprise 〔 sə'praɪz 〕 *n.* 使人驚訝的事
  have sb. over 請某人到家裡作客　　*be busy + V-ing* 忙著～
  promote 〔 prə'mot 〕 *v.* 促銷；推銷　　latest 〔'letɪst 〕 *adj.* 最新的

20. (**C**) M：I need twenty more dollars to buy a cheeseburger meal.

男：我需要 20 多元去買一份起士漢堡餐。

W：Here. You can have all the change from my pocket.

女：這裡。你可以拿我口袋裡的所有零錢。

M：How much is it?

男：有多少？

W：I don't know. Count it. I'm sure there's more than twenty dollars there.

女：我不知道。你算一下。我很確定有超過 20 元。

Question：What does the man want to do? 男士想做什麼？

(A) Buy a bus ticket. 買一張公車票。

(B) Buy a pair of pants. 買一條褲子。

(C)　Buy a cheeseburger.　<u>買一個起士漢堡。</u>

* dollar〔ˋdɑlɚ〕*n.* 元　　　cheeseburger〔ˋtʃiz͵bɝgɚ〕*n.* 起士漢堡
meal〔mil〕*n.* 一餐　　　change〔tʃendʒ〕*n.* 零錢
pocket〔ˋpɑkɪt〕*n.* 口袋　　count〔kaʊnt〕*v.* 算
sure〔ʃʊr〕*adj.* 確定的　　ticket〔ˋtɪkɪt〕*n.* 票
pair〔pɛr〕*n.* 一對　　　pants〔pænts〕*n. pl.* 褲子；長褲

21.（**C**）In order for a small business to be successful, it must
solve a problem, fulfill a need or offer something the
market wants.　There are a number of ways you can
identify this need, including research, focus groups, and
even trial and error.

一間小企業為了要成功，它必須是可以解決問題、滿足需求，或
是提供市場需要的東西。有一些方式你可以辨認出這個需求，包
含調查研究、焦點人群，甚至嘗試錯誤。

Question：What is the speaker talking about?
說話者在談論什麼？

(A)　Attending a new school.　進入一個新學校。

(B)　Moving to a foreign country.　搬到國外。

(C)　Starting a business.　<u>開創一個企業。</u>

* *in order to V.* 為了~　　successful〔səkˋsɛsfəl〕*adj.* 成功的
solve〔sɑlv〕*v.* 解決　　problem〔ˋprɑbləm〕*n.* 問題
fulfill〔fʊlˋfɪl〕*v.* 滿足　　need〔nid〕*n.* 需求
offer〔ˋɔfɚ〕*v.* 提供　　market〔ˋmɑrkɪt〕*n.* 市場
a number of 一些　　way〔we〕*n.* 方法
identify〔aɪˋdɛntə͵faɪ〕*v.* 辨別
research〔ˋrisɝtʃ〕*n.* 研究；調查　　focus〔ˋfokəs〕*n.* 焦點
focus group 焦點人群【代表大眾，其觀點用於市場調查】
trial〔ˋtraɪəl〕*n.* 試驗　　error〔ˋɛrɚ〕*n.* 錯誤
trial and error 嘗試錯誤；反覆實驗
attend〔əˋtɛnd〕*v.* 上（大學等）　　foreign〔ˋfɔrɪn〕*adj.* 外國的
country〔ˋkaʊntrɪ〕*n.* 國家

TEST 13 詳解

聽力測驗（第 1-21 題，共 21 題）

第一部分：辨識句意（第 1-3 題，共 3 題）

1. (**A**) (A)  (B)  (C)

This is a book about a bird. 這是一本關於一隻鳥的書。

* parrot〔'pærət〕*n.* 鸚鵡　　ant〔ænt〕*n.* 螞蟻
grasshopper〔'græs,hɑpə〕*n.* 蚱蜢　　fox〔fɑks〕*n.* 狐狸
goat〔got〕*n.* 山羊

2. (**C**) (A)  (B)  (C)

Maureen is practicing her flute. 莫琳正在練習她的長笛。

* Maureen〔mə'rin〕*n.* 莫琳
practice〔'præktɪs〕*v.* 練習；學習　　flute〔flut〕*n.* 長笛

3. (**A**) (A)  (B)  (C)

Kim will work on the computer from 8:00 a.m. to 10:00 a.m. 金從早上八點到十點會用電腦工作。

　* **a.m.** 午前；上午（= *ante meridiem*）

第二部分：基本問答（第 4-10 題，共 7 題）

4. (**A**) I'm a student at Gordon Junior High. Where do you go to school? 我是戈登國中的學生。你在哪個學校上學？

　(A) I attend Harper Elementary. 我在哈波小學上學。

　(B) I usually stay home on weekends. 我周末通常在家。

　(C) I have dance class on Friday nights.

　　　我星期五晚上有舞蹈課。

　* junior〔'dʒunjɚ〕*adj.* 少年的

　　junior high 國中（= *junior high school*）

　　attend〔ə'tɛnd〕*v.* 上（大學等）

　　elementary〔ˌɛlə'mɛntərɪ〕*n.* 小學（= *elementary school*）

　　on weekends 每逢週末

5. (**B**) Why were you late for class this morning, Bill?

　　　比爾，為什麼你今天早上上課遲到？

　(A) The sandwich had mayonnaise on it.

　　　三明治上有美乃滋。

　(B) The bus got stuck in a traffic jam. 公車遇到塞車。

　(C) The cold wind makes my head hurt.

　　　這陣冷風讓我頭痛。

　* **be late for class** 上課遲到　　sandwich〔'sænwɪtʃ〕*n.* 三明治

　　mayonnaise〔ˌmeə'nez〕*n.* 美乃滋　　stuck〔stʌk〕*adj.* 卡住的

　　get stuck 受困　　traffic〔'træfɪk〕*n.* 交通；車輛

　　jam〔dʒæm〕*n.* 果醬；阻塞　　**traffic jam** 塞車

　　wind〔wɪnd〕*n.* 風　　head〔hɛd〕*n.* 頭

　　hurt〔hɝt〕*v.* 感到痛

6. (**A**) Danny has been down in the dumps lately. We should do something to try and cheer him up. 丹尼最近心情低到谷底了。我們該試試做些事情，讓他開心起來。

(A) Let's take him out for dinner. 我們帶他去吃晚餐吧。

(B) Let's find a better place to sit.
我們找個比較好的地方坐吧。

(C) Let's not make any mistakes.
讓我們不要犯任何一個錯誤吧。

* down〔daʊn〕*adj.* 情緒低落；消沉
dump〔dʌmp〕*n.* 垃圾場
be down in the dumps 垂頭喪氣；心情低落
lately〔'letlɪ〕*adv.* 近來；最近
cheer sb. up 使某人開心起來　　*take sb. out* 帶某人外出
mistake〔mə'stek〕*n.* 錯誤

7. (**C**) Could you please keep an eye on my bag? I'll be back soon. 你可不可以幫我看一下包包？我很快就回來。

(A) Yes, I was there. 對，我當時在那裡。

(B) No, I didn't. 不，我沒有。

(C) Sure, no problem. 當然，沒問題。

* *keep an eye on sth.* 照顧；看守
sure〔ʃʊr〕*adv.* 當然　　*no problem* 沒問題

8. (**C**) There's a new Indian restaurant in the neighborhood. Would you like to try it sometime?
附近有家新的印度餐廳。你改天想試試看嗎？

(A) I speak Chinese. 我說中文。

(B) I was born in Canada. 我在加拿大出生。

(C) I don't really care for Indian food.
我不是很喜歡印度料理。

* Indian〔'ɪndɪən〕*adj.* 印度的
neighborhood〔'nebə،hud〕*n.* 附近　***would like to V.*** 想要~
sometime〔'sʌm،taɪm〕*adv.* 在（將來或過去）某一時候；改天
Canada〔'kænədə〕*n.* 加拿大　***care for*** 喜歡

9. (**B**) What did John Parker ask you? 約翰・派克問了你什麼事？

(A) He gave her some directions. 他跟她指路。

(B) He asked to borrow a pencil. 他要借枝鉛筆。

(C) He took it to the cafeteria. 他帶它去自助餐館。

* directions〔də'rɛkʃənz〕*n. pl.*（路的）指引；指示
borrow〔'baro〕*v.* 借（入）　　pencil〔'pɛnsl̩〕*n.* 鉛筆
cafeteria〔،kæfə'tɪrɪə〕*n.* 自助餐館

10. (**A**) How was your hike in the mountains last weekend?
你上禮拜的登山健行好玩嗎？

(A) I didn't go. 我沒去。

(B) They weren't there. 他們不在那裡。

(C) She said she was happy. 她說她很快樂。

* hike〔haɪk〕*n.* 健行　***in the mountains*** 在山裡
weekend〔'wikɛnd〕*n.* 週末

第三部分：言談理解（第 11-21 題，共 11 題）

11. (**A**) W：Have you ever attended one of the big summer music
festivals in Taiwan?

女：你在台灣參加過大型夏季音樂祭嗎？

M：Unfortunately, no. Have you?

男：很遺憾地，沒有。妳有嗎？

W：Nope. But I'm planning to attend Spring Scream in
Kenting this year.

女：沒有。但我今年計畫要去參加墾丁的春吶。

M : Really? When is it?

男：真的嗎？它在什麼時候？

W : It's in April. Are you interested in going? Maybe we could go together.

女：它在四月。你有興趣要去嗎？也許我們可以一起去。

Question : What is true about the speakers?

關於說話者，何者為真？

(A) Neither have ever been to a music festival in Taiwan.

兩位都沒有去過台灣的音樂祭。

(B) Both have been to music festivals in Taiwan.

兩位都去過台灣的音樂祭。

(C) The man has been to several music festivals in Taiwan. 男士已經去過幾場台灣的音樂祭。

* attend〔əˋtɛnd〕v. 參加　　festival〔ˋfɛstəvḷ〕n. 節慶；表演會
unfortunately〔ʌnˋfɔrtʃənɪtlɪ〕adv. 不幸地；遺憾地
nope〔nop〕adv. 不（= no）　　plan〔plæn〕v. 計畫；打算
scream〔skrim〕n. 尖叫；吶喊　　Kenting〔ˋkɛntɪŋ〕n. 墾丁
be interested in 對…感興趣　　maybe〔ˋmebɪ〕adv. 或許；可能
neither〔ˋniðɚ〕pron. 兩者皆非　　**have been to** 去過～
both〔boθ〕pron. 兩者

12. (**B**) M : That was Principal Martin on the phone. We need to have a talk with Fiona when she gets home.

男：剛剛通話中的是馬丁校長。等費歐娜回來的時候，我們需要跟她談談。

W : What happened? Did she cause trouble at school again today?

女：發生什麼事了？她今天又在學校惹麻煩了嗎？

M : No, she didn't even go to school today.

男：沒有，她今天甚至沒有去上學。

W : That's not good. Where was she?

女：那真是不乖。她在哪？

M : Nobody knows. That's what we need to find out.

男：沒人知道。那是我們需要去查清楚的事情。

Question : Who did the man speak to on the phone?

這個男士在電話中跟誰說話？

(A) Fiona. 費歐娜。

(B) Principal Martin. 馬丁校長。

(C) Fiona's mother. 費歐娜的媽媽。

* principal〔ˋprɪnsəpḷ〕 *n.* 校長　　***be on the phone***　講電話
have a talk　談一談　　Fiona〔fiˋonə〕 *n.* 費歐娜
cause〔kɔz〕 *v.* 導致；引起　　trouble〔ˋtrʌbḷ〕 *n.* 問題；麻煩
at school　在學校　　***go to school***　上學
find out　發現；查清楚

13. (**C**)　W : Deborah and William have invited over 300 people to their wedding reception next month.

女： 黛博拉和威廉已邀請超過 300 百人來參加他們下個月的婚宴。

M : Three hundred?!? That's a lot of people. Where is the reception going to be held?

男： 三百?!? 那很多人。宴席辦在哪裡？

W : At the Grand Ballroom in downtown Cooper City.

女： 在庫柏市中心的大禮堂。

M : I'll bet that's going to cost them a fortune. Who's paying for it?

男： 我敢說那會花他們一大筆錢。誰會付錢呢？

W : Deborah's parents, I guess. It's always been Deborah's dream to have a big wedding, and she's their only child.

女：黛博拉的父母，我猜。黛博拉一直很想有個盛大的婚禮，
而且她又是獨生女。

Question：How many people are expected to attend
Deborah and William's wedding reception?
預期有多少人會來參加黛博拉及威廉的婚宴？

(A) 100. 一百。

(B) 200. 二百。

(C) 300. 三百。

* Deborah〔'dɛbərə〕*n.* 黛博拉
invite〔ɪn'vaɪt〕*v.* 邀請；招待　　wedding〔'wɛdɪŋ〕*n.* 婚禮
reception〔rɪ'sɛpʃən〕*n.* 接待；招待會
wedding reception 婚宴　　hold〔hold〕*v.* 舉辦
grand〔grænd〕*adj.* 宏偉的；豪華的
ballroom〔'bɔlrum〕*n.* 舞廳
downtown〔'daʊntaʊn〕*n.* 市中心
bet〔bɛt〕*v.* 打賭；打包票　　***I'll bet*** 我敢肯定；我敢保證
cost〔kɔst〕*v.* 花費　　fortune〔'fɔrtʃən〕*n.* 一大筆錢
pay for 為⋯付錢　　parents〔'pɛrənts〕*n. pl.* 父母；雙親
guess〔gɛs〕*v.* 猜；想　　***only child*** 獨生子
expect〔ɪk'spɛkt〕*v.* 預期　　attend〔ə'tɛnd〕*v.* 出席；參加

14. (**B**) W：Excuse me, sir. Didn't you tell me that this dish had
no meat in it?
女：不好意思，先生。你不是告訴我說這道菜裡面沒有肉嗎？

M：Yes. Did I make a mistake?
男：是的。我出了什麼差錯嗎？

W：Apparently so. There's definitely some kind of meat
in this sauce.
女：似乎是這樣。醬料裡面確實是有某種肉。

M：I'm sorry. I didn't realize that.

男：我很抱歉。我沒有察覺到。

W : Could you bring me something else? I'm a vegetarian.

女：你可以給我別的嗎？我是素食者。

M : I'll take this dish away and bring you a menu.

男：我會把這盤菜拿走並給妳一份菜單。

Question : What do we know about the woman?

　　　　　關於女士我們知道什麼？

(A) She is allergic to shellfish.　她對有殼海鮮過敏。

(B) She doesn't eat meat.　她不吃肉。

(C) She wants a refund.　她想要退款。

* **excuse me**　【用於引起注意】對不起　　sir〔sɚ〕n. 先生
  meat〔mit〕n. 肉　　**make a mistake**　犯錯
  apparently〔ə'pærɛntlɪ〕adv. 似乎；看上去
  definitely〔'dɛfənɪtəlɪ〕adv. 確實地　　kind〔kaɪnd〕n. 種類
  sauce〔sɔs〕n. 醬料　　realize〔'rɪə,laɪz〕v. 察覺；了解
  bring〔brɪŋ〕v. 帶來　　vegetarian〔,vɛdʒə'tɛrɪən〕n. 素食者
  take away　拿走；帶走　　dish〔dɪʃ〕n. 盤子；菜
  menu〔'mɛnju〕n. 菜單　　allergic〔ə'lɝdʒɪk〕adj. 過敏的
  be allergic to　對…過敏　　shellfish〔'ʃɛlfɪʃ〕n. 貝類；蝦蟹類
  refund〔'rɪ,fʌnd〕n. 退款

15. (**A**) W : Don't you have everything you need for your trip already? What are we doing here?

女：你不是已經有你出遊所需的所有東西了嗎？我們在這裡做什麼？

M : I need some waterproof wool socks.

男：我需要一些防水的羊毛襪。

W : I know you have at least one pair. I bought them for you last year.

女： 我知道你至少有一雙。我去年幫你買的。

M： Yes, but it's better to have more than one pair, in case one gets wet.

男： 對，但最好要帶超過一雙，以免其中一雙弄溼了。

W： They're waterproof!

女： 他們是防水的喔！

M： Well, better safe than sorry.

男： 嗯，有備無患。

W： I just don't understand why you're taking so much stuff on a two-day hike when it's not even supposed to rain. Plus, your boots are waterproof.

女： 我就是不懂你為什麼兩天的遠足要帶這麼多東西，甚至是在應該不會下雨的時候。再者，你的靴子是防水的。

Question： Why is the woman surprised?

為什麼女士很驚訝？

(A) The man wants to buy more clothing.

男士想買多一點衣物。

(B) The man left his wallet at home.

男士把他的皮夾留在家。

(C) The man already has five pairs of shoes.

男士已經有五雙鞋子了。

* waterproof (ˈwɔtɚˈpruf) *adj.* 防水的
  wool (wul) *n.* 羊毛　　socks (sɑks) *n. pl.* 襪子
  at least 至少　　pair (pɛr) *n.* 一對；一雙
  in case 以免唯恐　　wet (wɛt) *adj.* 潮溼的
  better safe than sorry 有備無患；小心一點總比事後難過來的好
  understand (ˌʌndɚˈstænd) *v.* 理解；懂
  stuff (stʌf) *n.* 東西　　hike (haɪk) *n.* 健行；遠足
  suppose (səˈpoz) *v.* 假定；認為　　*be supposed to V.* 應該～
  plus (plʌs) *adv.* 加上；而且　　boots (buts) *n. pl.* 靴子

surprised〔 sə'praɪzd 〕*adj.* 驚訝的
clothing〔'kloðɪŋ 〕*n.* 衣服；衣物   wallet〔'wɑlɪt 〕*n.* 皮夾
at home 在家裡

16. (**B**) W : Is that the new iPhone 7?

女：那是新的 iPhone 7 嗎？

M : Yep. Check it out.

男：對。來看看吧。

W : Hmm. The screen is a little bit bigger than the
iPhone 6S', isn't it?

女：嗯。這螢幕比 iPhone 6S 的大一點，不是嗎？

M : Just a little.

男：只大了一點。

W : How much did it cost?

女：它要多少錢？

M : Well, there are three different versions of the phone,
depending upon capacity. This has 64 gigabytes,
which is the mid-range. I paid $299.

男：嗯，這款手機依照容量有三種不同的版本。這支是 64GB，
是中價位的。我付了 299 美元。

Question : What does the woman notice about the phone?
關於手機，女士注意到什麼？

(A) It has more capacity. 它有更多的容量。

(B) The screen is larger than the iPhone 6S screen.
<u>此螢幕比 iPhone 6S 的還大。</u>

(C) The price is just about right. 價格差不多剛好。

* yep〔 jɛp 〕*adv.* 是（＝yes）   ***check it out*** 看一看
hmm〔 hm 〕*interj.* (表示遲疑、停頓) 嗯
screen〔 skrin 〕*n.* 螢幕   ***a little*** 一點點
cost〔 kɔst 〕*v.* 花（錢）   well〔 wɛl 〕*interj.* 嗯

there + be 有　　version〔'vɝʒən〕 *n.* 版本

depending upon 根據；依據

capacity〔kə'pæsətɪ〕 *n.* 容量；能力

gigabyte〔'gɪgə,baɪt〕 *n.* 億萬位元組 (= *GB*)

mid-〔mɪd〕 *adj.* 在…中間　　range〔rendʒ〕 *n.* 範圍

mid-range *adj.* 中檔的；中價位的

notice〔'notɪs〕 *v.* 注意　　price〔praɪs〕 *n.* 價格

just about 幾乎；差不多 (= *almost*)

17. (**B**)　M : Why have you been coming home late this week?

男：妳這個禮拜爲什麼這麼晚回家？

W : I've been walking Tina's dog while she's out of town.

女：蒂娜不在鎮上的時候，我一直在幫她遛狗。

M : That's nice of you.　I didn't know Tina had a dog.

男：妳人眞好。我不知道蒂娜有養狗。

W : There are a lot of things you don't know about Tina.
Maybe you should try talking to her next time she
comes over.

女：蒂娜還有很多你不知道的事。也許下次她來時，你該試著跟
她講些話。

M : Eh, I'm not that interested in getting to know your
friends.

男：嗯，我對認識妳的朋友沒有那麼有興趣。

Question : Who is the man probably talking to?

男士可能在跟誰說話？

(A)　His brother.　他的兄弟。

(B)　His sister.　他的妹妹。

(C)　His friend, Tina.　他的朋友蒂娜。

* ***walk a dog*** 遛狗　　***out of town*** 出城

　town〔taʊn〕 *n.* 城市；鎮　　***a lot of*** 許多；大量

maybe〔'nebi〕*adv.* 或許；可能   ***try + V-ing*** 試看看～
come over 順便來訪   that〔ðæt〕*adv.* 那麼；那樣地
be interested in 對…感興趣   ***get to V.*** 有機會～；得以～
probably〔'prɑbəblɪ〕*adv.* 很可能

18. (**A**) M : I've just read something interesting. There was a
study about religion and childhood development, and
it showed that children from highly religious
backgrounds are actually meaner than kids who grow
up without religion.

男：我剛讀了些有趣的東西。有個關於宗教及兒童發展的研究，
它顯示具有高度宗教背景的兒童，實際上比沒有宗教信仰的
兒童還要壞。

W : That's odd. You'd think the religious kids would be
nicer.

女：那眞奇怪。你會覺得有宗教信仰的孩童會更善良。

M : Well, it turns out to be the opposite.

男：嗯，結果是相反的。

Question : What are the speakers talking about?

說話者在討論什麼？

(A) Children and religion. 兒童與宗教。

(B) Health and fitness. 健康與保健。

(C) Society and crime. 社會與犯罪。

* just〔dʒʌst〕*adv.* 剛剛
  interesting〔'ɪntrɪstɪŋ〕*adj.* 有趣的
  study〔'stʌdɪ〕*n.* 研究   religion〔rɪ'lɪdʒən〕*n.* 宗教
  childhood〔'tʃaɪld,hʊd〕*n.* 童年
  development〔dɪ'vɛləpmənt〕*n.* 進化；發展
  show〔ʃo〕*v.* 顯示   highly〔'haɪlɪ〕*adv.* 非常；很
  religious〔rɪ'lɪdʒəs〕*adj.* 宗教的；有宗教信仰的

background〔'bæk,graʊnd〕*n.* 背景
actually〔'æktʃʊəlɪ〕*adv.* 事實上；實際上
mean〔min〕*adj.* 卑鄙的；壞的　　grow〔gro〕*v.* 成長
grow up 長大　　odd〔ɑd〕*adj.* 奇怪的；不尋常的
turn out 結果　　opposite〔'ɑpəzɪt〕*n.* 相反的事物
health〔hɛlθ〕*n.* 健康　　fitness〔'fɪtnəs〕*n.* (健康) 良好
society〔sə'saɪətɪ〕*n.* 社會　　crime〔kraɪm〕*n.* 罪

19. (**C**)　M : Is this where you usually have lunch?

　　　男：這是妳平常吃午餐的地方嗎？

　　　W : It's one of the places I frequently eat at, but I'm not
　　　　　here every single day.

　　　女：這是我常去吃的其中一個地方，但我不是每天都來這吃。

　　　M : What do you usually order?

　　　男：妳通常點什麼？

　　　W : I generally rotate between a few dishes.　Sometimes
　　　　　the daily special is good.　Today it's a chicken sub
　　　　　sandwich.　Those are always tasty.

　　　女：我一般都在幾道菜中輪著點。有時每日特餐很好。今天
　　　　　是雞肉潛艇堡。那些總是很好吃。

　　　M : What about the tuna salad?

　　　男：那麼鮪魚沙拉呢？

　　　W : I'm not a big fan of the tuna salad here.　I think they
　　　　　use too much mayonnaise.

　　　女：我沒有很愛這的鮪魚沙拉。我認為他們美乃滋用太多了。

　　　Question : Where is the conversation taking place?

　　　　　　　　這段對話是在哪裡發生的？

　　　(A) In a library. 在圖書館。

　　　(B) In a kitchen.　在廚房。

　　　(C) In a restaurant. 在餐廳。

* usually (ˈjuʒʊəlɪ) *adv.* 通常　　have (hæv) *v.* 吃
frequently (ˈfrikwəntlɪ) *adv.* 頻繁地
single (ˈsɪŋl̩) *adj.* 單一的　　order (ˈɔrdɚ) *v.* 點（菜）
generally (ˈdʒɛnərəlɪ) *adv.* 通常；一般地
rotate (roˈtet) *v.* 輪流　　*a few* 一些
sometimes (ˈsʌmˌtaɪmz) *adv.* 有時候
daily (ˈdelɪ) *adj.* 每日的　　special (ˈspɛʃəl) *n.* 特色菜
sub (sʌb) *n.* 潛艇堡（= *submarine sandwich*）
tasty (ˈtestɪ) *adj.* 好吃的　　tuna (ˈtunə) *n.* 鮪魚
fan (fæn) *n.* 擁護者；迷；粉絲
mayonnaise (ˌmeəˈnez) *n.* 美乃滋　　*take place* 發生
library (ˈlaɪˌbrɛrɪ) *n.* 圖書館

20. (**B**)　M：How often do you exercise?

　　　男：妳多常運動？

　　　W：I go to the gym twice a week, and I usually ride my
　　　　　bicycle every day, unless it's raining.

　　　女：我一星期去健身房兩次，我通常每天騎我的腳踏車，除非
　　　　　下雨才不騎。

　　　M：So would you consider yourself to be fairly active?

　　　男：所以妳會認為妳自己相當積極在運動嗎？

　　　W：I guess so.　I mean, I could probably go to the gym
　　　　　more often, but I have a lot going on between work
　　　　　and school.　What about you?

　　　女：我想是吧。我的意思是，我可能可以更常去健身房，但工
　　　　　作學業中有很多事情要顧。你呢？

　　　M：Oh, I'm terribly out of shape.　Ever since I broke my
　　　　　ankle, I've had a hard time getting back into the gym.

　　　男：啊，我非常不健康。自從我的腳踝骨折後，我就很難再回
　　　　　到健身房運動。

　　Question：What are they mainly talking about?

他們主要在談論什麼？

(A) Their study habits. 他們的讀書習慣。

(B) Their exercise habits. 他們的運動習慣。

(C) Their eating habits. 他們的飲食習慣。

* ***how often*** 多常；多久一次
  exercise〔'ɛksə‚saɪz〕v. 運動
  gym〔dʒɪm〕n. 體育館；健身房（= *health club*）
  twice〔twaɪs〕adv. 兩次　unless〔ʌn'lɛs〕conj. 除非
  consider〔kən'sɪdə〕v. 考慮；認為
  fairly〔'fɛrlɪ〕adv. 相當地
  active〔'æktɪv〕adj. 積極的　guess〔gɛs〕v. 猜
  mean〔min〕v. 意思是　***a lot*** 大量的；許多的
  go on（尤用於進行時態）發生
  have a lot going on 很忙；要趕做很多事情（= *be very busy*）
  What about…? …如何？
  oh〔o〕interj.（表示驚訝、痛苦等）啊
  terribly〔'tɛrəb!ɪ〕adv. 很；非常
  shape〔ʃep〕n. 外型；形狀；身體狀況
  out of shape 變形；不健康
  ever since 自從（= *since*）　break〔brek〕v. 折斷；使碎裂
  ankle〔'æŋk!〕n. 腳踝
  have a hard time + V-ing 很難去…（= *have difficulty* + V-ing）
  get back 恢復　mainly〔'menlɪ〕adv. 主要地；大部分地
  habit〔'hæbɪt〕n. 習慣

21. (**A**) Think about giving your old smart phone to someone who needs it in your life: you'll put a smile on their face and give your phone new life. Maybe your child is ready for their first smart phone, but not a brand new one. Perhaps your best friend just shattered the screen on his uninsured smart phone.

考慮一下，把你的舊智慧型手機送給你生命中某個需要它的人：你會使他們的臉上有笑容，並讓你的手機有新生命。或許你的小孩已經準備好要用他們的第一支智慧型手機，但不是一支全新的。也許你最好的朋友剛砸碎他那支沒有保固的智慧型手機的螢幕。

Question : Who is the intended audience of the speaker?
誰是說話者所預期的聽眾？

(A) People who are buying new smart phones.
正要買智慧型手機的人。

(B) People who have recently lost their smart phones.
最近弄丟智慧型手機的人。

(C) People who will never use a smart phone.
永遠不會用智慧型手機的人。

* **think about** 想；考慮
  smart phone 智慧型手機 (= smart-phone)
  smile〔smaɪl〕n. 微笑
  put a smile on one's **face** 使某人開心
  (= please = make sb. happy)
  maybe〔'mebi〕adv. 或許　　**be ready for** 準備好
  brand〔brænd〕n. 品牌
  brand new adj. 全新的 (= completely new)
  shatter〔'ʃætɚ〕v. 砸碎；使粉碎
  screen〔skrin〕n. 螢幕
  uninsured〔͵ʌnɪn'ʃʊrd〕adj. 沒有保險的
  intended〔ɪn'tɛndɪd〕adj. 預期的
  audience〔'ɔdɪəns〕n. 觀眾；聽眾
  recently〔'risṇtlɪ〕adv. 最近
  lost〔lɔst〕v. 丟失；喪失【lose 的過去式】

TEST 14 詳解

聽力測驗 (第 1-21 題，共 21 題)

第一部分：辨識句意 (第 1-3 題，共 3 題)

1. (**C**) (A)　　　　　　(B)　　　　　　(C)

Jay will have piano lessons on Wednesdays and Fridays.
杰禮拜三和禮拜五有鋼琴課。

* piano〔pɪˋæno〕*n.* 鋼琴　　lessons〔ˋlɛsn̩z〕*n. pl.* 課程

2. (**B**) (A)　　　　　　(B)　　　　　　(C)

Catherine came home late and her father is upset.
凱薩琳晚回家，她爸爸很生氣。

* Catherine〔ˋkæθərɪn〕*n.* 凱薩琳　　upset〔ˋʌpsɛt〕*adj.* 生氣

3. (**C**) (A)　　　　　　(B)　　　　　　(C)

George is fond of bird watching. 喬治很喜歡賞鳥。

* fond〔fɑnd〕 *adj.* 喜歡的　　*be fond of* 喜歡；愛好
bird watching 賞鳥

第二部分：基本問答（第 4-10 題，共 7 題）

4. (**A**) It's hotter in here than it is outside! Why don't you turn on a fan or something?

這裡裡面比外面還要熱！你為何不打開電風扇之類的？

(A) I like it this way. 我喜歡這樣子。

(B) They said it was true. 他們說這是真的。

(C) We have to leave soon. 我們必須快點離開。

* *turn on* 打開　　outside〔'aut'saɪd〕 *adv.* 在外面；向外面
fan〔fæn〕 *n.* 電風扇　　*have to V.* 必須~

5. (**C**) Remember to put your jacket on before you go out.

出去前記得穿上你的夾克。

(A) I was. 我當時是那樣。

(B) I am. 我是。

(C) I will. 我會。

* remember〔rɪ'mɛmbɚ〕 *v.* 記得　　*put on* 穿上
go out 外出

6. (**B**) How long does it take to drive from Taipei to Taichung?

從台北開車到台中要多久？

(A) On Friday, if it's not raining.

在禮拜五，如果沒下雨的話。

(B) Two hours or so, depending on traffic.

兩小時左右，要看交通狀況。

(C) 11:00, on the dot. 準時十一點。

* take〔tek〕v. 花 (時間)　　drive〔draɪv〕v. 開車
rain〔ren〕v. 下雨　　*or so* 大約
depend〔dɪˈpɛnd〕v. 視⋯而定　　*depending on* 取決於
traffic〔ˈtræfɪk〕n. 交通　　*on the dot* 準時

7. (**B**) Do you take public transportation to work?

你搭乘大衆運輸工具上班嗎？

(A) Yes, I'm fine. 是，我很好。

(B) Yes, I ride the bus to work. 是，我搭公車上班。

(C) Yes, I'll be here tomorrow. 是，我明天會在這裡。

* public〔ˈpʌblɪk〕adj. 公共的；大衆的
transportation〔ˌtrænspɚˈteʃən〕n. 運輸
ride〔raɪd〕v. 搭乘

8. (**A**) I feel awful. I'm staying home from school.

我覺得很不舒服。我要待在家裡不去上學了。

(A) Good idea. Your cold seems a lot worse today.

好主意。你的感冒今天似乎更糟了。

(B) Take your time. There's no rush. 你慢慢來。不用急。

(C) Thanks. I'll see you next time. 謝謝。下次再見。

* awful〔ˈɔful〕adj. 糟糕的；不舒服的
stay〔ste〕v. 停留；留下
cold〔kold〕n. 感冒　　seem〔sim〕v. 似乎
a lot (強調比較級) 非常 (= *much*)
worse〔wɝs〕adj. 更糟的；更嚴重的
take one's time 慢慢來；不用急　　rush〔rʌʃ〕n. 匆忙；緊急

9. (**A**) Do you celebrate Single's Day in Taiwan?

你在台灣有慶祝光棍節嗎？

(A) No, it's a Chinese thing. 沒有，那是中國人的東西。

(B) I was there last year. 我去年在那裡。

(C) No wonder you're so busy. 難怪你這麼忙。

* celebrate (ˈsɛləˌbret) v. 慶祝　　single (ˈsɪŋgl) n. 單身的人
  Single's Day 單身節；光棍節【每年 11 月 11 日流傳於中國大陸年輕
  人的娛樂性節日，以慶祝自己仍是單身一族為傲】
  no wonder 難怪

10. (**C**) Let's take Jimmy to Disneyland next weekend.
我們下周末一起帶吉米去迪士尼樂園吧。

(A) They didn't recognize me. 他們不認得我。

(B) I didn't think it was all that funny.
我不覺得它有這麼好笑。

(C) That would make him very happy. 那會讓他很開心。

* **Let's ~**　一起 ~ 吧
  Disneyland (ˈdɪznɪlænd) n. 迪士尼樂園
  weekend (ˈwikˈɛnd) n. 週末
  recognize (ˈrɛkəgˌnaɪz) v. 認出　　**all that** 那麼
  funny (ˈfʌnɪ) adj. 有趣的

第三部分：言談理解（第 11-21 題，共 11 題）

11. (**C**) W：You're new here, aren't you?
女：你是新來的，不是嗎？

M：Yes. My name is Oliver.
男：是。我的名字是奧利弗。

W：Hi, Oliver. I'm Serena. Nice to meet you. Are you
on your way to class right now?
女：嗨，奧利佛。我是薩琳娜。很高興認識你。你現在要去上課
的途中嗎？

M：No, I'm done for the day. I'm just walking around,
getting familiar with the campus.

男：不，我今天課上完了。我只是到處走走，熟悉一下校園。

W : Have you been to the library yet? The media center
is great. I highly recommend it.

女：你去過圖書館了嗎？多媒體中心很棒。我非常推薦那裡。

M : Thanks. Can you point me in the direction of the
library?

男：謝謝妳。妳可以指給我圖書館的方向嗎？

Question : Where are the speakers?

這些說話者在哪裡？

(A) At work. 在上班。

(B) At home. 在家。

(C) At school. 在學校。

* new〔nju〕adj. 剛來的　　Oliver〔'ɑləvɚ〕n. 奧利佛
Serena〔sə'rinə〕n. 薩琳娜
on one's way to 在去…的路上　　*right now* 立即；馬上
done〔dʌn〕adj. 完成的　　*walk around* 到處走走
familiar〔fə'mɪljɚ〕adj. 熟悉的＜with＞
campus〔'kæmpəs〕n. 校園　　*have been to* 去過
library〔'laɪ,brɛrɪ〕n. 圖書館　　media〔'midɪə〕n. pl. 媒體
center〔'sɛntɚ〕n. 中心　　highly〔'haɪlɪ〕adv. 高度地；非常地
recommend〔,rɛkə'mɛnd〕v. 推薦　　point〔pɔɪnt〕v. 給～指路
direction〔də'rɛkʃən〕n. 方向

12. (**B**) M : Hey, Monica. What were you and Lorraine arguing
about?

男：嘿，莫妮卡。妳跟蘿倫在吵什麼？

W : She has owed me money for a while now. Like, not a
small amount, either. I simply asked her to repay the
loan. She didn't take it very well.

女：她欠我錢好一陣子了。唉，也不是小數目。我只是要她還錢。
她不能接受。

M：You can say that again! She seemed very upset.

男：我同意！她似乎很生氣。

W：Well, you know, she just bought a new iPhone, and then I heard she's going on a vacation to Hawaii. If she can afford those things, I think she can afford to pay me back.

女：嗯，你知道的，她剛買了新 iPhone，然後我聽說她要去夏威夷度假。如果她可以付的起這些，我想她也能夠還我錢。

M：I agree. That's why I never loan money to friends. It never ends well. How much does she owe you?

男：我同意。這就是為什麼我從不借錢給朋友。這從來沒有好結果。她欠你多少錢？

W：Never mind. It's not important.

女：算了。這不重要。

Question：Why is Monica unhappy?
為什麼莫妮卡不開心？

(A) Lorraine stole her boyfriend. 蘿倫搶了她的男朋友。

(B) Lorraine owes her money. 蘿倫欠她錢。

(C) Lorraine broke her phone. 蘿倫弄壞了她的手機。

* Lorraine〔loˋren〕n. 蘿倫　　argue〔ˋɑrgju〕v. 爭吵
owe〔o〕v. 欠錢　　*for a while* 一陣子
like〔laɪk〕interj.（用在話語填補思考下文時出現的停頓）像是；
　嗯（= *well*）
amount〔əˋmaunt〕n. 總數；總額
either〔ˋiðɚ, ˋaɪðɚ〕adv. 也（不）
simply〔ˋsɪmplɪ〕adv. 簡單地；只是
repay〔rɪˋpe〕v. 還（錢）　　loan〔lon〕n. 借款　v. 借（錢）

take ~ well 接受~   *You can say that again.* 我同意。
seem〔sim〕*v.* 似乎   upset〔ˋʌpsɛt〕*adj.* 情緒不好的
just〔dʒʌst〕*adv.* 剛剛   *go on a vacation* 去度假
Hawaii〔həˋwaɪ〕*n.* 夏威夷   afford〔əˋford〕*v.* 付的起
pay back 還錢   end〔ɛnd〕*v.* 結束
never mind 不用在意；沒關係
stole〔stol〕*v.* 偷【steal 的過去式】

13. (**A**) W : Do you know who will be taking Ms. Yang's place
when she has her baby?

女：你知道楊女士去生小孩子的時候，誰會替代她的位子嗎？

M : Somebody told me that Mr. Mao will be her
replacement.

男：有人告訴我毛先生會代替她。

W : Mr. Mao, the PE teacher?

女：毛先生，那個體育老師？

M : Yes.

男：對。

W : How is he going to teach a history class?

女：他要怎麼教歷史課？

M : From what I was told, he actually has a master's
degree in political science.

男：就我所被告知的，他實際上有政治學的碩士學歷。

W : Oh. I didn't know that.

女：噢。我不知道有這回事。

Question : What do we know about Ms. Yang?

關於楊女士，我們知道些什麼？

(A) She will be taking a leave of absence. 她將會請假。

(B) She will be teaching a PE class. 她將要去教體育課。

(C) She has a master's degree in political science.

　　她有政治學的碩士學歷。

* ***take place*** 取代；代替　　Ms.〔 mɪz 〕 *n.* …女士

have〔 hæv 〕 *v.* 有；生 (小孩)

have a baby 生小孩 (= *give birth to a baby*)

replacement〔 rɪ'plesmənt 〕 *n.* 取代；替代

Mr.〔'mɪstɚ〕 *n.* …先生　　***PE*** 體育 (= *physical education*)

history〔'hɪstərɪ 〕 *n.* 歷史　　actually〔'æktʃʊəlɪ 〕 *adv.* 事實上

master〔'mæstɚ 〕 *n.* 碩士　　degree〔 dɪ'gri 〕 *n.* 學位

political〔 pə'lɪtɪkḷ 〕 *adj.* 政治的

political science 政治學 (= *politics*)

oh〔 o 〕 *interj.* (表示驚訝、恐懼等) 噢；啊

leave〔 liv 〕 *n.* 離開；請假

absence〔'æbsṇs 〕 *n.* 缺席；不在

leave of absence 准假；休假

14. (**C**) M : Hi, I'm calling to ask about the aquarium's new summer hours. I heard that you'll be staying open late some evenings.

男：你好，我打來問水族館新的夏季開放時間。我聽說你們某幾天會開到很晚。

W : Yes, from May 31 until August 15 we will be open until 10:30 P.M. on Friday and Saturday nights. We are going to have special behind-the-scenes tours of the aquarium's facilities at that time.

女：是的，從 5 月 31 日到 8 月 15 日，我們週五、週六會開到晚上 10:30。我們那時將會有特別水族館設備的幕後導覽。

M : That sounds neat! Is there an additional charge to join one of these tours?

男：聽來很棒！參加其中的導覽有額外收費嗎？

W : No, the cost is included in admission. However, we
expect the aquarium will be quite crowded, so we
suggest that you buy advance tickets on our website.
That way you'll be able to avoid the lines.

女：沒有，費用已經包含在入場費裡了。但是，我們預測那時水
族館會很擁擠，所以我們建議你到我們網站上買我們的預售
票。這樣你就能夠避開排隊人潮。

Question：What does the woman recommend?

女士建議什麼？

(A) Arriving early to an event. 早點到達那個活動。

(B) Signing up for a membership program.
註冊一個會員活動。

(C) Buying tickets online. 線上購票。

* aquarium (ə'kwɛrɪʌm) *n.* 水族館
hours (aʊrz) *n. pl.* (活動、業務等的) 時間
stay (ste) *v.* 保持   open ('opən) *adj.* 開放的；營業的
special ('spɛʃəl) *adj.* 特別的
behind (bɪ'haɪnd) *prep.* 在…之後   scene (sin) *n.* 場景
behind-the-scenes *adj.* 幕後的   tour (tʊr) *n.* 旅遊；導覽
facilities (fə'sɪlətɪz) *n. pl.* 設備   sound (nit) *v.* 聽起來
neat (nit) *adj.* 很好的   additional (ə'dɪʃənl̩) *adj.* 額外的
charge (tʃɑrdʒ) *n.* 收費   cost (kɔst) *n.* 費用
include (ɪn'klud) *v.* 包含   admission (əd'mɪʃən) *n.* 入場費
however (haʊ'ɛvɚ) *adv.* 然而   expect (ɪk'spɛkt) *v.* 預計
crowded ('kraʊdɪd) *adj.* 擁擠的   suggest (sə'dʒɛst) *v.* 推薦
advance (əd'væns) *adj.* 預先的   ticket ('tɪkɪt) *n.* 票
be able to V. 能夠~   avoid (ə'vɔɪd) *v.* 避開
line (laɪn) *n.* 排隊   recommend (ˌrɛkə'mɛnd) *v.* 建議；勸告
arrive (ə'raɪv) *v.* 到達   event (ɪ'vɛnt) *n.* 事件；活動
sign up 註冊   membership ('mɛmbɚˌʃɪp) *n.* 會員

program〔'progræm〕*n.* 活動

online〔'ɑnlaɪn〕*n.* 網路上;線上

15. (**A**) W : Um, you're not going to park your bicycle right here on the sidewalk, are you?

女:欸,你沒有要把你的腳踏車停在這人行道上吧,有嗎?

M : I was planning on it.

男:我原本計畫這麼做。

W : There must somewhere else you could leave it.

女:一定還有其他你可以放腳踏車的地方。

M : What's wrong with right here?

男:停這裡有什麼問題嗎?

W : It's blocking the entrance to my shop. My customers will have to walk around it.

女:它擋住我店的入口。我的顧客必須繞過它走。

M : Maybe if the city provided us with bicycle racks, we wouldn't have this problem.

男:也許市政府如果有提供給我們腳踏車架,就不會有這問題。

W : Please move your bicycle, sir.

女:先生,請移走你的腳踏車。

Question : Where is this conversation taking place?

這對話是在哪裡發生?

(A) In front of the woman's shop. 在女士的店門前。

(B) At a bicycle rack. 一個腳踏車架旁。

(C) On the sidewalk. 在人行道上。

* um〔ʌm〕*interj.* (說話時表示猶豫) 嗯

be going to V. 打算;計劃   park〔pɑrk〕*v.* 停放 (車輛等)

sidewalk〔'saɪd,wɔk〕*n.* 人行道   **plan on** 想要

leave〔liv〕*v.* 放置   block〔blɑk〕*v.* 封鎖;堵住

entrance（ˈɛntrəns）*n.* 入口　　shop（ʃɑp）*n.* 商店
customer（ˈkʌstəmɚ）*n.* 顧客　　*have to V.* 必須~
walk around 繞過~走　　maybe（ˈmebi）*adv.* 或許；可能
the city 市政府（= *the government of a city*）
provide（prəˈvaɪd）*v.* 提供
provide sb. with sth. 提供某人某物　　rack（ræk）*n.* 架子
move（muv）*v.* 移動　　sir（sɚ）*n.* 先生
conversation（ˌkɑnvɚˈseʃən）*n.* 對話
take place 發生；舉行　　*in front of* 在…前面

16. (**C**) Good evening, ladies and gentlemen. My name is Jeff Bennett, general manager of the Twilight Theater. First, let me welcome you to this evening's performance of Shadows and Sunbeams. It gives me great pleasure to see another sold out audience, and in fact, every show since opening night has sold out. During the intermission, please feel free to buy snacks and drinks sold in the lobby or browse the merchandise in our theater gift shop. All proceeds from this evening's sales will help fund arts programs for disadvantaged, inner-city youth. So, thank you all in advance. Now, without further ado, let the show begin!

晚安，各位先生女士。我的名字是傑夫·班奈特，我是暮光劇院的總經理。首先，讓我歡迎你來到今晚的表演──陰影與陽光。我很高興看到另一場滿座的觀眾，而事實上，從開幕夜到現在每場秀的門票都已經賣光了。在中場休息時間，請您隨意在大廳選購零食飲料，或是在我們劇院的禮品店瀏覽商品。今晚所有的銷售收入將會資助給弱勢、市中心貧民區年輕人的藝術計畫。所以，先謝謝你們。現在，就不再贅言，開始今晚的演出！

Question : What does the speaker say is special about the
play? 關於這齣劇，說話者說了什麼特別的？

(A) It features several famous actors.

它的特色是有許多知名演員。

(B) It was recently made into a movie.

它最近被拍成電影。

(C) Every ticket has been sold since opening night.

自從開幕夜，每張票都賣出。

* general〔'dʒɛnərəl〕*adj.* 普遍的；概括的
  general manager 總經理
  twilight〔'twaɪˌlaɪt〕*n.* 黃昏；暮光　　theater〔'θiətə〕*n.* 劇院
  performance〔pə'fɔrməns〕*n.* 表演
  shadow〔'ʃædo〕*n.* 陰影　　sunbeam〔'sʌnˌbim〕*n.* 陽光
  pleasure〔'plɛʒə〕*n.* 愉悅　　***sold out*** *adj.* 票已售完的；滿座的
  audience〔'ɔdɪəns〕*n.* 觀眾　　***in fact*** 事實上；實際上
  since〔sɪns〕*prep.* 自從
  opening〔'opənɪŋ〕*adj.* 開場的；開幕的　　***sell out*** 銷售一空
  intermission〔ˌɪntə'mɪʃən〕*n.* 中場休息　　***feel free*** 隨意
  snack〔snæk〕*n.* 點心　　drink〔drɪŋk〕*n.* 飲料
  lobby〔'lɑbɪ〕*n.* 大廳　　browse〔brauz〕*v.* 瀏覽；隨意逛逛
  merchandise〔'mɜtʃənˌdaɪz〕*n.* 商品　　gift〔gɪft〕*n.* 禮物
  gift shop 禮品店　　proceeds〔'proˌsidz〕*n. pl.* 收入
  sales〔selz〕*n. pl.* 銷售額　　fund〔fʌnd〕*v.* 提供～資金
  arts〔ɑrts〕*n. pl.*（總稱）藝術
  program〔'proˌgræm〕*n.* 計畫；活動
  disadvantaged〔ˌdɪsəd'væntɪdʒd〕*adj.* 弱勢的
  inner-city *adj.*（市中心周圍）貧民區的
  youth〔juθ〕*n.* 年輕人　　***in advance*** 預先；事先
  ado〔ə'du〕*n.* 騷擾；忙亂
  without further ado 立刻；不再囉嗦
  　（= *without delaying or wasting any time*）

feature〔'fitʃə〕*v.* 以…爲特色
several〔'sɛvərəl〕*adj.* 幾個的
famous〔'feməs〕*adj.* 有名的
actor〔'æktə〕*n.* 演員　　recently〔'risṇtlɪ〕*adv.* 最近

17. (**C**) W : Hello?

女：哈囉？

M : Hi, Ms. Kao?

男：嗨，高女士嗎？

W : Yes.

女：我是。

M : This is Wayne Chien from Three Brothers Furniture. We're going to be delivering the dining set you bought yesterday.

男：我這裡是三兄弟家具的簡韋恩。我們要運送妳昨天買的餐桌組。

W : Right. You're supposed to have been here by now. You said 10 o'clock.

女：對啊。你們現在應該在這裡了。你當時講是 10 點。

M : I know. I'm sorry. I'm calling to let you know that our truck broke down, which is why we're late. I'm making other arrangements to have the dining set delivered as soon as possible. Will you be home around noon?

男：我知道。我很抱歉。我打來是告訴妳我們卡車壞了，這也就是爲什麼我們會遲到。我正在做其他安排儘快把餐桌組運送過去。妳中午左右會在家嗎？

W : Yes, I'll be here.

女：是，我會在這。

Question : What did Ms. Kao do yesterday?

高小姐昨天做了什麼事？

(A) She bought a sofa. 她買了一個沙發。

(B) She bought a refrigerator. 她買了一台冰箱。

(C) She bought a dining set. 她買了一組餐桌組。

* furniture〔'fɝnɪtʃɚ〕n. 家具　　deliver〔dɪ'lɪvɚ〕v. 運送
dine〔daɪn〕v. 用餐　　set〔sɛt〕n. 組
dining set 餐桌椅組　　**be supposed to V.** 應該要～
by now 現在　　truck〔trʌk〕n. 卡車
break down 停止運作；壞了
arrangements〔ə'rændʒmənt〕n. pl. 安排；調配
as soon as possible 盡快
around〔ə'raʊnd〕prep. 大約；將近
noon〔nun〕n. 中午　　sofa〔'sofə〕n. 沙發
refrigerator〔rɪ'frɪdʒə,retɚ〕n. 冰箱

18. (**C**) The Internet is used for many things, but one of the most popular is online shopping. With just a few clicks of a computer mouse, you can view a wide variety of goods sold locally or overseas. Once you have found something to buy, you can quickly and easily arrange payment and delivery. One of the best things about online shopping is that prices are generally lower than those in regular stores. Smart shoppers can expect savings of up to 70%.

網路被用來做很多事情，但其中最熱門之一是網路購物。只要點幾下電腦滑鼠，你就可以看到在當地及海外銷售的各種商品。一旦你找到要買的東西，你可以快速且輕易地準備付款及運送。網路購物其中一個最棒的是，它的價格通常比一般的商店來的低。聰明的消費者預期可以節省多達百分之 70 的價格。

Question : What is the speaker mainly talking about?

這位說話者主要在談論什麼？

(A) Saving money. 存錢。

(B) Surfing the Internet. 上網。

(C) Online shopping. 網路購物。

* Internet ('ɪntəˌnɛt) *n.* 網際網路　use (juz) *v.* 使用

popular ('pɑpjələ) *adj.* 熱門的

online ('ɑnlaɪn) *adj.* 線上的

shopping ('ʃɑpɪŋ) *n.* 買東西；購物　**a few** 幾個的

click (klɪk) *n.* 點擊　mouse (maʊs) *n.* 滑鼠

view (vju) *v.* 觀看；檢視　wide (waɪd) *adj.* 廣泛的

a variety of 各種的　goods (gʊdz) *n. pl.* 商品；貨物

locally ('lokḷɪ) *adv.* 當在地

overseas ('ovəˌsiz) *adv.* 當海外　once (wʌns) *conj.* 一旦

quickly ('kwɪklɪ) *adv.* 立即；馬上

easily ('izɪlɪ) *adv.* 容易地；輕易地

arrange (ə'rendʒ) *v.* 安排；準備

payment ('pemənt) *n.* 付款

delivery (dɪ'lɪvərɪ) *n.* 運送　price (praɪs) *n.* 價格

generally ('dʒɛnərəlɪ) *adv.* 普遍地；通常

regular ('rɛgjələ) *adj.* 一般的　smart (smɑrt) *adj.* 精明的

shopper ('ʃɑpə) *n.* 顧客；購物者

expect (ɪk'spɛkt) *v.* 預測

saving ('sevɪŋ) *n.* 節省下來的錢

mainly ('menlɪ) *adv.* 主要地　save (sev) *v.* 節省；存 (錢)

surf (sɝf) *v.* 上 (網)

19. (**C**) W : I am so excited. My sister just had a baby. Now, I'm an aunt. Do you have any nieces or nephews?

女：我很興奮。我姊妹剛生了小孩。現在我是姑姑了。你有姪女或姪子嗎？

M : I never mentioned it? Hmm. I guess I didn't. Anyway, yes, I have a niece and two nephews.

男：我從沒提過嗎？嗯，我想我沒有。不過，是的，我有一個姪女及兩個外甥。

W : How many siblings do you have?

女：你有幾個兄弟姊妹？

M : A brother and a sister. My brother has a six-year-old daughter, and my sister has seven-year-old twin boys.

男：一個哥哥及一個姊姊。我哥有個六歲的女兒，我姊有一對七歲雙胞胎男孩。

Question : Who has a six-year-old daughter?

誰有六歲大的女兒？

(A) Gloria. 葛洛麗雅。

(B) Nick's sister. 尼克的姊姊。

(C) Nick's brother. 尼克的哥哥。

* excited〔ɪk'saɪtɪd〕*adj.* 興奮的；激動的
  have a baby 生小孩（= *give birth to a baby*）
  aunt〔ɑnt〕*n.* 姑姑；阿姨　　niece〔nis〕*n.* 姪女；甥女
  nephew〔'nɛfju〕*n.* 姪子；外甥　　mention〔'mɛnʃən〕*v.* 提到
  sibling〔'sɪblɪŋz〕*n. pl.* 兄弟姊妹　　twin〔twɪn〕*adj.* 雙胞胎的
  Gloria〔'glɔrɪə〕*n.* 葛洛麗雅

20. (**B**) Should you work for the student newspaper? The experience itself is valuable. It allows you to explore different aspects of the paper. For example, at the Spectrum I was a writer, an editor, a photographer and even did some graphic design. Even if you are not going to go into the newspaper world, it gives you great experience with writing and time management.

你應該爲校刊工作嗎？這經驗是很寶貴的。它讓你可以探索報紙的不同面向。例如，在光譜刊物裡，我當過作家、編輯、攝影師，甚至還做了些平面設計。即使你沒有打算要投入報業，它也可以給你很好寫作及時間管理的經驗。

Question : What is the woman's attitude toward working for the student newspaper?

對於爲校刊工作，女士的態度是什麼？

(A) Negative. 負面的。

(B) Positive. 正面的。

(C) Neutral. 中立的。

* ***work for*** 爲…做事　　***student newspaper*** 學生報；校刊
  experience〔ɪk'spɪrɪəns〕*n.* 經驗
  valuable〔'væljəbļ〕*adj.* 寶貴的
  allow〔ə'laʊ〕*v.* 容許；使可以
  explore〔ɪk'splor〕*v.* 探索　　aspect〔'æspɛkt〕*n.* 層面
  paper〔'pepɚ〕*n.* 報紙（= *newspaper*）
  for example 例如；譬如
  spectrum〔'spɛktrəm〕*n.* 光譜　　editor〔'ɛdɪtɚ〕*n.* 編輯
  photographer〔fə'tɑgrəfɚ〕*n.* 攝影師
  graphic〔'græfɪk〕*adj.* 圖形的　　design〔dɪ'saɪn〕*n.* 設計
  graphic design 平面設計　　***go into*** 進入
  management〔'mænɪdʒmənt〕*n.* 管理
  negative〔'nɛgətɪv〕*adj.* 負面的；否定的
  positive〔'pɑzətɪv〕*adj.* 正面的　　neutral〔'njutrəl〕*adj.* 中立的

21. (**A**)　W : This is a great park. People seem to be enjoying themselves.

女：這是個很棒的公園。人們似乎很愉快。

M : I come here often. It's the one place in the city where I can relax.

男：我常來這裡。這裡是我在這個城市中可以放鬆的地方。

W : I can see why.　It's a wonderful place to spend a Saturday afternoon.

女：我可以了解為什麼。它是個度過週六下午的好地方。

M : Let's grab one of the empty picnic tables near the pavilion.　We can have our lunch there.

男：我們快佔一個靠近涼亭沒人用的野餐桌。我們可以在那吃我們的午餐。

W : There's one, under the big tree.

女：有一個，在大樹下。

Question : Where are the speakers?

說話者在哪裡？

(A) At a public park.　在一個公園。

(B) At a museum.　在一間博物館。

(C) At a restaurant.　在一間餐廳。

* ***enjoy*** *oneself* 感到快樂；過得愉快
relax〔rɪ'læks〕v. 放鬆　　see〔si〕v. 看到；了解
wonderful〔'wʌndəfəl〕adj. 很棒的
grab〔græb〕v. 抓；奪取
empty〔'ɛmptɪ〕adj. 空的；沒人的
picnic〔'pɪknɪk〕n. 野餐　　pavilion〔pə'vɪljən〕n. 涼亭
have〔hæv〕v. 吃　　lunch〔lʌntʃ〕n. 午餐
public〔'pʌblɪk〕adj. 公共的
museum〔mju'zɪʌm〕n. 博物館
restaurant〔'rɛstərənt〕n. 餐廳

TEST 15 詳解

聽力測驗（第 1-21 題，共 21 題）

第一部分：辨識句意（第 1-3 題，共 3 題）

1. (**A**) (A)   (B)   (C)

They are watching a baseball game. 他們正在看一場棒球賽。
   * baseball〔'bes,bɔl〕*n.* 棒球   game〔gem〕*n.* 比賽

2. (**C**) (A)   (B)   (C)

Tom was a vampire for Halloween.
湯姆在萬聖節時當吸血鬼。
   * vampire〔'væmpaɪr〕*n.* 吸血鬼
     Halloween〔,hælo'in〕*n.* 萬聖節

3. (**A**) (A)   (B)   (C)

Ms. Stevenson is washing the window.
史蒂芬森女士正在洗窗戶。

* Ms. 〔 mɪz 〕 *n.* …女士   window 〔ˈwɪndo 〕 *n.* 窗戶

第二部分:基本問答 (第 4-10 題,共 7 題)

4. (**A**) How much would it cost for a burger and a side of fries?
一個漢堡加點一份薯條要花多少錢?

(A) That will be $1.50. 要一點五美元 ?

(B) At six o'clock. 在六點鐘。

(C) Always on Fridays. 總是在禮拜五。

* cost 〔 kɔst 〕 *v.* 花 (錢)   burger 〔ˈbɝgɚ 〕 *n.* 漢堡
side 〔 saɪd 〕 *n.* 額外的食物;配菜
fries 〔 fraɪz 〕 *n. pl.* 薯條 (= *French fries*)
o'clock 〔 əˈklɑk 〕 *adv.* …點鐘

5. (**B**) How much did you pay for that sweater?
你花多少錢買那件毛衣?

(A) Two weeks. 兩個禮拜。

(B) Ten dollars. 十美元。

(C) Twelve kilos. 十二公斤。

* *pay for* 為了…付錢   sweater 〔ˈswɛtɚ 〕 *n.* 毛衣
kilo 〔ˈkilo 〕 *n.* 公斤

6. (**A**) Are you going to play in tomorrow's basketball game?
你會去打明天的籃球賽嗎?

(A) Probably not. 可能不會。

(B) See what she says. 看看她說什麼。

(C) He's in Taiwan. 他在台灣。

* *be going to V.* 即將;將要   probably 〔ˈprɑbəblɪ 〕 *adv.* 可能

7. (**C**) Ms. Wang, I'm so nervous. Would you tell me how I did on the test? 王老師，我很緊張。你可以告訴我我考的如何嗎？

   (A) Don't worry, Mike. You have little time.
     不用擔心，麥克。你時間不多。

   (B) That's OK, Steve. Don't mention it.
     沒關係，史蒂夫。不用客氣。

   (C) I'm sorry, Phil. You'll have to wait until I have graded all the tests.
     <u>我很抱歉，菲爾。你必須等到我打完所有考試成績。</u>

   * nervous〔'nɝvəs〕*adj.* 緊張的   worry〔'wɝi〕*v.* 擔心
     mention〔'mɛnʃən〕*v.* 提到
     Don't mention it. 別提這個；不客氣。   ***have to V.*** 必須～
     until〔ən'tɪl〕*conj.* 直到   grade〔gred〕*v.* 打…的分數

8. (**A**) Would it be convenient for you to give me a ride to the shopping mall? 你方便載我去購物中心嗎？

   (A) I'm sorry, but I'm running late for an appointment.
     <u>我很抱歉，但是我約會遲到了。</u>

   (B) I'm looking for a new pair of sunglasses.
     我正在找一付新的太陽眼鏡。

   (C) I'm fine. How are you? 我很好。你好嗎？

   * convenient〔kən'vinjənt〕*adj.* 方便的   ride〔raɪd〕*n.* 搭乘
     give sb. a ride 載某人一程；給某人搭便車
     shopping〔'ʃɑpɪŋ〕*n.* 買東西；購物   mall〔mɔl〕*n.* 購物中心
     run late 遲到   appointment〔ə'pɔɪntmənt〕*n.* 約會
     look for 尋找   pair〔pɛr〕*n.* 一副
     sunglasses〔'sʌnglæsɪz〕*n. pl.* 太陽眼鏡

9. (**A**) We've been waiting almost an hour. When will our pizza be ready?
   我們已經等了幾乎一個小時。我們的披薩什麼時候會好？

(A) It's coming out of the oven right now. 它現在出爐了。

(B) She's in the kitchen at the moment. 她現在在廚房裡。

(C) I'm tired and hungry. 我又累又餓。

* wait〔wet〕*v.* 等待　　pizza〔'pitsə〕*n.* 披薩
　ready〔'rɛdɪ〕*adj.* 準備好的　　oven〔'ʌvən〕*n.* 爐子；烤箱
　right now 現在　　***at the moment*** 現在
　tired〔taɪrd〕*adj.* 累的　　hungry〔'hʌŋgrɪ〕*adj.* 飢餓的

10. (**C**) Have you ever tried to learn a foreign language?
你有沒有試著學過一個外國語言？

   (A) Green Island sounds like fun. We should go.
綠島聽起來很有趣。我們應該去。

   (B) Mornings are the best time to reach him. Try again tomorrow. 早上是最好聯絡他的時間。明天再試一次。

   (C) German, in high school. It was very difficult.
德語，高中的時候。它非常難。

* ***try to V***. 試圖~　　learn〔lɜn〕*v.* 學習
　foreign〔'fɔrɪn〕*adj.* 外國的
　language〔'læŋgwɪdʒ〕*n.* 語言　　island〔'aɪlənd〕*n.* 島
　Green Island 綠島【位於台灣臺東縣外海】
　sound〔saʊnd〕*v.* 聽起來
　reach〔titʃ〕*v.* 接觸；（用電話）聯絡
　German〔'dʒɜmən〕*n.* 德語

第三部分：言談理解（第 11-21 題，共 11 題）

11. (**A**) M：My mom made some holiday cookies. Would you like to try some?

男：我媽做了一些假日餅乾。妳想要試吃一些看看嗎？

W：Sure! I love cookies. What kind are they?

女：當然！我很愛餅乾。他們是哪種餅乾？

M : These are oatmeal raisin, these are chocolate chip, and these are peanut butter.

男：這些是燕麥葡萄，這些是巧克力脆片，而這些是花生醬。

W : (chewing) The oatmeal raisin are delicious! Best cookies ever!

女：(咀嚼中) 這個燕麥葡萄真好吃！有史以來最好吃的餅乾！

M : Here, take some more. Try the peanut butter. That's my favorite. Don't be shy.

男：來，拿多一些。試試看花生醬的。那是我的最愛。別客氣。

Question : Which cookie did the woman try?

女士試了哪些餅乾？

(A) Oatmeal raisin. 燕麥葡萄。

(B) Chocolate chip. 巧克力脆片。

(C) Peanut butter. 花生醬。

cookie ('kʊkɪ) *n.* 餅乾

holiday cookie 假日餅乾【因應某些節日所做的餅乾，像是聖誕節有
  聖誕樹、雪人形狀的餅乾】

would like to V. 想要～   sure (ʃʊr) *adv.* 當然

kind (kaɪnd) *n.* 種類   oatmeal ('ot,mil) *n.* 燕麥

raisin ('rezn) *n.* 葡萄乾   chip (tʃɪp) *n.* 碎片

peanut ('pi,nʌt) *n.* 花生   butter ('bʌtə) *n.* 奶油；像奶油之物

chew (tʃu) *v.* 咀嚼   delicious (dɪ'lɪʃəs) *adj.* 好吃的

shy (ʃaɪ) *adj.* 害羞的；不好意思的

12. (**C**) M : I just received a text message. Jack isn't coming to the party.

男：我剛收到一個簡訊。傑克沒有要來派對。

W : Why not?

女：為什麼不來？

M : I don't know. All it says is, "Sorry, can't make it tonight. Have fun."

男：我不知道。簡訊只有說：「抱歉，今晚趕不過去。好好玩喔。」

W : That's odd. He seemed really excited about it.

女：那真奇怪。他之前似乎很期待這個派對。

M : Something must have come up.

男：一定發生了什麼事。

Question : Why won't Jack attend the party?

為什麼傑克不會參加這個派對？

(A) He's not feeling well. 他現在不舒服。

(B) He can't find a ride. 他搭不到便車。

(C) It's impossible to say. 無法判斷。

* receive〔rɪ'siv〕v. 收到　　text〔tɛkst〕n. 文字
  message〔'mɛsɪdʒ〕n. 訊息　　***make it*** 成功；能出席
  have fun 玩得愉快　　odd〔ɑd〕adj. 奇怪的
  seem〔sim〕v. 似乎　　excited〔ɪk'saɪtɪd〕adj. 興奮的
  must have + p.p. 當時一定～　　***come up*** 出現；發生
  attend〔ə'tɛnd〕v. 參加；出席　　well〔wɛl〕adj. 健康的
  ride〔raɪd〕n. 便車　　say〔se〕v. 說；判斷
  It's impossible to say. 很難說；天曉得。

13. (**B**) W : Mr. Robinson, today's your lucky day.

女：羅賓森先生，今天是你的幸運日。

M : Excuse me?

男：不好意思？

W : I was able to upgrade your seat to business class.
You're now in row 3, seat C. That's an aisle seat, by
the way.

女：我能幫你的位置升級到商務艙。你現在在第三排，座位 C。
另外，那是一個靠走道的位置。

M : Wow! What did I do to deserve the upgrade?

男：哇！我是做了什麼可以得到升等。

W：You didn't do anything. We had some last-minute cancellations, so there are plenty of seats in business class.

女：你什麼也沒做。我們有些最後幾分鐘的座位取消，所以商務艙還有許多位子。

M：Thanks, but I don't have to pay extra, do I?

男：謝謝，但我不需要額外付費，要嗎？

W：Nope. Here's your boarding pass. Have a nice flight.

女：不用。這是你的登機證。祝你飛行愉快。

Question：What does the woman tell the man?

女士告訴男士什麼事？

(A) He's receiving an award. 他將要得獎。

(B) He's getting a better seat.

他將會得到一個更好的位子。

(C) He's taking a later flight. 他將會搭晚一點的班機。

* Mr. (ˈmɪstɚ) n. …先生　　Robinson (ˈrɑbɪnsn̩) n. 羅賓森
  lucky (ˈlʌkɪ) adj. 幸運的　　*excuse me* 對不起；請再說一遍
  be able to V. 能夠~　　upgrade (ʌpˈgred) v. n. 升級
  seat (sit) n. 座位　　class (klæs) n. 等級
  business class 商務艙　　row (ro) n. 排
  aisle (aɪl) n. 走道　　*by the way* 順帶說
  wow (wau) interj. (表示驚訝、喜悅等) 哇
  deserve (dɪˈsɝv) v. 應得　　last-minute adj. 最後一分鐘的
  cancellation (ˌkænsl̩ˈeʃən) n. 取消　　*plenty of* 很多
  have to V. 必須~　　extra (ˈɛkstrə) adv. 額外地
  nope (nop) adv. 不 (= *no*)
  board (bɔrd) v. 上 (飛機、船等)
  pass (pæs) n. 通行證　　*boarding pass* 登機證
  flight (flaɪt) n. 飛行；班機　　receive (rɪˈsiv) v. 收到
  award (əˈwɔrd) n. 獎；獎品

14. (**B**) If you want to start a travel business but don't have a lot of money, consider basing the business out of your home as a way to keep expenses to a minimum. If you have an Internet connection, you have access to items such as airline schedules and travel packages, and you can help clients make travel arrangements over the phone or via email. However, if you intend to focus on corporate travel, a brick-and-mortar building will give you a more professional presence.

如果你想要開始旅遊事業但沒有很多錢，可以考慮以你家做為辦公室的方法將開支降到最低。如果你有網路連結，你能夠取得像是航班時刻表及旅遊套裝行程，而且你可以透過電話及電子郵件幫客戶安排旅行。然而，如果你想要專注於公司旅遊，一間實體的建築物可以讓你有一個比較專業的外表。

Question：Who would be most interested in this information? 誰會對這則資訊最感興趣？

(A) People who are seeking cheap airfares.
在找便宜機票的人。

(B) People who are interested in starting a business.
有興趣創業的人。

(C) People who are traveling around the world.
到世界各地旅遊的人。

* travel〔ˋtrævl̩〕*n.* 旅行　　business〔ˋbɪznɪs〕*n.* 事業；營業
a lot of 許多；大量　　consider〔kənˋsɪdɚ〕*v.* 考慮
base〔bes〕*v.* 以…為基礎　　*out of* 從…；來自
expense〔ɪkˋspɛns〕*n.* 費用
minimum〔ˋmɪnəməm〕*n.* 最小量
keep…to a minimum 將…減到最低
Internet〔ˋɪntɚ͵nɛt〕*n.* 網際網路
connection〔kəˋnɛkʃən〕*n.* 連結

access〔'æksɛs〕*n.* 接近的機會;使用 < *to* >
item〔'aɪtəm〕*n.* 項目;物品　*such as* 像;諸如
airline〔'ɛr‚laɪn〕*n.* 航空公司　schedule〔'skɛdʒul〕*n.* 時間表
package〔'pækɪdʒ〕*n.* 套裝行程　client〔'klaɪənt〕*n.* 客戶
arrangement〔ə'rendʒmənt〕*n.* 安排
over the phone 透過電話　via〔'vaɪə〕*prep.* 經由
however〔hau'ɛvɚ〕*adv.* 然而　intend〔ɪn'tɛnd〕*v.* 意圖
focus on 集中;專注於
corporate〔'kɔrpərɪt〕*adj.* 集團的;大公司的
brick〔brɪk〕*n.* 磚塊　mortar〔'mɔrtɚ〕*n.* 水泥
brick-and-mortar *adj.* 磚塊水泥的;實體的
professional〔prə'fɛʃənl̩〕*adj.* 專業的
presence〔'prɛzn̩s〕*n.* 外表　*be interested in* 對…感興趣
seek〔sik〕*v.* 尋找;追求　cheap〔'pækɪdʒ〕*adj.* 便宜的
airfare〔'ɛr‚fɛr〕*n.* 機票費用　*around the world* 世界各地

15. (**B**) If you want to help protect the ocean you love from
pollution, Heal the Bay can help. From volunteering with
your friends and family at one of our monthly beach
cleanups, choosing your favorite beach for a year of
cleanups to helping orchestrate an event for your own
company, there are many ways you can protect what you
love. To learn more about beach cleanups, please visit
our website at www.healthebay.com.

如果你想幫助保護你熱愛的海洋不受到污染,治療海灣可以提供
幫助。有很多方法可以保護你愛的海洋,從與你朋友和家人自願
加入我們每月的淨灘、選擇你最喜愛的海灘一年清理一次,到替
自己的公司精心策劃活動。關於淨灘,要了解更多請參訪我們的
網站 www.healthebay.com。

Question : What does the woman instruct listeners to do?
女士教導聽者去做什麼?

(A) Make a phone call. 打一通電話。

(B) Visit a website. 參觀一個網站。

(C) Write a letter. 寫一封信。

* protect〔prə'tɛkt〕v. 保護　　ocean〔'oʃən〕n. 海洋
protect…from~ 保護…免於~
pollution〔pə'luʃən〕n. 汙染
heal〔hil〕v. 治癒；使恢復健康　　bay〔be〕n. 海灣
volunteer〔,vɑlən'tɪr〕v. 自願（做）
monthly〔'mʌnθlɪ〕adj. 每月的；每月一次的
cleanup〔'klin,ʌp〕n. 大掃除　　**beach cleanup** 淨灘
favorite〔'fevərɪt〕adj. 最喜愛的
orchestrate〔'ɔrkɪs,tret〕v. 精心安排　　event〔ɪ'vɛnt〕n. 活動
company〔'kʌmpənɪ〕n. 公司　　visit〔'vɪzɪt〕v. 參觀；拜訪
website〔'wɛb,saɪt〕n. 網站　　instruct〔ɪn'strʌkt〕v. 教導
make a phone call 打電話

16. (**C**) W：Your Chinese is very good. In fact, it's better than mine, and I'm a native speaker! How did you become fluent?

女：你的中文很棒。事實上，比我的好，而我還是中文為母語的人！你的中文如何變流利的？

M：I studied at the Mandarin Training Center in Taichung. And I've lived in Taiwan for 10 years.

男：我在台中的華語訓練中心研讀。而且我已經在台灣住了十年。

W：Wow! What do you think helped more, going to school or living in Taiwan?

女：哇！你覺得哪一個比較有用？去上中文課或是住在台灣？

M：Both, actually. School gave me the knowledge, and life gave me a chance to use it.

男：實際上，兩者都有用。學校交給我知識，而住在台灣的生活給我機會去活用知識。

Question：What do we know about the man?

關於男士，我們知道什麼？

(A) He's an English teacher. 他是一位英文老師。

(B) He lives in Taichung. 他現在住在台中。

(C) He speaks fluent Chinese. <u>他說一口流利的中文。</u>

* Chinese〔tʃaɪ'niz〕*n.* 中文　　**in fact** 事實上
native〔'netɪv〕*adj.* 天生的　　**native speaker** 說母語的人
fluent〔'fluənt〕*adj.* 流利的　　Mandarin〔'mændərɪn〕*n.* 華語
training〔'trenɪŋ〕*n.* 訓練　　center〔'sɛntɚ〕*n.* 中心
wow〔waʊ〕*interj.*（感到驚訝、喜悅等）哇
actually〔'æktʃʊəlɪ〕*adv.* 實際上
knowledge〔'nɑlɪdʒ〕*n.* 知識　　chance〔tʃæns〕*n.* 機會；良機

17. (**B**) M : Would you like to play tennis tomorrow before breakfast?

男：明天吃早餐之前妳會想要打網球嗎？

W : I have a dentist's appointment at 9:00 a.m., so probably not.

女：我早上九點預約牙醫，所以可能不了。

M : Hmm, I see. We could try to play in the afternoon, but the courts are usually crowded after lunch until early evening.

男：嗯，我知道了。我們可以試試在下午打，但是球場通常在午餐後直到傍晚前都很擁擠。

W : I have a yoga class at 1:30, so I wouldn't be able to make it in the afternoon, either.

女：一點半我有瑜珈課，所以我下午也不能趕到。

M : How about Friday morning?

男：那星期五早上呢？

W : Let's play it by ear.

女：我們見機行事吧！

Question : What will the woman most likely do tomorrow
　　　　 morning?　女士明天早上最有可能做什麼？

(A) Play tennis.　打網球。

(B) Visit the dentist.　<u>看牙醫。</u>

(C) Attend a yoga class.　上瑜珈課。

* ***would like to V***.　想要～　　tennis〔'tɛnɪs〕*n.* 網球
　 dentist〔'dɛntɪst〕*n.* 牙醫
　 appointment（ə'pɔɪntmənt）*n.*（會面的）約定
　 a.m. 午前；早上（= *ante meridiem*）
　 probably〔'prɑbəblɪ〕*adv.* 大概；或許　　***try to V***. 嘗試～
　 court〔kort〕*n.*（網球等）場地　　usually〔'juʒʊəlɪ〕*adv.* 通常地
　 crowded〔'kraʊdɪd〕*adj.* 擁擠的　　yoga〔'jogə〕*n.* 瑜珈
　 class〔klæs〕*n.* 上課　　***be able to V***. 能夠～
　 make it 成功；及時趕到　　either〔'iðɚ〕*adv.* 也（不）
　 How about…? …如何？　　***play it by ear*** 隨機應變；見機行事
　 attend（ə'tɛnd）*v.* 出席；上（課）

18. (**C**)　M : Hi, I saw your advertisement for a two-bedroom
　　　　　 apartment for rent on Fox River Drive.　I'm calling
　　　　　 to find out when it's available.

　　　　 男：嗨，我在福斯河道上看到妳要出租兩房公寓的廣告。我致電
　　　　　　 想知道什麼時候可以租？

　　　　 W : We need a tenant who can move in on April first.
　　　　　 It's a great living space.　In fact, it's the only
　　　　　 two-bedroom in the building that faces the river.　It's
　　　　　 gorgeous.　Would you like to schedule a viewing?

　　　　 女：我們需要一位可以在四月一日搬進來的房客。這間公寓是個
　　　　　　 很棒的生活空間。事實上，這間是這棟建物唯一一間面河的
　　　　　　 兩房公寓。這是極好的。你想要排時間來看屋嗎？

　　　　 M : Yes, please.　How about tomorrow in the early
　　　　　 evening?

男：好，拜託妳。那麼明天傍晚可以嗎？

W : Sure. Come to the building tomorrow at 7:00 P.M. I'll meet you by the front gate.

女：沒問題。明天晚上七點到這棟大樓來。我會在前門旁接你。

Question : What does the man ask about the apartment?

關於公寓，男士問了什麼？

(A) How many rooms it has. 這公寓有多少房間。

(B) How much it costs. 這公寓要花費多少錢。

(C) **When it is available.** 這公寓什麼時候可以租。

* advertisement (͵ædvɚˈtaɪzmənt) *n.* 廣告；宣傳
apartment (əˈpɑrtmənt) *n.* (一戶) 公寓
rent (rɛnt) *n.* 出租　*for rent* 供出租　fox (fɑks) *n.* 狐狸
drive (draɪv) *n.* (私人住宅的) 車道　*find out* 發現；查明
available (əˈveləbl) *adj.* 可用的；可得到的
tenant (ˈtɛnənt) *n.* 房客　*move in* 搬進
living (ˈlɪvɪŋ) *adj.* 生活的　　space (spes) *n.* 空間；房間
building (ˈbɪldɪŋ) *n.* 建築物；房屋　　face (fes) *v.* 面向
gorgeous (ˈgɔrdʒəs) *adj.* 極好的
schedule (ˈskɛdʒul) *v.* 安排；預定　*would like to V.* 想要～
viewing (ˈvjuɪŋ) *n.* 參觀；觀賞　*How about…?* …如何？
sure (ʃur) *adv.* 當然　*P.M.* 午後；下午 (= *post meridiem*)
meet (mit) *v.* 和～見面；迎接
by (baɪ) *prep.* 在…旁邊；靠近　　front (frʌnt) *adj.* 前面的
gate (get) *n.* 大門；出入口

19.(**B**) OK, everybody listen up! I'm going to divide the classroom into four groups. Now listen very carefully. Those who were born in January, February, and March, you're Group A. Those who were born in April, May, and June, you're Group B. Those in July, August, and September, you're Group C. The rest of you are Group D. Now, remember your group letter, because in a minute, we're going to rearrange the classroom into those four sections.

好，大家聽好了！我將要把課堂分成四組。現在仔細聽好。在一月、二月、三月出生的人，你們是 A 組。在四月、五月、六月出生的人，你們是 B 組。在七月、八月、九月出生的人，你們是 C 組。其餘的人是 D 組。現在，記住你們組別的字母，因為在一分鐘後，我們將教室重新安排成這四組。

Question：What is the woman doing? 女士正在做什麼？

(A) Assigning some homework. 分配一些功課。

(B) Dividing the students into groups. 把學生分組。

(C) Explaining the examination process. 解釋考試流程。

* **listen up** 注意聽著　　**be going to V**. 將要～
　 divide〔də'vaɪd〕v. 分；分割＜into＞
　 classroom〔'klæs,rum〕n. 教室；課堂
　 carefully〔'kɛrfəlɪ〕adv. 小心地　　rest〔rɛst〕n. 剩餘的人或物
　 letter〔'lɛtə〕n. 字母；文字　　minute〔'mɪnɪt〕n. 分鐘
　 rearrange〔,riə'rendʒ〕v. 重新排列
　 section〔'sɛkʃən〕n. 部分；組　　assign〔ə'saɪn〕v. 分配；分派
　 explain〔ɪk'splen〕v. 解釋
　 examination〔ɪg,zæmə'neʃən〕n. 檢查；調查
　 process〔'prɑsɛs〕n. 過程；步驟

20. (**C**) M：Hi, what seems to be the problem?

　　　　　　男：嗨，似乎是有什麼問題嗎？

　　　　　 W：Hello. Yes, well, my car's engine has been making a strange sound, and it hasn't been driving like normal. It's also driving very slow, even when I floor the gas pedal.

　　　　　　女：哈囉。是的，嗯，我車子的引擎一直發出一個奇怪的聲音，而且駕駛起來不太正常。甚至當我把油門踏板踩到底，它還是開得非常慢。

M : I see. Have you checked the oil recently?

男：我了解了。妳最近有查看過機油嗎？

W : I wouldn't even know where to look.

女：我根本不知道要看哪裡。

M : OK, is that it——the Ford Focus?

男：好。那是妳的車嗎，福特焦點？

W : Yes, that's my car.

女：是的，那是我的車。

M : Give me the keys and I'll have a look at it.

男：請把鑰匙給我，我來看一下。

Question : Who is the woman probably talking to?

女士可能在跟誰說話？

(A) A priest. 一位牧師。

(B) A lawyer. 一位律師。

(C) An auto mechanic. 一位汽車技師。

* seem〔sim〕*v.* 似乎　　problem〔'prɑbləm〕*n.* 問題
  well〔wɛl〕*interj.* 嗯　　engine〔'ɛndʒən〕*n.* 引擎
  strange〔strendʒ〕*adj.* 奇怪的　　sound〔saʊnd〕*n.* 聲音
  drive〔draɪv〕*v.*（車）行駛　　normal〔'nɔrml̩〕*n.* 標準；常態
  slow〔slo〕*adv.* 慢地　　floor〔flor〕*v.* 踩足（汽車）的油門
  gas〔gæs〕*n.* 汽油　　pedal〔'pɛdl̩〕*n.* 踏板
  gas pedal 油門（踏板）　　**I see.** 我知道了；我了解了。
  check〔tʃɛk〕*v.* 檢查　　oil〔ɔɪl〕*n.* 機油；潤滑油
  recently〔'risn̩tlɪ〕*adv.* 最近；近來　　**have a look at** 看一看
  priest〔prist〕*n.*（基督教）牧師　　lawyer〔'lɔjɚ〕*n.* 律師
  auto〔'ɔto〕*n.* 汽車　　mechanic〔mə'kænɪk〕*n.* 機械工；技工

21. (**C**) W : Have you ever been on a cruise ship?

女：你坐過郵輪嗎？

M : No, I'd get seasick. I don't do well on boats.

男：沒有，我會暈船。我不適合在船上。

W : Me, too. I have a terrible time with motion sickness.

女：我也是。動暈症讓我很痛苦。

M : My dad told me there are pills I could take that would solve the problem, but… I'm happy here on dry land.

男：我爸告訴我有種藥丸我吃之後可以解決這種問題，但…我在乾燥的陸地上很開心。

W : I have a problem with my inner ear that makes almost any kind of travel an unpleasant experience.

女：因為我的內耳有問題，這幾乎讓任何類型的旅行都是一個不愉快的經驗。

Question : Which speaker has trouble with seasickness?

　　　　哪一個說話者有暈船的問題？

(A) The man.　男士。

(B) The woman.　女士。

(C) Both speakers.　兩位說話者。

* cruise〔kruz〕*n.* 巡航　　***cruise ship*** 郵輪
seasick〔'si,sik〕*adj.* 暈船的　　***do well*** 進展良好
have a terrible time 過得不好；感到不適
motion〔'moʃən〕*n.* (物體的) 運動；移動
sickness〔'sɪknɪs〕*n.* 噁心
motion sickness 動暈症【動暈最常發生在海上，其他在火車、交通
　　工具或乘坐飛機時，也有可能發生，即我們常聽到的暈車或暈船】
pill〔pɪl〕*n.* 藥丸　　solve〔salv〕*v.* 解決
have a problem with 在…有問題
inner〔'ɪnɚ〕*adj.* 內部的；裡面的　　***inner ear*** 內耳
kind〔kaɪnd〕*n.* 類型　　travel〔'trævl〕*n.* 旅行
unpleasant〔ʌn'plɛznt〕*adj.* 使人不愉快的
experience〔ɪk'spɪrɪəns〕*n.* 經驗；體驗
have trouble with 在…有問題
seasickness〔'si,sɪknɪs〕*n.* 暈船